RAIL CITY

CHICAGO USA

BY GEORGE H. DOUGLAS

SAN DIEGO   Howell -North Books   CALIFORNIA

385
D

For information write to:

Howell-North Books
P.O. Box 3051
La Jolla, California 92038

Library of Congress Cataloging in Publication Data

Douglas, George H.
  Rail city, Chicago, U.S.A.

  Bibliography: p.
  Includes index.
  1. Railroads — Illinois — Chicago.   I. Title.
HE2781.C4D68   385′.09773′11   81-6361
ISBN 0-8310-7150-8   AACR2

1 2 3 4 5 6 7 8 9   84 83 82 81

For Philip Douglas

Table of Contents

List of Tables and Charts

Acknowledgments

No book of this sort could be undertaken without the help of many individuals and institutions. But a person who does a book about railroads is never forced to go it alone; indeed he finds at every hand eager helpers and contributors, a fact which has provided this author with the delights of many new associations and friendships.

This book almost certainly would never have seen the light of day had I not relied on the Chicago-area railroads themselves, most especially the public relations and information officers of those roads who provided many of the pictures and otherwise put their resources at my disposal. Of the individuals involved, I am especially indebted to: J. A. Hagle of the Burlington Northern; Bill Burk of the Santa Fe; Thomas J. Judge of the Chicago and North Western; Robert W. O'Brien and Jack E. Rudman of the Illinois Central Gulf; Jim Scribbins of the Milwaukee Road, and Debbie Marciniak of Amtrak. Readers of this book will find large numbers of the pictures attributed to these sources, and the individuals named above were more than generous in looking them up and having them reproduced.

I have been heavily reliant on a number of Chicago rail experts and authorities, the most prominent being: Jim Adams of the Midwest Railway Historical Society, Andrew C. Koval, a member of several of the city's rail organizations and a tireless worker in my behalf; and Charles Stats, Chairman of the Chicago Chapter of the Railway and Locomotive Historical Society.

The chapter in this book dealing with Chicago's extensive system of interurban railways would not have been possible without the help and generosity of William D. Middleton, surely the country's most prolific author on this subject.

I owe a large debt of gratitude to a number of my colleagues at the University of Illinois, most especially Robert M. Sutton, Director of the Illinois Historical Survey; also Robert W. Harbeson, Donald L. Kemmerer, Robert W. Mayer and Walter L. Creese. At the same institution I am grateful for the superlative typing help I received from Marlyn Ehlers, Irene Wahlfeldt and Louise Steele, and for the photo duplication services of Robert Silver.

A number of institutions have been especially useful as sources of pictures and other research materials. I could not have gotten very far without the resources of the Chicago Historical Society, where Jane Stevens was particularly helpful in locating pictures from the large graphic archives of that institution. Also, I am indebted to the Newberry Library of Chicago, the Chicago Public Library, the De Golyer Foundation Library, the Illinois State Historical Library, the Library of Congress and the Smithsonian Institution (most especially to John H. White, Jr., Curator of the Division of Transportation).

The work of many photographers—some of their names now lost to posterity—is represented in this volume. On the other hand, I have been fortunate in having been able to rely on the large picture collection of railroad photographer Bob Lorenz and the very handsome collection of pictures taken in Chicago during the Second World War by Jack Delano. This latter collection is safely housed in the Library of Congress, and is readily available to the public. Rosalind Douglas has offered advice on architectural photographs.

Among the other individuals who have been of assistance are: Herbert H. Harwood, Jr., M. M. Adams of the Erie-Lackawanna Railroad; Alicia D. Stamm of the American Historic Buildings Survey; Norman J. Perrin; Mike Cassidy; Richard W. Smith of the Joint Council of Dining Car Employees, R. D. Bunton of the Chicago, South Shore and South Bend Railroad; Mary Michals and Mark Johnson of the Illinois State Historical Library; Ann C. Altemose of the Indiana State Library; Professor Carl W. Condit of Northwestern University; Patricia Ann Kelly of the Evanston Historical Society; Martha K. Jones of the Bensenville Community Public Library; Don L. Hofsommer of the Lexington Group in Transportation History; F. Clayton Snyder; Walter P. Feret of the Chicago and Northwestern Historical Society; William Dillman of Esmark Inc.

Leslie F. Orear of the Illinois Labor History Society; Patricia Shymanski of the Historic Pullman Foundation; James W. Phillips of the De Golyer Foundation Library; Jane Hamlin of the Geneva Historical Society, Mary E. Neff of the Waukegan Historical Society; Janet Cyrwus of Northwestern University; Lisa Bradshaw of the Research Services Office of the University of Illinois; James J. D. Lynch, Jr., of the Pennsylvania Railroad Technical and Historical Society; Diane C. Bartoloma of the Inland Steel Corporation; and Elsie Jacobsen of the Historical Society of Oak Park and River Forest.

Introduction

Chicago, it has been said, is the most American of cities. It is youthful, brash, energetic, reckless. It is a zesty giant not yet grown to maturity—a city that never seems to grow old even in the face of adversity, a city constantly turning some fresh face on the world.

Chicago was built by the railroads—so we have been told over and over in textbooks of American history. And the railroads, more than any of the city's other institutions, stamped Chicago with its most enduring characteristics—energy, restlessness, constantly changing human drama, the pulsating beat of motion, of travel, of people coming together and moving from place to place. The railroad has grown old now, some will say, and has given way to other modes of transportation. In Chicago itself the railroad offers evidence aplenty of the forms of decay—abandoned spurs and sidings, hundreds of miles of tracks choked with weeds, tattered freight houses, demolished passenger terminals, great name trains that have faded into the dark recesses of history.

But, in spite of it all, the railroad is still there, and it is as important to Chicago as it was in 1848 when a little woodburning locomotive called the *Pioneer* carried the first load of freight into the city from the Des Plaines River on the Galena and Chicago Union Railroad, predecessor of the now-mighty Chicago and North Western Railway. The city remains what Carl Sandburg called it, "player with railroads," "the nation's freight handler," "city of the big shoulders." Its thousands of miles of railroad tracks are still there; so too are its millions of carloads of freight passing through endless exchanges, transfers, and the tangled web of rail yards. Even if the railroad's presence is somewhat obscured since the disappearance of the iron horse, it continues to serve as the city's lifeblood—the arteries and capillaries which make life possible in a great metropolis.

The spirit of a place is in its memories. Chicago has always been a city of railroad memories. Historians will have theirs. They will remember William Butler Ogden and his long struggle to convince Chicagoans of the value of the railroad. They will remember the diminutive depot by the river where Ogden and John B. Turner, early presidents of the city's first railroad, watched from a cupola with a marine telescope for the arrival of the line's revenue cars. They will remember the great railroad wars of the 1850s, and the rush to reach Chicago from all points of the compass. They will remember the great Pullman strike of 1894.

But the memories that are most important are of a more personal nature. For so many years the railroad was *the* way to reach Chicago, and the railroad served up the essence of the city itself. Young Theodore Dreiser recalled his first trip to Chicago from his native Indiana in the 1880s as the very substance of adventure, as the most intense and wonderful experience of his life. Passing by the smooth, green fields and the soft, foggy groves near Valparaiso, he recalled his first glimpse of industrialized America. "In South Chicago the train was boarded by a crowd of Italians, Huns, Poles, Czechs, all chattering in their own tongue, their pipes smelling vilely." Then "the thousands of telephone and telegraph poles, the miles and miles of railroad yards and sidings, then the city itself and the great Union Depot on Canal Street, with its hurly burly of trunks and porters and bags, lines of busses and cabs outside."

Writers by the score have had their own impression of Chicago, the railroad town. John Gunther, Chicago born and bred, recalled the "automobile-like horns of the Illinois Central suburban trains," perhaps as they slipped through the fog by the lakeside during some early winter's night. Lucius Beebe, born to the comforts of Boston's Back Bay, recalled Chicago as the departure of the elegant *Twentieth Century Limited* from the grim and chaotic La Salle Street Station. He remembers boarding that greatest of all American name trains on a bleak winter's evening "while car tonks were thawing out the brake rigging with flares," and while "immaculate porters stood rigidly at attention as of old. . . . Through the gloom of the train shed, the cut flowers showed in the windows of the warmly lit club cars."

Many of those who experienced the railroad atmosphere, or came to Chicago by train, were not moved to thoughts of nostalgia. Some were impressed merely by smoke, and soot, and grime. But even these were impressed by some kind of strength, of magnitude, of greatness. The railroad in Chicago was always bigger than life. Chicago is a vast territory—everything from Racine to La Porte is Chicago, and over every mile of this vast territory one finds signs of railroad activity, or industries served by railroads or belt lines.

Chicago is a city of enormous railroad yards, of thousands of industrial sidings, of round-the-clock workers, of ever-changing moods. It is a city of exchanges, of spaghetti-bowl crossings, of interlocking towers. A city where the rails meet the waters. It is a city of drawbridges, sometimes keeping trains captive. It is a city of Winter, and one cannot help but think of the countless track workers attempting to keep switches unstuck as the most treacherous of winds and ice blow in off Lake Michigan.

Even if the railroad age is thought to be past, the visitor to Chicago cannot help but notice that thousands of humans still enter the city by railroad. Many of the long-distance passenger trains are gone, but passengers are not. Every weekday they come—the commuters—across the bridges at Madison or Adams, threading their way to the Loop from the trains of Union and Chicago and North Western Stations; they come back the same way in the evening, in waves, thousands upon thousands of railroad riders, all attesting to the fact that the railroad is not, after all, dead.

What follows is a history of Chicago as a railroad town. It is, of course, *a* history, not *the* history. That is to say, what I offer my readers is an essay, a series of historical sketches, which attempt to capture the flavor and spirit of a city and the instrument which brought it to greatness. A formal history of the railroad in Chicago would probably be of small value, and, except in my coverage of the very early period, I have not attempted anything of the sort. No, what matters to the general reader is a rendering of the things with the greatest commonality of interest. To this end I have offered a text and have selected pictures not for narrow technical concerns, but for the light they shed on everyday life and the broad sweep of human experience. Railroads are exciting. Chicago is exciting. It is my belief that these two lively partners grew up together and have provided some sparkling pages in the history of the United States.

CHAPTER 1

Old Roads to Fort Dearborn

Chicago was created by the railroads. Daniel H. Burnham, Chicago's great architect and city planner, had reason to know about that. He had spent years trying to figure out a way to draw the city's railroad passenger terminals into one convenient location—all to no avail. In 1910 the sheer immensity of such a project would stagger even the most forceful imagination. No one who visited Chicago during the days of steam, during the days of the iron horse, could fail to see that it was the railroad that had brought Chicago into being. It was always the most obvious and striking characteristic of the place. By sound, sight and smell, Chicago was a railroad town.

Chicago had to wait a long time for the railroad that created it. Before the railroad's coming, Chicago didn't amount to very much of anything at all. To be sure, the locale of present-day downtown Chicago had a long history of travel and human activity, but nothing that would hint at the present magnitude of things. In 1671 French missionaries established a meager outpost of French civilization on the site, called the Mission of the Guardian Angel. But this little endeavor was short-lived, and by the time of the American Revolution it was long gone.

But the spot itself obviously had something "natural" about it—there was a meeting of the waters as the Indians had discovered long before the paleface made his appearance. And Indian trails abounded near Chikagou (its name in the Potawatomi language)—in fact, trails in all directions. From ancient times, Chicago was a place where all roads seemed to meet. A site for powwows—for meetings and conventions, just as it is today.

But Chicago played no part in the early history of the United States. At a time when Boston and Philadelphia were already thriving metropolises, Chicago was nothing. There was no fort, there was no trading post, no holy father to save souls and baptize babies. An early traveler reported that the site of Chicago "offered but few features upon which the eye could dwell." The extensive collection of waters was unchecked by islands, and the scenery was uniform and monotonous, consisting of prairie and dismal swamp with here and there a few patches of scrubby woods.

Because of the original unattractiveness of the site, Chicago drew few early visitors during the period after the United States took over the Old Northwest—certainly few who wanted to stay. In 1800 there were only 2,500 people living in what came to be known as the Illinois country, and nearly all of these were in the southern part of the future state. Northern Illinois was far off the beaten track, and had few attractions. The outposts of civilization were to the south and huddled along the Mississippi River, below what is now St. Louis. These towns, with names like Cahokia, Kaskaskia and Prairie du Rocher were originally French. When the Anglo-Americans came in, it was because they had journeyed along the convenient waterways that led from the East.

Around 1800 there were only two ways for Americans to arrive in the Illinois country, and neither of these led anywhere near Chicago. One way was the Wilderness Road, over the Cumberland Gap to the Falls of the Ohio, after which the westward trip was made by flatboat. The other easy way to go (and by today's standards

2

Until long after the American Revolution, Chicago was far from the beaten path. Taking up residence anywhere in what was called the "Old Northwest" was not to be contemplated lightly by the faint at heart.

(University of Illinois Library)

it was far from easy) was by pack trail through the mountains to Pittsburgh or Wheeling and then down the Ohio River. Direct overland travel to Illinois was not dreamed of. It made no sense.

There was really very little reason for a settlement to exist at the mouth of the Chicago River in 1800. Nevertheless, a little fort was established there in 1803, and soon became known as Fort Dearborn. It was named after General Henry Dearborn, the Revolutionary War hero who was Secretary of War under Thomas Jefferson and the man who signed the order causing the fort to be built. The only excuse for having a fort at that site was as protection against the Indians and against the few trouble-making Britishers still left in the vicinity.

The original site of Fort Dearborn can be seen at the southwest corner of Michigan and Wacker in today's Chicago, and is identified by bronze markers on the sidewalk.* It was a place lacking in everything but military significance. The fort was out of reach and out of touch. Even the soldiers who were sent down from Detroit by an overland route took a long time on the way—35 days to be exact. It wasn't on the way to anything. The nearest post office was in Fort Wayne, 150 miles away. For a number of years after its establishment, the mail was brought into Fort Dearborn once a month by foot messenger—a very precarious occupation, since there were still plenty of hostile Indians around, to say nothing of wolves and bear.

As long as the only way to reach Chicago was by primitive trail there was no way that it could attract the amenities of civilized life, no way that a city could grow. The river towns along the Mississippi and Ohio soon prospered with a great increase of boat traffic either from the East or up from New Orleans, but Fort Dear-

*The markers are correctly placed, but are confusing to those who look at old prints which show the fort to be on the north bank of the river. In 1803 the mouth of the river was down by Madison Street.

The first house in Chicago was built by John Kinzie who came to Chicago in 1804 to trade with the Indians. In the early days, however, Kinzie lived in the fort. This house was probably not built until after the War of 1812.

(University of Illinois Library)

The original Fort Dearborn began to take form after 1803. Originally nothing but a fort surrounded by a log palisade, this little stronghold soon made civilian settlement possible. In time it also made possible one of the great cities of the world.

(Chicago Public Library)

4

born remained an outpost at the very edge of civilized life. For several decades the civilian population of Fort Dearborn remained close to zero, but even when it began to rise, the growth rate was for a long time unspectacular. A noted Chicago historian gives the following figures for the rise in the population of Chicago between 1829 and 1848:*

1829	30	1839	4,200
1830	40	1840	4,470
1831	60	1841	5,752
1832	150	1842	6,248
1833	350	1843	7,580
1834	1,800	1844	8,000
1835	3,265	1845	12,088
1836	3,820	1846	14,169
1837	4,170	1847	16,859
1838	4,000	1848	20,023

*Bessie Louise Pierce, *A History of Chicago*, Vol. I. New York: Alfred A. Knopf, 1937, p. 44.

The sudden spurt in growth seen in this table from 1834 on was due to the then-recent opening of the Erie Canal, which introduced a new and convenient means of transportation between the East and the West. The Erie Canal opened to travelers an all-water route between New York and Chicago, and for at least seven months of the year many weeks of travel time could be cut off the usual overland trip to the West.

At this time, one could not yet hope to travel west of Chicago by water, but the port of Chicago became almost immediately a focal point of interest. Between 1830 and 1833 gross tonnage on the Great Lakes tripled, and in the year 1833, for example, it was estimated that a

Travel to Chicago was far from luxurious for many years after the construction of the first settlements. This old sketch shows a Frink and Walker stage about to depart from the terminal at Lake and Dearborn Streets, probably about 1844. There were a number of stagecoach operators at this time, but Frink and Walker owned the largest fleet, with more than 2,000 miles of mail routes in the Midwest.

(Chicago Historical Society)

hundred passengers left Buffalo for the West, and perhaps a fifth of these eventually reached Chicago. Some were in transit for points farther west, but others stayed, swelling the population of the town, and immediately giving the place a name on the map.

And there was something else afoot at this time. Not only did Chicago quickly become the western terminus of Great Lakes travel, "canal fever" was spreading over the land. Successes like those of the Erie Canal in New York State suggested to the citizens of Illinois that they could have a canal of their own connecting the Chicago and Illinois rivers. Shortly after the War of 1812, President James Madison proposed just such a waterway to Congress, and every governor of Illinois following its admission to statehood in 1818 urged the construction of this canal. All believed it to be a matter of utmost importance. In fact, the canal project is responsible for Chicago and the northern counties of Illinois being included in the state of Illinois today. Had it not been for the hoped-for benefits of this scheme, the northern counties of Illinois might well have melted into Wisconsin.

Long before the coming of the railroad, Chicago was an important port and center of shipping. The proposed construction of the Illinois and Michigan Canal, that would link the Great Lakes and the Mississippi, had a great deal to do with rapid settlement and rising land values in the city, most especially along the Chicago River.

(Chicago Public Library)

A fanciful early drawing entitled "American Progress," originally published in Crofutt's *New Overland Tourist and Pacific Coast Guide* in 1883, vividly illustrates the significance Americans had come to place on transportation in all its forms. Chicago, and the vast Midwest generally, had been witnesses to all of these forms of transportation in the course of only a few decades.
(University of Illinois Library)

Even so, the canal was a long time in coming. It did not actually open until 1848, and by that time its usefulness had diminished a great deal since the advent of the railroad. The promise of the canal, the believed importance of it, was of more significance to Chicago than the actual event itself.

All of a sudden overland travel reentered the picture. If all waterways were pointing toward Chicago, so were all roads. When Fort Dearborn was built in 1803, it took weeks of travel along primitive paths to get from the Indiana settlements to Chicago. Now real roads, even if very primitive ones, needed to be constructed. "Hubbard's Trace," north of Danville,

became a state road in 1834, and almost immediately began serving as the main artery of travel from the Wabash country to Chicago. This old state road in time became State Street, perhaps the best-known street in Chicago to this day.

This same year activity increased in the northwestern corner of Illinois at Galena. Fresh discoveries of lead near Galena made the heart of the "Black Hawk country" an almost immediate goal for miners and speculators. Since travel on the Mississippi was not possible all year round, it was soon perceived that some kind of road between Galena and Chicago was absolutely essential. A wagon road opened the way between Galena and Chicago in 1832. At this time, and for the next decade, Galena rivaled Chicago as the queen city of northern Illinois. In this period its mining operations were the most extensive in the West and its trade actually surpassed that of Chicago until 1842.

Another wagon trail of this period was that between Bloomington and Chicago, long known as the "Old Chicago Trail." This trail was broken in 1833, the same year that Chicago was officially organized as a town. To Chicagoans this road was known as Archer's Road. And just as the northerly end of "Hubbard's Trace" became State Street, so Archer's Road became Archer Avenue, to this day one of Chicago's more prominent thoroughfares.

Soon there would be other roads leading everywhere, eventually improved to provide for the passage of stagecoaches, wagons, and freight traffic of all sorts. But none of this meant that Chicago had yet become a place of sophistication and refinement, a real city. As late as 1833 an English traveler referred to Chicago as "one chaos of mud, rubbish and confusion." For another decade the main characteristic of the future great metropolis was one of uncouth drovers coming into town in muddied wagons, pushing before them cattle, sheep and hogs from the Salt Creek country or elsewhere in the hinterlands. The town itself was mostly one of rude log cabins and mud huts.

Still, in spite of the primitive quality of the place in the 1830s, almost everybody around the country, including Chicagoans, knew that the dirty bustling town was marked for bigger things. In 1833 the United States government built a lighthouse there and the following year appropriated $25,000 for the construction of a decent harbor at Chicago. In the few years preceding the Panic of 1837 there was a land-lot craze in Chicago, with lots being sold for as much as $22,000. This made Chicago a place of infinite attractiveness both to Eastern speculators and to new residents, who continued to pour into the city, even after the bubble had burst and prices were deflated.

No matter what happened in the financial circles of the nation, and in spite of the agonies of boom and bust, it was clear by the late 1830s that Chicago was going to amount to something big, and very shortly. By 1840 Chicago was still a place of log cabins and muddy streets, with pigs and chickens following rude Western barbarians up and down the byways. But the young people growing up in these very log cabins would live to see the day when their home town would become one of the largest cities of the world.

The agency that would bring this great metropolis into being was just around the corner.

CHAPTER 2

The Coming of the Railroad: A Man and His Dream

In the year 1835 there was neither a mile of railroad, nor a charter to build one anywhere in the state of Illinois. But railroads were beginning to sprout up in the East, and enthusiasm for them spread widely as soon as their advantages were understood. As early as 1831, in fact, there were a few people around who thought that northern Illinois would be better off with a railroad than a canal. No less a personage than James M. Bucklin, chief engineer of the projected Illinois and Michigan Canal, had surveyed two alternate routes: one for the canal, which he thought would cost $100,000 a mile; and one for a railroad, which he thought would cost only $25,000 a mile.

Unfortunately, in the early 1830s, canals were in the ascendancy. Railroads were still objects of mystery and suspicion, whereas the canals had already proved themselves to some extent. For a while there was a certain amount of hot debate about the relative merits of canal versus railroad, but for the time being the canal won. Construction on the Illinois and Michigan Canal was therefore begun in 1836—though lack of funds, political wranglings and various misadventures would delay its completion until 1848, by which time the competing railroads were almost strong enough to kill off the canal.

The railroad idea did not stay dead very long in Illinois. As early as 1832, the year of the Black Hawk War, Alexander M. Jenkins, Speaker of the Illinois House of Representatives, proposed a "central" Illinois railroad that would link the waters of the Ohio and Mississippi rivers in southern Illinois (at Cairo) with the proposed Illinois and Michigan Canal. For a few years nothing came of this, but by 1835 people were becoming enthusiastic about the railroad. In that year a bill to grant a charter for a "central" railroad was introduced in the legislature, and among its supporters were Speaker Jenkins, a young legislator from Sangamon County named Abraham Lincoln, and Judge Sidney A. Breese of Carlyle (who later on, as United States Senator from Illinois, supported the land-grant idea which, in time, made the actual construction of the Illinois Central Railroad possible). The bill creating the charter for the first railroads in Illinois was passed very quickly on the strength of this support, in January 1836.

Unfortunately, for all of the railroad fever, railroads did not immediately spring into existence. They existed mostly in men's minds and on fancy-looking charter paper. The Panic of 1837 dashed a great many hopes, and among these were the extravagant railroad schemes that had taken hold of people's imaginations. Before the Panic set in there had been a number of charters granted (including one for the first railroad in Chicago), but these all came to nought when the money supply dried up. Charters, charters everywhere, but nary a penny to lay a mile of track.

By the time the Panic of 1837 came along, only one short line of railroad had actually been funded in Illinois. This was a 24-mile stretch between the Illinois River at Meredosia and Jacksonville in the central part of the state. (The

William Butler Ogden, the man who dreamed of a great Chicago. Ogden was not only the first Mayor of the City of Chicago but the founder and moving spirit behind the city's first railroad, the Chicago and Galena Union Railroad (forerunner of the Chicago and North Western). A greater visionary and organizer of men and ideas Chicago has probably never known.

(University of Illinois Library)

eventual aim of this railroad was to bisect the state from East to West.) The first rail ever laid in the State of Illinois went down on May 9, 1838, in Meredosia in Morgan County, but no regular train service was begun until the following year. During this period, 12 miles of tracks were built from Meredosia to Morgan City.

The first locomotive engine ever to turn a wheel in the State of Illinois was the "Rogers," built by the Rogers Locomotive and Machine Works of Paterson, New Jersey. The "Rogers" came from New Jersey to the middle of Illinois by water. It was shipped to New Orleans by sailing vessel and then came up the Mississippi and Illinois rivers by barge to Meredosia, where it was first placed on the track and put in operation on November 8, 1838.

But where in the rail scene did this trifling little line leave Chicago? As yet, nowhere. Nonetheless, when the first round of charters was drawn up in 1836, Chicago was not left out. Certain of its citizens were already conscious of the future possibilities of railroads and they drew up a charter for a railroad to be called the Galena and Chicago Union Railroad. Their purpose was to build a railroad from Chicago out into the prairie country, towards, if not to, the Mississippi River, at some spot near the lead mines of Galena. The charter specifically called for a railroad "from Galena in Jo Daviess County to the Town of Chicago," and fixed the capital stock at $100,000.

The idea was a good one, but alas, it still remained nothing but a piece of paper. After a year a survey of a feasible route was authorized, and an engineer by the name of James Seymore carried out a preliminary survey between the foot of North Dearborn Street and the Des Plaines River. But it did not lead to construction. Later on, additional funds were obtained to make a complete survey of the whole railroad, but the Panic of 1837 had put construction out of the question. The Galena and Chicago Union Railroad would remain nothing but an idea for a long time to come. It was not precisely that all faith had been lost in the idea of a railroad from Chicago to Galena, it was just that no one had a major commitment to the project. Someone was needed who would push for the railroad in a big way, and Chicago just didn't seem to have anyone who cared that much.

But quite suddenly it did. The time for Chicago's first great visionary was at hand. This role was dynamically filled by William Butler Ogden, a newcomer to the city, but also the first of Chicago's citizens to be totally committed to the railroad. While most of the elders of the city were hemming and hawing over the relative advantages of canals, plank roads, toll roads, and the like, as a way to link Chicago and the inland territories, Ogden immediately perceived that the railroad was precisely what Chicago needed.

William Butler Ogden had been born in Delaware County, New York, in 1805, and had grown to maturity in that state while Eleazar Lord and Benjamin Loder were pushing forward their rail route between the Hudson River and the Great Lakes—the railroad that later became the Erie. Ogden had seen that railroad built, and he knew its virtues—unlike most Chicagoans of the 1830s, to whom a railroad was nothing but a distant mechanical toy.

Ogden's reason for coming to Chicago had nothing to do with the railroad, but with the land boom. His brother-in-law Charles Butler had come to Chicago from New York in 1832 and had purchased 182 acres of land on the north side of the Chicago River. It immediately became obvious to Butler that this land was going to become extremely valuable, and that speculation in Chicago real estate would quickly make any Eastern investor wealthy. With this belief he tempted his brother-in-law, William Butler Ogden, to come to Chicago to look after and subdivide this acreage and perhaps do a little speculating of his own.

Ogden came, although in the beginning he was contemptuous of the sort of wild land speculation that was going on in the West in general and in Chicago in particular. Ogden was clearly a solid citizen and he almost immediately became one of the leading lights of the town. He involved himself in real estate and financial transactions of all sorts, and within a few years had set up a general land agency to care for and sell real estate in Illinois, Wisconsin, western Michigan and northern Indiana. His wisdom and leadership qualities were widely recognized, and he was elected the first Mayor of Chicago when the city was incorporated in 1837. (The vote in that first primitive election was: William Butler Ogden, Democrat, 489; John H. Kinzie, Whig, 289.)

But it was Ogden the land developer, not Ogden the politician, who was responsible for the birth of the railroad. Ogden was not rooted to his office in Chicago. His pursuit of real estate deals had him wandering up and down the countryside in what was then known as the Old Northwest—especially northern Illinois and southern Wisconsin. Ogden knew what was going on out there. He knew what the farmers were thinking; he knew what had to be done. Almost immediately, he was struck by the obvious necessity of an efficient form of inland transportation. There had to be better ways for farmers to get their products to market, and there had to be a place for great markets to grow—a central marketplace and transportation hub. And what better place than the rapidly growing village at the mouth of the Chicago River—Ogden's own town of Chicago.

Thus it was that Ogden's mind turned to the possibility of doing something to revitalize that half-dead charter of the Galena and Chicago Union Railroad. The charter was there; some surveying had been done. Now all that was necessary was to open up the subscription books and start raising the capital. Surely the money would start flowing in as soon as the Chicago city fathers and the farmers out in the hinterlands had in their heads the same dream that Ogden was now dreaming daily—the railroad as the chosen form of transportation; railroads all leading to a very convenient rail center—Chicago. And why shouldn't it be Chicago?

All this was easier said than done. As it turned out, the money did not come pouring in. Somebody had to go out and convince the populace that the railroad was a good idea and not just a will-o'-the-wisp. What the railroad needed was a good spokesman, a good public relations man. That person was William Butler Ogden.

Ogden's involvement did not start immediately after his election as Mayor of Chicago. In fact, 10 long years were to pass before anything was really done to revive the sickly charter of the Galena. The company had been established in 1836, and continued to elect presidents and hold meetings, but nary a mile of railroad track was laid. Not, that is, until February 17, 1846, when Ogden assumed the presidency of the railroad and immediately began to do what should have been done a decade earlier—raise the funds necessary for construction. Under Ogden's leadership, the Galena Company issued a prospectus, and on August 10, 1847, opened stock books for subscriptions for the capital stock in the company, announcing a firm intention to build a road that would be part of a "great line of railroad between the Atlantic and the Mississippi."

Ogden and the Galena directors were firmly convinced that the railroad's time had come, and that all they had to do was sit back and wait for the subscriptions to roll in. But once more they were in for a rude disappointment. There did seem to be a mild interest, but within the city of Chicago itself, hardly any at all. Butler and another strong railroad partisan by the name of Jonathan Young Scammon held meetings, met with merchants and leading citizens, traveled everywhere. But they discovered, much to their surprise, that other Chicagoans were not as impressed with the idea of the railroad as they were themselves and as they assumed everyone else would be.

There were some new flies in the ointment too. One was a flash-in-the-pan scheme that had caught the public's imagination in the early 1840s—the plank road. Plank roads had been introduced in Canada in 1836, and the idea quickly spread to the United States. It went over big in northern Illinois. The first plank road out of Chicago was built in 1848 and forged through the nine-mile swamp to Riverside. The road cost $16,000 to build, and when it was opened the receipts for the first month were $1,600.* In no time at all there sprang up a whole network of these plank roads near Chicago, and they proved very popular with travelers and farmers who were sick and tired of having their wagons stuck in the mud. The main justification for the railroad had been that it would help farmers bring their products to market, but already there was this new development, which promised to do the same thing at reasonable expense.

Plank roads were usually constructed of oak or walnut—whatever was available locally—and were generally eight feet wide, laid on crossties. For a few years they were almost universally thought to be the answer to the transportation problems of the Midwest. Within two years of their construction the Chicago roads were paying dividends of 30 to 40 percent. This, said the editor of the Chicago *Democrat*, was "the best investment afloat."

Over the long term, however, plank roads were not to be quite so successful. They were very useable when first built, but they deteriorated quickly, and the owning companies had given little if any thought to maintenance costs. Few plank roads lasted more than 10 years. In the swampland they floated away, or were buried in mud, making travel as bad as that endured on the older roads they were supposed to replace. Or the planks themselves were carried away by settlers who used them to build their log cabins. Even if these physical problems could

---

*Plank roads were toll roads: the toll for a four-horse team was 37½ cents; for a single team 25 cents; and for a horseback rider 12½ cents.

have been overcome, there would be no speedy means of conveyance over the roads, and the load weight for wagons was severely restricted.

These defects were not immediately obvious, however. So, when Ogden and his colleagues went to the merchants of Chicago in 1848, at the height of the plank roads' popularity, they met with determined opposition. Chicago was doing just fine with plank roads. Sometimes as many as two hundred wagons a day were coming into the city. Chicago was becoming the great transportation hub of the Midwest, and the plank roads were making it that way. Furthermore, Chicago merchants were afraid of the railroad, afraid that it would allow farmers to ship their products to the city while staying home themselves. This would be bad for business. Chicago was a retail town, too, it was argued. The whole idea was to force the farmers to come to Chicago—to patronize local stores, saloons and watering places.

And there was another objection. Chicago merchants felt that the railroad might not only prevent the farmers from coming to town, but that it might also keep them from sending their products to Chicago at all. Other towns, railroad towns, might spring up and divert traffic from Chicago. No, the railroad was a distant threat to Chicago both as a retail town and as a transportation center! Everybody was thriving, everybody was getting rich. Why argue with success?

But Ogden knew he was right. He knew that Chicago wasn't going to go anywhere in the middle of the nineteenth century without the kind of transportation that had a solid future. He knew that he could get his railroad subscrip-

tion books fattened up if only he could persuade the right people to listen. And, for the moment, the only people who would listen were the farmers. Hang the dullards in the city! Ogden got out on the road with his horse and buggy and visited every village and hamlet along the proposed route. He talked to farmers in their homes, at town meetings, at any crossroads where he could find anyone willing to listen,—always talking up the railroad as the only modern and efficient means of shipment.

Yes, the farmers listened. They agreed with Ogden. By April 1, 1848, Ogden and his friends had located 126 subscribers, and had sold stock worth $351,800, mostly to people who lived in the area through which the railroad would pass. But Ogden didn't even wait for all that money to start rolling in. Almost immediately, he had the route surveyed and set workmen to the job of laying rails. If you wanted to prove the value of the railroad, he thought, there was nothing better than to build one and show what it could do. Even before he had the money in his hands, William Butler Ogden, the newly elected president of the Galena and Chicago Union Railroad, was letting contracts for the construction of a railroad. The contract for the first seven miles west of Chicago was let in the fall of 1847; the contract for the second section, another 31 miles to the west, was let in March 1848. By the fall of this same year, Ogden was ready to start operating his railroad.

According to the *Chicago Journal*, "the first shipment of goods over the Galena Railroad was made by one W. Smith, whose store was at 143 Water Street, and who forwarded a number of boxes of goods for DuPage County by the train

Chicago's first railway locomotive was this 10-ton woodburning midget *Pioneer* built in Philadelphia by the Baldwin Locomotive Works. Its wheels first turned in Chicago on October 24, 1848. In spite of its diminutive size, the locomotive remained in service on the Chicago and North Western for many years. It is now on permanent exhibit at the Chicago Historical Society.

(Smithsonian Institution)

which left here on December 18, 1848." Right after this the freight started coming in. Before the railroad was built further west than the Des Plaines River, farmers were bringing their products to the Des Plaines depot for shipment to Chicago. In a matter of weeks there were big carloads of wheat waiting at the Des Plaines depot for forwarding to Chicago. Almost immediately, Chicago merchants, who had enacted an ordinance that would have prevented the Galena from building any kind of depot within the city limits of Chicago, had a change of heart. When they heard of those carloads of wheat waiting for transport to their city, they suddenly lifted the ordinance and begged to get into the act as stockholders and shippers. In a matter of months, plank roads were out and the railroad

was in. Railroad fever spread everywhere, and Chicagoans pointed with pride to their erstwhile mayor, now destined to be their very own railroad pioneer. Ogden had been right all along: Chicago was a natural as the rail capital of the Midwest.

In the long sweep of history, the growth of the Galena and Chicago Union Railroad does not seem to have been swift or spectacular. The line moved westward, slowly, tentatively. Little feeder lines were built, and changes were made in the determination of where the line would end. But from a technical point of view the little railroad was ready for business from the start. Tracks were laid rapidly, and the company quickly took steps to acquire equipment and build facilities along the right-of-way. By the end of 1849 it had already acquired three loco-

Chicago's first locomotive engineer was John Ebbert, shown here in formal portrait with his wife. Ebbert continued in the employ of the C&NW for many years and lived to exhibit the *Pioneer* at the great Columbian Exhibition in 1893.

(Midwest Railway Historical Society)

The first permanent passenger station of the Chicago and North Western was this stone structure on Wells Street. It was built in 1852-53, but enlarged and improved in 1863. It was, however, destroyed in the Chicago fire of 1871. It was then temporarily replaced by a wooden shed until the opening of a large and impressive station at the same site in 1881.
(Chicago and North Western Railroad)

and Turner saw no need to press on to that Mississippi River town. Instead, in the late 1850s and early 1860s the Galena line drove on to the Mississippi River at Fulton. Another spur left this main line at a place called Turner's Junction and struck out for Freeport. This line, in turn, connected with another branch to Beloit, Wisconsin. This same line, perhaps more than any other, was to put big thoughts in Ogden's mind. The State of Wisconsin was now anxious to get into the railroad business and chartered a railroad to run between Beloit and Madison. In due course, this road, which from the very first was assumed to be a feeder line for the Galena, came

under the influence of the larger road to the south.

But there was even more happening in Wisconsin, which brought William Butler Ogden back to railroading in a big way. While men like Scammon, Turner and Newberry were keeping the Galena spinning forward like a top, Ogden was watching with fascination as the State of Wisconsin was chartering some new lines that showed great signs of promise. One was the Chicago, St. Paul and Fond du Lac Railroad, the ultimate purpose of which was to connect Chicago and Green Bay. This road succeeded in firing Ogden's imagination, and in the financial Panic of 1857 he managed to lay hands on it. Here again he was taking over a railroad that was not completely built and not well managed, but it represented the inception of a great new dream.

It was a dream not just of Green Bay, but also of the land to the north generally. The great steel reserves of northern Minnesota were now well known. Northern Wisconsin and Minnesota were growing apace. The little hamlet of Pig's Eye on the Mississippi had changed its name to the more civilized St. Paul, and showed signs of becoming a metropolis to be reckoned with. And, yes, things were bustling still farther to the West—in Iowa and the Nebraska Territory. Ogden's new railroad venture must have stirred him to thoughts of even greater glory in these western farmlands.

When Ogden, with the help of his famous New York lawyer, Samuel J. Tilden, acquired the Fond du Lac line in 1859, he quite wisely selected for it a new name that expressed his desires for the future—the Chicago and North Western Railway Company. Under this title the Fond du Lac was reorganized on June 7 of that year. In a way, the few years that followed seemed to be repetitions of the early years of the Galena, with Ogden using his great powers of persuasion out along the proposed line to raise the money to build a railroad all the way to Green Bay. At first people up near Green Bay weren't sure that they wanted to have a railroad. But it wasn't long before Will Ogden *told* them what they wanted.

Almost overnight, William Butler Ogden was the most celebrated railroad man in the West. He was the first person anyone thought of when they envisioned railroads crossing the wide-open spaces. When the Union Pacific Railroad was chartered in 1862, with the aim of building a railroad from Nebraska to Nevada, it was only natural that William Butler Ogden should be elected president of that railroad also. Two years later there appeared the first great railroad consolidation in the land. Two Ogden railroads, the Galena and Chicago Union Railroad and the Chicago and North Western Railway, joined into one, dropping the undescriptive Galena name in favor of the more venturesome and visionary name—the Chicago and North Western Railway. And the first president of this great new consolidated line was William Butler Ogden. From being boss of a 7-mile railroad in 1848, William Butler Ogden found himself in charge of a vast 860-mile system that was already nearly bursting at the seams with the promise of even larger growth.

This vast network of rails all led to Chicago. Chicago was the place where one began the trek west—the jumping-off place. A great and awe-inspiring network of rails spread out from Chicago, almost like those which had emanated from New York, Philadelphia and Baltimore a generation earlier. Strictly speaking, all of these later roads were constructed into Chicago; it was only the original Galena line which started from Chicago and built outward. However one puts it, Chicago was the hub, the center from which the western railroad industry was growing.

Of course not all of the early railroad endeavors in Chicago were those of the North Western. Long before the great North Western consolidation of 1864, the Illinois Central had

THE CHICAGO & NORTH-WESTERN RAILWAY CREATED

The following circular, issued by President William Butler Ogden, announced the union of the Galena & Chicago Union Railroad and the Chicago and North-Western Railway into a new 860-mile system on June 3, 1864:

OFFICE CHICAGO & NORTH-WESTERN RAILWAY COMPANY
CHICAGO, June 10, 1864.

NOTICE

WHEREAS, The Galena & Chicago Union Railroad Company and the Chicago and North-Western Railway Company were, on the 3rd of June, 1864, duly consolidated into one Company, under the name, style and title of the "Chicago & North-Western Railway Co."

And whereas, The Board of Directors of said consolidated Company have duly elected and appointed the following general officers, to-wit:
W. B. OGDEN, President.
PERRY H. SMITH, Vice-President.
GEORGE H. DUNLAP, General Superintendent.
WILLIAM H. FERRY, Acting Director of the Galena Division.
GEORGE P. LEE, Treasurer.
HENRY TUCKER, Assistant Treasurer.
JAMES R. YOUNG, Secretary.

Now, therefore, by authority and direction of the Board of Directors of said Consolidated "Chicago & North-Western Railway Company," notice is hereby given to all officers and employees of said Company, and to all parties having business relations with said Company, that the lines of road heretofore comprising the Galena & Chicago Union Railroad Company, and the lines of railroad operated by said Company under lease or otherwise, and the lines of railroad heretofore comprising the Chicago & North-Western Railway Company, together with all the property, assets and effects of said respective companies, having been consolidated as aforesaid into one Corporation and Company, under the management and control of one Board of Directors and of the officers above named; the orders and instructions of said officers will be observed and respected accordingly.

W. B. OGDEN.
President Chicago & North-Western Railway Co.

made its entry into Chicago (although this was not yet the Illinois Central main line, but only a "branch." Other roads were arriving as well.

Still, it was the North Western and its predecessors that brought the flavor and ambience of a railroad town to Chicago. Under the leader-

ship of Ogden, the North Western became a big owner of Chicago real estate and the prominence of its properties near the Chicago River was a singular characteristic of the city in the late nineteenth century.

Before the Great Fire of 1871 destroyed a great many railroad properties, the North Western had built a number of interesting buildings in Chicago. Their appearance and proliferation was indicative of the rapid growth of the railroad at this time in American history. The very first railroad building to be erected in Chicago was an engine house and shop built on a lot owned by the company on the north branch of the Chicago River. This building, erected in 1848 at a cost of $1,200, had space in it for two engines. The shop was supplied by water from an aqueduct that sloped down to the river. In a report to the board of directors and president that year, the second fiscal year of the company, the superintendent of the road reported that the company owned the following equipment: "six four-wheeled and six eight-wheeled platform cars, three four-wheeled and four eight-wheeled covered freight cars, two hand and small gravel

cars and one second-hand engine with which to continue the construction of the road and to transport all of its traffic." Two more locomotives would arrive during the year 1849, and this would pretty well stretch the resources of this very primitive engine house.

More building in Chicago was to come in 1850. At this time the North Western built a freight house of 50 by 100 feet, along with an addition to the engine house, a smith shop, a car shop and a wharf on the river next to the company's facilities whereby freight-waterway transfers could be made with ease. None of these buildings would be adequate for very long, however. In the summer of 1849 the Galena acquired its first passenger car, and passenger service commenced almost immediately. Additional cars were acquired, and passenger service between Chicago and St. Charles, Ill., was in full swing by December of that year.

The new passenger business made it imperative that something be done with the original depot to make it suitable for all the purposes of the company. This building, which stood on a triangular piece of land west of Canal and south of Kinzie streets, was at first intended for freight alone. In 1849 it was elongated, the west end being used for freight, the nearer-in east end being used for passengers. A second floor was also added and this served for company offices. Early pictures of this building with the additions show that it also contained a cupola or observatory. Legend has it that North Western executives like Ogden and John B. Turner could look out to the vast open prairie to the west and monitor railroad operations out of the city. It is said that John Turner had a large marine telescope with which he could look down the line. In the flat and open country of that now-distant time, he could detect the presence of a train as distant as Austin, six miles away, and announce to eager shippers and spectators the arrival of the company's revenue cars.

In looking back historically over the origins and development of Chicago's own railroad, the Chicago and North Western Railway, it is sometimes easy to forget that the consolidation of 1864 merged *several* railroads which had properties and depots in Chicago. In the period before 1880, at which time a great central terminal was built on Wells Street, North Western trains arrived at a number of different terminals. Trains

Before the great acts of consolidation, there were several passenger stations serving lines that would in time become part of the Chicago and North Western System. This curious looking depot was called the Kinzie St. Depot and was built in 1856. It brought passengers from the Chicago, St. Paul, and Fond du Lac Railroad to the edge of the north branch of the Chicago River. The station remained in service until the opening of the Wells Street Station in 1881. This building was then moved to another location and was used as a warehouse until well into the twentieth century. (Chicago and North Western Railroad)

24

Like most railroads in the nineteenth century, the Chicago and North Western did not quickly abandon useful locomotives. Its very first locomotive, the *Pioneer,* remained in service for many years, and may be seen here with a construction gang in 1869.
(University of Illinois Library)

from the west (on the old Galena line) came in at one terminal, while trains from the north (the Chicago, St. Paul & Fond du Lac Railroad) arrived at another. Altogether there were seven different stations in use for passenger service before the construction of the Wells Street Station.

The depots built before the 1871 Chicago Fire to accommodate trains from several different directions were a strong reminder of another major role played by the North Western in Chicago history. The North Western has always been a great commuter railroad, and, to this day, maintains the largest volume of commuter business in the Chicago area. Commuter traffic

dates back a long way. It might be safe to say there could have been some small commuter traffic to the west on the Galena, right after it started in the passenger business in 1849. The first of the present North Western lines to get into commuting on a large scale was the present North line, which was not yet a part of the North Western at the time of the consolidation in 1864. By the time this line was taken over by the North Western it was already doing a brisk business serving commuters in the little communities between Chicago and Evanston (now all a part of Chicago). This line was also beginning to serve a number of communities in Lake County up to the Wisconsin border. Originally this North line was called the Chicago and Milwaukee Railroad, and it extended train service to Waukegan by 1854 and to Milwaukee the following year. This line had built its own Chicago terminal in 1855, as would be expected. When the road was acquired by the North Western its terminal was abandoned in favor of the larger, consolidated terminals of the parent company.

William Butler Ogden gave up the presidency of the Chicago and North Western Railway in 1868, four years after he had brought together his two beloved railroads in a single 860-mile system. But in the first four years after the consolidation many hundreds of miles of new rail lines were either constructed, or, like the Chicago and Milwaukee Railroad, added by further consolidation. Although Ogden lived to see the day when nearly all of the railroad's Chicago properties were destroyed by fire (he had retired

to a mansion in New York by this time), he was one of the first to say, after the Great Fire of 1871, that Chicago should be rebuilt and on a greater, more modern, more magnificent scale than anything dreamed of before. In Ogden's mind the reason for this was obvious. You could burn down a railroad's depots and freight houses, but you couldn't burn down a railroad. By 1871 there were not just one or two or several lines leading to Chicago, but lines by the dozens. When Chicago burned to the ground it was not gone at all; its reason for being was still there. In no time the trains were running again; new and better depots were going up; and people were saying, now more than ever, that Chicago *had* to be rebuilt because it was the city's destiny to be the rail center of America. The rails all led to Chicago, so there must be a Chicago for them to enter. Nothing could have been more natural or necessary. The next decade would see an even

This is a map of the Galena and Chicago Union Railroad at the time of the consolidation with the Chicago and North Western Railroad in 1864. At the time of the merger the total extent of the Galena was 294 miles.

(Chicago and North Western Railroad)

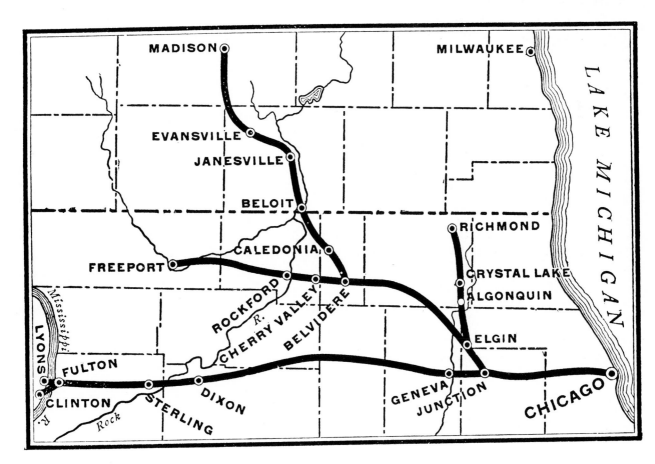

In the very beginning the Midwestern roads had to import their locomotives. But after a while they did a little locomotive building of their own. Here is the *John B. Turner*, which the Chicago and North Western built in its own shops in 1867. The locomotive not only bears the name of the line's distinguished early president, but also displays his portrait on the side of the lantern.

(John H. White, Jr.)

more incredible growth in railroad traffic and mileage. Ogden died on August 3, 1877, and thus did not see his city's resurgence. But of course he had known it was coming. He always knew what was coming for Chicago. He knew this because he dreamed and willed it. As a Chicago historian of the next decade wrote:

To the Citizens of Chicago and the People of the Northwest: Would you behold William Butler Ogden's monument, look around you!

—History of Chicago, *by A. T. Andreas (1884)*

CHAPTER 3

How the Big Roads Came

In the years immediately after the first laying of rail on the Galena and Chicago Union Railroad one might have expected a great spurt of railroad activity both to and from the burgeoning lakeside metropolis of Chicago. That is what everyone wanted, what everyone expected. But reality was somewhat different. Consider the case of John Murray Forbes, for example. Forbes, a shrewd New Englander who was taking control of the destinies of the Michigan Central, saw that a rail route between Detroit and Chicago was preferable to the tedious water route. He and a number of his colleagues and competitors put up the immediate cry, "On to Chicago!" But getting to Chicago was not as easy as it seemed.

The history of the railroad in Chicago in the three or four decades after 1848 is a rather curious one. Some railroads made their way to Chicago with astonishing quickness. Such was the case with the Illinois Central, although Chicago was at first only one end of a "branch" line. The main line ran from the southern tip of Illinois to Dunleith near Galena. Other railroads that later became famous names in the Chicago rail scene were not so quick to arrive. These included the three great Eastern roads—the New York Central, the Pennsylvania, and the Baltimore and Ohio—all of which were chartered to serve only their own Eastern regions. To get to Chicago they had to acquire other railroads west of the Appalachians, and many of these were poorly financed or poorly managed. That very early Eastern railroad, the Erie, had to overcome both its eccentric 6-foot gauge and the financial escapades of such chaps as "Uncle Dan'l" Drew, Jim Fisk and Jay Gould. Still other railroads, like

the Santa Fe, had to fight back the competition and found their entry into the great rail center blocked for many long years.

No railroad (other than the Chicago and North Western) has been more closely identified with Chicago than the Illinois Central. The Illinois Central got off the ground a bit later than Mr. Ogden's little prodigy, but when it did, it nearly exploded into being. In a few short years it had breathed life into the whole state of Illinois and brought thousands of new residents pouring into the state from all points of the compass.

The Illinois Central story is a remarkable one in the history of the United States because, like no other railroad before it, the railroad created the territory through which it ran. When the Baltimore and Ohio struck out from Baltimore the aim was to make transportation possible to the settlements in the West. The Illinois Central, on the other hand, was conceived as a way of cutting through the vast wilderness of the state and making human habitation possible—and desirable. The Illinois Central project was an act of colonization.

This giant colonization effort was not the dream of a small group of visionaries and local supporters but an act of the Congress of the United States. A bill sponsored in the United States Senate by Senator Stephen A. Douglas made possible a railroad that would be built by the sale of 11,500,000 acres of unoccupied public lands in the state. The idea was that the railroad could sell the lands granted to it and use the proceeds for construction. The land thus sold would presumably be settled and thus add to the taxable wealth of the State of Illinois. The largesse

"Chicago the crossroads of transportation" was already a popular notion in 1850. But in that year the city had only a single rail line, the still diminutive Galena and Chicago Union Railroad. But all this would soon change. Two years later, in 1852, a number of lines from the East, West and South were fighting each other for entry to the city, and the railroad age was underway with a vengeance.

(Harvard University Press)

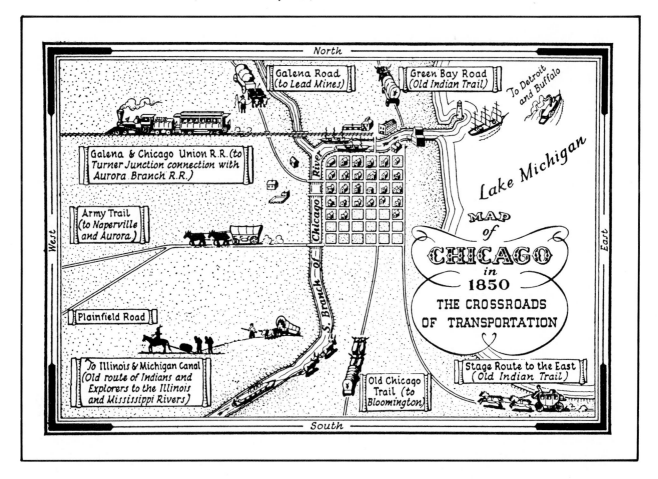

of the United States government would thus be a double advantage to the State of Illinois.

The act, as finally signed by President Millard Fillmore on September 20, 1850, called for a railroad that would extend from a place near the junction of the Ohio and Mississippi rivers to the western end of the Illinois and Michigan Canal at Peru or La Salle, with two branches from there, one to the northwest corner of the state opposite Dubuque, Iowa, and another to Chicago. When a charter for this railroad was later granted by the Illinois legislature, there was authority to build and operate a railroad 705

miles in length—and this would be a railroad twice the length of any railroad existing in the United States at that time.

Among the provisions of the gift of public lands from the United States (and some of these would cost the Illinois Central Railroad dearly in

The Illinois Central was the largest enterprise in railroading during the 1850s. It began as an act of colonization, as this broadside shows, and perhaps no railroad in American history was more clearly responsible for the growth and development of the territory through which it ran.

(Illinois Central Gulf)

THE FINEST FARMING LANDS

CORN COTTON FRUITS & VEGETABLES

EQUAL TO ANY IN THE WORLD!!!

MAY BE PROCURED

AT FROM $6 TO $12 PER ACRE,

Near Markets, Schools, Railroads, Churches, and all the blessings of Civilization.

1,200,000 Acres in Farms of 40, 80, 120, 160 Acres and upwards, in ILLINOIS, the Garden State of America.

The Illinois Central Railroad Company offer, on LONG CREDIT, the beautiful and fertile PRAIRIE LANDS lying along the whole line of their Railroad, 700 MILES IN LENGTH, upon the most Favorable Terms for enabling Farmers, Manufacturers, Mechanics, and Workingmen, to make for themselves and their families a competency, and a home they can call Their Own.

ILLINOIS

Is about equal in extent to England, with a population of 1,722,666, and a soil capable of supporting 20,000,000. No State in the valley of the Mississippi offers so great an inducement to the settler as the State of Illinois. There is no part of the world where all the conditions of climate and soil so admirably combine to produce those two great staples, CORN and WHEAT.

CLIMATE.

Nowhere can the industrious farmer secure such immediate results from his labor as on these deep, rich, loamy soils, cultivated with so much ease. The climate from the extreme southern part of the State to the Terre Haute, Alton and St. Louis Railroad, a distance of nearly 200 miles, is well adapted to Winter

WHEAT. CORN, COTTON, TOBACCO,

Peaches, Pears, Tomatoes, and every variety of fruit and vegetables are grown in great abundance, from which Chicago and other Northern markets are furnished from four to six weeks earlier than their immediate vicinity.

THE ORDINARY YIELD

of Corn is from 50 to 80 bushels per acre. Cattle, Horses, Mules, Sheep and Hogs are raised here at a small cost, and yield large profits. It is believed that no section of country presents greater inducements for Dairy Farming than the Prairies of Illinois, a branch of farming to which but little attention has been paid, and which must yield sure profitable results.

AGRICULTURAL PRODUCTS.

The Agricultural products of Illinois are greater than those of any other State. The Wheat crop of 1861 was estimated at 35,000,000 bushels, while the Corn crop yields not less than 140,000,000 bushels, besides the crop of Oats, Barley, Rye, Buckwheat, Potatoes, Sweet Potatoes, Pumpkins, Squashes, Flax, Hemp, Peas, Clover, Cabbage, Beets, Tobacco, Sorghum, Grapes, Peaches, Apples, &c., which go to swell the vast aggregate of production in this fertile region. Over Four Million tons of produce were sent out of Illinois during the past year.

CULTIVATION OF COTTON.

The experiments in Cotton culture are of very great promise. Commencing in latitude 39 deg. 30 min. (see Mattoon on the Branch, and Assumption on the Main Line), the Company owns thousands of acres well adapted to the perfection of this fibre. A settler having a family if young children can turn their youthful labor to a most profitable account in the growth and perfection of this plant.

THE ILLINOIS CENTRAL RAILROAD

Traverses the whole length of the State, from the banks of the Mississippi and Lake Michigan to the Ohio. As its name imports, the Railroad runs through the centre of the State, and on either side of the road along its whole length lie the lands offered for sale.

CITIES, TOWNS, MARKETS, DEPOTS.

There are ninety-eight Depots on the Company's Railway, giving about one every seven miles. Cities, Towns, and Villages are situated at convenient distances throughout the whole route, where every desirable commodity may be found as readily as in the oldest cities of the Union, and where buyers are to be met for all kinds of farm produce.

EDUCATION.

Mechanics and working men will find the free school system encouraged by the State, and endowed with a large revenue for the support of the schools. Children can live in sight of the school, the college, the church, and grow up with the prosperity of the leading State of the Great Western Empire.

For Prices and Terms of Payment,

ADDRESS LAND COMMISSIONER, Ill. Central R. R. Co., Chicago, Ill.

Roswell B. Mason, the resourceful Chief Engineer of the Illinois Central Railroad, who drove his line to completion through the wilderness with record-breaking speed. Sometimes with as many as 10,000 men under his control, Mason had to contend with drunken brawls, Indians, camp followers, payroll robbers and the maliciousness of competing railroad builders. But the great "central" railroad of Illinois was built, and on time.
(Illinois State Historical Library)

after the granting of the charter the Illinois Central had a number of engineers in the field. Construction was begun both at Cairo and Chicago (actually somewhat south of the city) on December 23, 1851. Within a few months the railroad would have in its employ thousands of workers in several different locations.

Recruiting workers was a big part of the problem. Although Illinois had a population of 900,000 in 1851, most of these people lived in the counties bordering the Mississippi, Wabash and Illinois rivers, or near Chicago and the Illinois and Michigan Canal. Most of the territory between Chicago and Cairo was unsettled and there was no way that a labor force could be gathered from the inhabitants of those wide-open spaces. Fortunately, Colonel Mason proved to have a genius for colonization. He obtained laborers from places as far away as New York and New Orleans. Ads were placed in newspapers in the East, and even in foreign countries. One contractor hired by Mason journeyed to Ireland and brought in a thousand lusty, brawling Irishmen, most of whom, one supposes, stayed on and settled a soil far more fertile than that of the Emerald Isle.

There were as many as ten thousand men at work on the Illinois Central at one time, and in the six-year period of construction it was estimated that at least one hundred thousand men were employed. Such masses, of course, meant trouble: fights, drunkenness, disease, fever, and

later years) were those stating that the railroad be completed in a period of six years, that it pay the State of Illinois seven percent of its revenues, that the Illinois Central would transport Federal property and troops at one-half the standard rate, and that it would carry the U.S. mails at 20 percent less than the standard rates.

Of most immediate concern was the provision that all 705 miles of the railroad be completed in six years. In meeting that goal the Illinois Central was fortunate in having Colonel Roswell B. Mason, one of the foremost railroad and canal builders of that day, as its Chief Engineer. Mason had come to the Illinois Central from work on the Erie Canal. He had also been Chief Engineer of the New York and New Haven Railroad and had supervised the construction of that road. But in Illinois he had to accept responsibilities of superhuman proportions. Shortly

the various summertime diseases such as the dreaded "milk sickness," to which Abraham Lincoln's mother had succumbed. There were problems of housing and transportation and of paying the workers. The laborers had to be paid in cash, and the paymasters had to get their funds to camp under heavy guard. But in spite of the troubles, these workers were the beginning of a giant colonization effort that was to accelerate many times over when the road itself was completed and the bargain farmland was made available.

The story behind the Illinois Central's entrance into Chicago and its acquisition of the magnificent waterfront properties for which it has always been memorable to both travelers and local residents is a fascinating one. The lakeside approach and terminal facilities were by no means predetermined. In fact they came about

by some rather curious circumstances. When the so-called "Chicago branch" of the Illinois Central was surveyed, an almost straight line of track was planned from Effingham County, two hundred miles in length, to the southern border of Cook County near Richton (the present southern end of the Illinois Central's commuter territory). What then? Where in the city of Chicago should the Illinois Central bring its terminal? Old surveyor's maps show that the ori-

The most remarkable thing about the Illinois Central's entrance into Chicago was its lake front approach. Present-day city planners would be horrified that a railroad would be permitted to intrude in such scenic environs, but the City of Chicago had no alternative. It needed the railroad to provide landfill, breakwaters and dikes for the protection of Michigan Avenue and its luxurious residences. But the result was not as unsightly as it might seem, as this picture looking north to the old Randolph St. Station would indicate.

(Illinois Central Gulf)

ginal plan was to pass the western shore of Lake Calumet and then proceed due north to dock facilities on the Chicago River, probably near or adjacent to the terminals of the Galena and Chicago Union Railroad. In an age when railroads were all attempting to forge links and connections in all directions, this seemed to make good sense.

But this original plan was never followed. Partly this was owing to the outcome of a nasty railroad war that broke out around the time of the first Illinois Central construction. Just as the Illinois Central was looking for a place to settle in Chicago, two rival railroads from the East, the Michigan Central and the Michigan Southern & Northern Indiana (both later absorbed into the New York Central System), were trying to break across the Illinois State line and win the symbolic prize of being the first Eastern road to get to Chicago. At this time there was no ready provision for granting charters to out-of-state railroads. To get out of that little difficulty, the Illinois Central agreed to award trackage rights to the Michigan Central Railroad. The Northern Indiana struck a deal with another newly formed railroad called the Rock Island to gain access to the city. The Rock Island interests had become very active, buying considerable acreage along the very right-of-way that the Illinois Central had hoped would provide a route to the heart of Chicago. Not only had they bought up much of the needed land, but they had also immediately begun to build.

The result of this little skirmish was that the Rock Island tracks were rapidly laid, and the first line from the East to arrive in Chicago was the Michigan Southern and Northern Indiana on February 20, 1852. In spite of the fact that it had been cheated of its chosen route, the Illinois Central wasn't far behind. Needing to get to the city by any route that was feasible, the Illinois Central engineers and management turned their attention to the eastern or lakefront route to Chicago. This alternative route would touch Lake Michigan five miles south of the Chicago River, then run north along the lakeshore to the southern limit of Chicago, which, at that time, was Twenty-third Street.

Where should the route go from there? Continue right along the lakeshore? Would the city fathers of Chicago permit such a thing? There were, after all, a great many people who were lukewarm about railroads in 1852 and not a few who were bitterly opposed to the railroads intruding themselves everywhere. Would there be any sympathy for a railroad that actually cluttered up the beautiful lakefront?

Chicago had no choice. In later years, enlightened city planners and beautifiers decried the fact that the Illinois Central had been able to grab the land next to the lake; they made persistent efforts to relocate the tracks. But in 1852 the Illinois Central happened to be the answer to one of the city's most persistent public problems. As far back as 1842, Alderman Eli S. Prescott had written to officials in Washington warning: "Unless something protective is immediately done, a large part of the Fort Dearborn Addition will soon be known as the bottom of the lake. The Fall storms have made the most tremendous and frightful inroads upon us." But the federal government did not come to the aid of the city, and on many occasions in the years that followed, Michigan Avenue itself was threatened

This is the depot that served the Illinois Central and Michigan Central Railroads before the Great Fire in 1871. It also contained the general offices of the IC. When it opened on June 12, 1856, a guest executive from one of the Eastern railroads exclaimed to Colonel Mason: "What under Heaven are you Westerners thinking about by building such a tremendous depot out here in Chicago? Why, sir, you'll never have use for half the room in this building." But in a matter of only a few years the building would be completely inadequate both as station and office.

(Illinois Central Gulf)

34

One of the reasons for the inadequacy of the early Central Station (shown here from the south) is that in addition to the Illinois Central and Michigan Central, it also served for a few years the trains of the Burlington and the Alton, which would not have a permanent terminal of their own until the 1880s.

(Chicago Historical Society)

by storms, its aristocratic residences repeatedly in danger of being washed away. Obviously the city was sorely in need of breakwater protection, but the treasury was in no condition to provide it.

Here at last was the answer. Let the railroad come in along the lakefront and it would obviously be compelled, for its own protection, to build and maintain breakwaters, dikes and other such devices, all of which, in the bargain, would protect city streets and houses from regular inundation. To be sure, there were citizens who protested what would surely be an aesthetic nuisance and eyesore, but they were few in number. There was just no alternative. So the city passed an ordinance on June 14, 1852, which granted to the Illinois Central Railroad a right-of-way 300 feet wide that was then located in the bed of Lake Michigan. This was not so generous as it might seem, of course, since the railroad, to use this right-of-way, had to provide landfill, construct trestles and otherwise insure protection to their right-of-way. Trains then, as now, could not run through water. And there were other disadvantages. However attractive the lakefront entrance, the Illinois Central acquired this location at the expense of losing what was then the commercial and industrial heart of the city. They were getting instead a scenic route flanked by parks, millionaire's residences, apartment houses and the like. Also, the railroad was forbidden to erect any structures between Randolph Street and Park Row (which might obstruct the view from the residences on Michigan Avenue). This restriction caused them to have to buy additional land north of Randolph Street for a station and other land for yards and shop facilities south of Park Row. Titles to these properties were all in private hands except 73,200 square feet of the old Fort Dearborn Reservation, which the Illinois Central bought from the U.S. War Department for $45,000.

Real estate investments like these were costly to the railroad, and they weren't the only problems involved with the acquisition of the lakefront entrance. For its own protection the railroad had to maintain walls and protective devices along the lakeshore south to what is now Hyde Park. All of this must have made the

Illinois Central route seem a mixed blessing in 1852—and perhaps it has been so ever since.

On the other hand, except for the area near downtown Chicago, the Illinois Central would soon come to enjoy other fruits of its route structure. The area of the south side as far as Lake Calumet was a wasteland in 1852, but before long it would be one of the great industrial areas of the Midwest. One of the first to foresee this was none other than U.S. Senator Stephen A. Douglas, who purchased 6,000 acres of swampy land from the Illinois Central near Lake Calumet (over the taunting cries of his friends, who told him he was buying "a useless frog-pond"). But Douglas was a man of vision and saw this land as ideal for industrial development. Before the passage of much time the Illinois Central right-of-way was to be surrounded by factories and

Chicago was obviously a bustling metropolis around the time of the Civil War, when this drawing was made. The scene shows a graceful arc of Illinois Central tracks, looking south from the Randolph Street Station.

(Illinois Central Gulf)

Stephen A. Douglas, the great Illinois statesman known to students of history, was also one of the prime movers of the Illinois Central Railroad. Moreover, he was a great promoter of Chicago, particularly the South Side, where he correctly envisioned the growth of a great industrial heartland. When he purchased 6,000 acres of land near Lake Calumet his friends scoffed at this indulgence, telling Douglas that he was investing in a "Frog Pond." But this "Frog Pond" would vastly contribute to Douglas' fortune even before his death in 1861, and would soon become an integral part of the most highly industrialized part of Chicago.

(Illinois Historical Survey)

Here is 63rd Street and Woodlawn as it appeared in the 1850s. Note the curious wooden post at the crossing. Woodlawn was obviously a pastoral setting in those days, but before long the little woodburning locomotives gave way to a brisk suburban service and the suburban community of Woodlawn was swallowed up into the city of Chicago.

(Illinois Central Gulf)

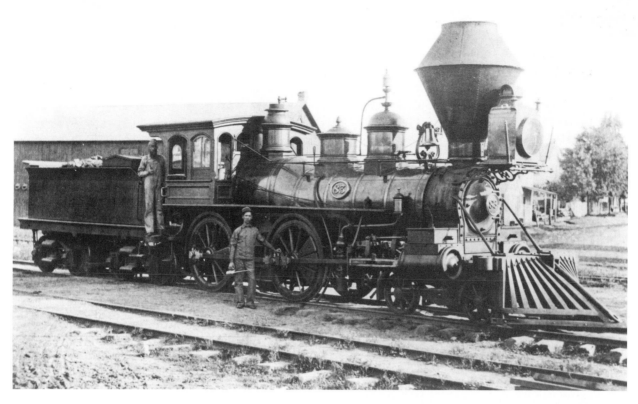

Typical of Illinois Central's locomotives during the Civil War period was No. 83, a 4-4-0 type with diamond stack, built by the Rogers Locomotive and Machine Works of Paterson, New Jersey.
(Smithsonian Institution)

industries of every description, including the great complex founded by George Mortimer Pullman for the manufacture of sleeping cars and other railroad equipment. If the Illinois Central had taken its eastern route as a kind of Hobson's choice, it found itself, in due time, the possessor of one of the most lucrative freight routes on any American railroad.

As we've already seen, the destiny of the Illinois Central in the Chicago area was linked to the development of other railroads under construction at that time. The stories of these early developments are so closely entwined that they can never be completely unraveled. Railroad building was very rapid in the 1850s, but everything was still on a small scale. It was only natural that all of the roads then in existence would be jockeying for position and vying with one another for routes and locations.

One of the earliest needs perceived by railroad men in the 1850s was that of a link between Chicago and the East—something that could shorten the long overland or water routes, and make possible an opening up of the West to the industrial and commercial powers of the East. There were active railroads east of the Alleghenies, to be sure, but the lines out in Michigan and Indiana were in a sorry state. The State of Michigan, for example, had chartered a whole bunch of railroads, but the Panic of 1837 had done in most of them. The two roads of which we have already spoken, the Michigan Central and the Michigan Southern, had fallen into a dilapidated condition and were never completed. The State of Michigan lacked funds to upgrade the properties, and to complete them to the point of their obvious destination—Chicago. Was there private money to do the job? Was there somebody with the vision?

As it turned out, there was. Three extraordinary railroad pioneers, all of whom would shortly play important roles in the history of Chicago-area railroads, now entered the scene. The first of these was a Detroit lawyer named James Frederick Joy, a New Englander and a graduate of Dartmouth College and the Harvard Law School. Joy had come to Detroit in 1836, where he became convinced of the great importance of the Michigan Central as an artery of transportation and a link between East and West. He swiftly became a strong advocate of convincing the State of Michigan to sell the road to private interests. Joy quickly found an ally in John W. Brooks, only 26 years old, but with past rail experience as Superintendent of the Auburn and Rochester Railroad. Joy and Brooks wanted to buy the broken-down Michigan Central, but where would they get the capital?

There was a little railroad activity in Michigan before the great rush to connect that state with Chicago. It was pretty primitive, however, and most of it resulted in financial disaster. Here, as early as 1837, a decade before Chicago railroading began, was the first train on the Erie and Kalamazoo Railroad. One can only wonder at the strange inspiration behind the "Gothic" passenger car.

(Author's Collection)

Taking on the burden of finding Eastern capital for rebuilding this far-away Western line, Brooks shortly found himself on the doorstep of a young but highly successful Yankee trader named John Murray Forbes. Forbes, only 32 years old at the time, was already a leader in Boston finance. He didn't personally have the $2,000,000 that the State of Michigan was asking for the Central, and which needed to be raised in six months, but he had all the right connections. What's more, with little difficulty, Brooks was able to convince Forbes that he would be investing in a gold mine. All this took place in the winter of 1845.

In a twinkling Forbes had raised not only the $2,000,000 needed to buy the Michigan Central, but in the next few years he was able to

Young John W. Brooks was only 26 years old when he formed an alliance with James Frederick Joy to get control of the Michigan Central. But he had already had solid railroading experience as superintendent of the Auburn and Rochester Railroad.
(University of Illinois Library)

James Frederick Joy, the Detroit lawyer who properly saw that the destiny of the Michigan Central was Chicago. He set about rebuilding the broken down Michigan Central and impelled it on to its ultimate destination. Joy would continue to be a great force in Chicago railroading as a founder and later president of the Burlington.

(Burlington Northern)

raise another $6,000,000 to rehabilitate the dilapidated line and complete its rails to Michigan City, Indiana (as far as it could hope to go at first, since the railroad had no charter from the State of Illinois).

The triumvirate that had achieved this spectacular feat in the four years between 1845 and 1849—Joy the lawyer, Brooks the railroad manager and Forbes the financier—were to move on to even more important achievements in railroad history as prime movers in the development of the Chicago, Burlington and Quincy Railroad—achievements that would in some ways dwarf those of the Michigan Central. But the completion of the Michigan Central to Michigan City was not the end of their experiences with that railroad. In some ways it was just the beginning, for the entry of their line into Chicago would soon involve them in one of the most bitter railroad wars of the time.

The heart of the trouble was that the Forbes interests had managed to complete the Michigan

Central to the western boundary of Michigan, but that was all. From here their passengers had to continue their journey to Chicago by steamboat. For this purpose they had a fine steamer called the *Mayflower*, and passengers were generally delighted about being able to complete the journey from Michigan City to Chicago by boat. Still, a steamboat was simply not a proper conveyance for a railroad; a railroad ought to be able to run its cars right into the city of Chicago.

For a while it did not seem urgent to find a means of entry into the great city on the lake; but suddenly there was a challenger in the field. This challenger was the Michigan Southern Railroad, which had now been taken over by New York financiers. Forbes and his associates had not paid any attention to the Michigan Southern because it was in an even more run-down condition than the Central and had only been extended 75 miles west of Toledo. But the charter was there, and now, with a big influx of money from New York, a lively competitor was rearing its ugly head. Moreover, if the Southern found a way to get to Chicago first, it might snare the lion's share of the traffic to the East and the Central might be left to starve. And there was more involved than the city of Chicago. Around 1850 main routes to the West were being proposed (and built), and the name of the game was finding allies and linkages to all parts of the country.

The Michigan Southern, later officially known as the Michigan Southern and Northern Indiana Railway, seemed to have the edge. The Southern had obtained an old Illinois plank road charter which they claimed (very dubiously) included the right to build a railroad. At the same time the Southern partisans had obtained a new charter for a railroad called the Rock Island and La Salle Railroad. They purchased this road in its entirety and changed its name to the Chicago and Rock Island Railroad. They thus assured themselves not only of a Chicago connection but of a Western outlet as well. The Rock Island ran nowhere near Chicago as yet, but with a strong impetus from the Eastern interests, track went down pell-mell toward an eventual juncture with the Michigan Southern.

The Forbes interests had to do something immediately or they would lose out. The smooth and polished James F. Joy was dispatched to Springfield to see what arrangements he could make at the Illinois state capital. One possibility that suggested itself was the acquisition of a charter from the State of Illinois that would allow the Michigan Central to build directly into Chicago. This seemed a remote possibility for an out-of-state carrier. But in the spring of 1851 came a better idea. The Illinois legislature was about to award the charter for the Illinois Central to some qualified private group. If the Forbes people could obtain this charter, if the Illinois Central became in effect part of their system, there would be no difficulty in building a branch line to the boundary of Indiana.

However, the Forbes interests never took over the Illinois Central. The two roads did form a secret alliance and entered into a kind of unofficial partnership. This was partly the by-product of financial aid arranged by Joy whereby the Michigan Central carried Illinois Central bonds worth $2,000,000 for two years, in return for Illinois trackage rights into Chicago.

In a way, the problem was not completely solved, since full legal permission to build from the Indiana line was never received. The Illinois Central did curve its tracks a bit to give the impression of a jog toward Indiana. But without having received a charter, the Michigan Central just laid the tracks and forged the all-important link that gave them access to Chicago—and the West!

One interesting footnote to this period of railroad warfare was a little story about the con-

When the Michigan Central arrived in Chicago, it accepted the hospitality of the Illinois Central and made use of that railroad's terminal facilities. This picture, taken about 1868, shows a Michigan Central train leaving the Central Station at Randolph Street. To the left are the original offices and works of the Pullman Palace Car Company at the corner of Randolph and Michigan. (These facilities were destroyed in the Chicago Fire of 1871.)
(Smithsonian Institution)

When the Michigan Southern Railroad pushed its way to Chicago in defiance of the Michigan Central, it forged a link with the Rock Island. Neither road would have been welcome over by the lakefront, so they were forced to build their own terminal facilities at Van Buren and La Salle Streets. Here is the first of the three La Salle Street Stations (actually this had been preceded by an earlier temporary one), an attractive stone structure, which was a victim of the Chicago Fire.

(University of Illinois Library)

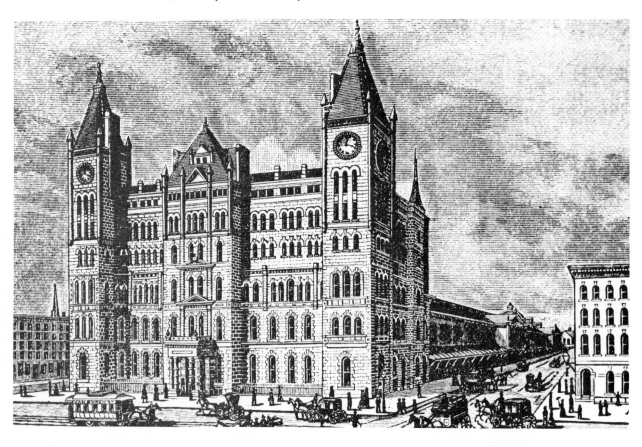

struction of Illinois Central tracks across those of the Michigan Southern. The Michigan Southern was on the spot with its East-West route and connection with the Rock Island, so the Illinois Central had to ask permission to build a crossing. But by now the Illinois Central was identified as an enemy to the Michigan Southern because of its alliance with the Michigan Central. So the answer was no, no crossing, and to emphasize the point the Southern put out a guard to prevent all unauthorized railroad construction. If the Illinois Central wanted to get across, let them build an overpass.

However, the Illinois Central's Roswell B. Mason was a very resourceful fellow. He had no intention of committing the company's treasury to thousands of dollars for such a silly and unnecessary expenditure. One dark night he had the lone Michigan Southern guard kidnapped, and at dawn the next day, there was a neat and perfect railroad frog; the Illinois Central tracks leaped over those of its competitor as nicely as you please.

For a while this led to some pretty reckless railroading, with trains of both roads running wildly over the crossing—that is, until 1853, when a terrible wreck killed 18 people. Public opinion was then aroused against the foolish practice of pretending that there was no such thing as a crossing, and that one's own

trains always have the right-of-way. Rules and regulations were established, and trains of both lines had to come to a stop at the rails of the other, and proceed only after establishing that there were no other trains approaching.

Rules and regulations of this sort would become a regular part of railroad administration from this point on, since railroads were spreading in greater profusion than ever before.

The railroad wars of the 1850s seem pretty remote and foolish today. Most of them were a mere prelude to much greater and more important rivalries in the years to come. The Michigan Southern and Northern Indiana won the battle to Chicago, its first train arriving on February 20, 1852, over the Rock Island tracks. But the Michigan Central arrived a mere three months later over Illinois Central tracks. The victory didn't seem important because both roads prospered mightily thereafter.

The trackage arrangements at that early period seem of little significance today. Historically, though, those early accords influenced later rail developments in numerous interesting ways. As far as Chicago is concerned, the link between the Rock Island and the Michigan Southern sealed a pact between those two roads which bound them together in their joint terminal facilities for over a century. When the various La Salle Street stations were built, their major tenants were and would continue to be the

Rock Island and the New York Central, successor to the Michigan Southern. The alliance was there from the beginning.

It is probably no small irony that these great competitors of the 1850s, the Michigan Central and the Michigan Southern, in time came under the sway of the Vanderbilt interests; both eventually became secure and indistinct parts of the New York Central System. In fact, the Michigan Southern, with its route through Toledo and along the south shore of Lake Erie to Buffalo, became the main line of the New York Central. The other route that was eventually forged from Detroit across southern Ontario to Buffalo was of secondary importance for the New York Central, but during the glory years of railroading it was never slighted. Sleek and beautiful passenger trains glided between Chicago and New York via this other, more northerly route, all watched over by the careful Vanderbilt management in New York.

What happened to the triumvirate of John Murray Forbes, John W. Brooks and James F. Joy? In time all moved on to greater triumphs in the West, specifically as part of the history of another great American railroad, the Chicago Burlington and Quincy. Today they must mainly be remembered for the history of that road, and for the development of the states of Iowa and Nebraska, rather than for their first little venture in forging the rail link between Detroit and Chicago.

The earliest origins of the Burlington, and its construction to Chicago, is a pertinent story and one that is mostly forgotten today. The railroad that now is known as the Burlington began as a quite small enterprise. It was started by a small but aggressive group of citizens in Aurora, Illinois, who perceived the need for a rail connection with Chicago. What they envisioned was nothing more complicated than a branch of the Galena Railroad, and what they built was a short stretch of railroad that linked Aurora with a place on the Galena line known as Turner's or Turner's Junction (named for the Galena's president, John B. Turner). For a few years what would be known as the Burlington was nothing but a little spur to convey the people and freight of Aurora to the Galena main line, 12 miles away.

It was inevitable that the little Aurora branch would grow. When the line opened to Aurora on October 4, 1850, the branch line had no rolling stock of its own. It had to hire the *Pioneer* and a single coach to make the connection with the Galena.* The West beckoned, however, and by October 20, 1854, 54 additional miles were opened from Aurora to Mendota. Another 79 miles were completed to Galesburg on December 7, 1854, and the following year construction was begun toward the Mississippi River from both Burlington and Quincy. It was obvious that the Burlington would be a major railroad of the West in the near future. For this reason it intrigued John Murray Forbes and James F. Joy, and became the repository of their financial investments after their work with the Michigan Central was completed.

One strange quirk in the development of the Burlington was its long-delayed arrival in Chicago over its own tracks. The entry to Chicago by

*Thus the *Pioneer* has the unique distinction of being the first locomotive on two great American railroads—the Chicago and North Western and the Chicago, Burlington and Quincy.

In the publicity-seeking days of the twentieth century the Rock Island Line started using the name "Rocket" for its "varnish" passenger runs. But the name was by no means a new one on the Rock Island. Here is the original Rock Island "Rocket" train of 1852, the year the railroad began its operations in Chicago.
(Illinois State Historical Library)

means of the Galena Road at Turner's Junction could hardly be totally satisfactory for a growing railroad. Furthermore, after a number of years of carrying the Burlington's cars, the Galena found its two-track line taxed to the limit with its own fast-growing traffic. As early as 1857 the Galena gave notice to the Burlington that it would shortly terminate the latter's trackage rights into Chicago, so the Burlington must find a new route of its own. Several times the Galena agreed to extend the trackage rights for a few years, but finally decided that the Burlington must make other arrangements by May 1, 1864. Still, it was not until 1862, with only two years to go, that Burlington's directors gave thought to building their own line from Aurora to Chicago.

John Murray Forbes and the other Burlington directors knew that they needed a line of their own into Chicago, and that they would save tremendously by operating over their own tracks (Forbes estimated the savings at $30,000 a year). Unfortunately, the Civil War had begun by this time, and the Burlington had all it could do to complete its Chicago spur before the Galena made good its threat to get rid of the Burlington traffic. Labor was scarce during the war. Inflation boosted costs far above the original estimates. Too, the winter of 1862-63 was very severe in Illinois and there were many long delays in construction. Although everyone thinks of the Illinois terrain as being without difficulty, such was not always the case in the early days of railroading. There was a formidable swamp between what today are Hinsdale and Western Springs, which froze over in 1862, holding up construction. In those days one could go between Western Springs and Hinsdale by boat, and in the winter one could skate over the frozen marshes. The Burlington just had to wait for the thaw. Even then, this area was full of obstacles for the builders. They had to dump carloads of rock and over 50,000 cubic yards of earth into the seemingly bottomless bog before they had any hope of laying down a secure rail.

Still, the Burlington pressed on to Chicago, with the last tie on the Chicago branch being laid on April 28, 1864—only a week before its trackage arrangements with the Galena were due to expire. The 36 miles of track cost a million dollars to build, way over the $800,000 Forbes had promised his directors in 1862.

Because of its long-standing alliance with the Illinois Central and the Michigan Central, the Burlington's new Chicago spur prompted it to seek terminal facilities with those roads. It shared the Illinois Central's waterfront terminal at Lake Street, but its tenancy was not of long duration. The Lake Street Station was destroyed in the Great Fire of 1871. For a few years thereafter the Burlington shared temporary facilities with the Illinois Central, but it moved to the Union Station at Canal and Adams Streets in 1881—where it has remained to this day.

Another railroad with a strong Chicago identification was the Rock Island. We have already seen that it came to Chicago long before

the Burlington. In a way the Rock Island got its start in much the same manner as did other Illinois railroads. It was an answer to terrible roads and winter impassability. The Rock Island was also the result of the strongly felt need of the citizens and commercial interests of Rock Island, Illinois, who wanted to be linked with eastern Illinois as a cure for their far-away isolation on the Mississippi River. The first charter of the railroad, adopted by the General Assembly of the State of Illinois on February 27, 1847, granted to the Rock Island and La Salle Railroad, the right to "survey, locate and construct . . . a railroad . . . from the town of Rock Island, on the Mississippi River . . . to the Illinois River at the termination of the Illinois and Michigan Canal."

As was so often the case, the charter did not immediately yield a railroad. But when activity did begin on the Rock Island in 1852, it began in earnest. By this time it was fated that the Rock Island would have to traverse the whole state of Illinois, not merely the part between the Mississippi and the now quickly fading canal. Indeed, building had begun in the eastern part of Illinois mainly because of those hoped-for opportunities to be derived from the link between the Michigan Southern and the Rock Island. The Rock Island's first job was to get that eastern traffic into Chicago.

But in the person of Henry Farnum the Rock Island had one of the great railroad builders of his day. In two brief years Farnum had built a railroad across the entire state of Illinois. First he made a connection with the Michigan Central for entry into Chicago in the spring of 1852. On October 10, 1852, the Rock Island reached Joliet. It reached Ottawa in February 1853 and La

Henry Farnum, the founder of the Chicago and Rock Island Railroad. The Rock Island began as a typical pragmatic railroad venture when citizens and businessmen of Rock Island felt isolated in the Western part of the state and anticipated rail travel to Chicago and the East. Henry Farnum would enjoy a greater distinction in the railroad world as the man who built the first railroad bridge across the Mississippi River, thus making possible transcontinental railroading.

(Illinois State Historical Library)

THE AMERICAN LOCOMOTIVE AT THE PARIS EXHIBITION.

Diameter of driving wheels, 5ft. 7in.	Distance from centre to centre of coupled wheels, 8ft. 6in.	Total grate bar surface, 16ft.	Width of ditto (exhaust), 2¼in.
Diameter of bogie wheels (engine and tender), 2ft. 6in.	Distance from centre to centre of bogie wheels, 5ft. 9in.	Diameter of cylinders, 16in.	Height of centre of boiler from rail, 6ft. 4in.
Diameter of driving axle, 6½in.	Length of boiler over all, 19ft. 11in.	Length of stroke, 22in.	Height of top of chimney from rail, 14ft. 2in.
Diameter of driving axle bearing, 6½in.	Diameter of ditto (outside), 4ft.	Length of connecting rod, 7ft. 3in.	Weight of engine (light), 27½ tons.
Diameter of bogie axle, 4½in.	Length of fire-box, 6ft. 2in.	Length of tubes, 10ft. 11in.	Ditto tender (light), 10 tons.
Diameter of bogie axle bearing, 4½in.	Total heating surface, 950ft.	Depth of fire-box, 5ft.	Thickness of plate in boiler shell, 7⁄16in.
Number of tubes (2in), 142.		Length of ports, 1ft. 4in.	Ditto fire-box, ⅜in.
		Width of ports (steam), 1¼in.	

Salle the following month. With great pageantry and fanfare the Rock Island reached the Mississippi River at the town of Rock Island on George Washington's Birthday in 1854. This was touted as "the espousal day of the Mississippi River and the Atlantic Ocean." It was not long before the Rock Island leaped the Mississippi River to another Farnum railroad on the Iowa side. The Rock Island would be the first of the great railroad bridge builders. It had to accomplish this feat amidst the howls and public outcries of the Mississippi steamboat interests. But the steamboaters' arguments were exploded by a brilliant lawyer from Springfield named Abraham Lincoln. Thus, it was only a matter of time before a new name for the Rock Island would be conjured in men's minds: the Chicago, Rock Island and Pacific Railroad Company.

Of the other railroads making their way to Chicago during the 1850s, the Alton has always played an important role in Illinois history. The Alton ran to Chicago from St. Louis, passing through Bloomington and Springfield. Its original entry into Chicago was by connection with the Rock Island at Joliet. It was on the Alton that Abraham Lincoln departed for Washington and his inauguration as president in 1861, and by which his funeral train returned in 1865. And in 1858 the Alton had become famous in railroad history as the first railroad to carry a sleeping

One of the most celebrated locomotives on the Rock Island was the *America,* which was built by the Grant Locomotive Works specifically for the Paris Exposition of 1867. It was later displayed in Chicago (May 1869) and then acquired by the Rock Island where it was put into service on the Council Bluffs Extension.

(John H. White, Jr.)

car manufactured by George M. Pullman. In the twentieth century, the Alton, a railroad with distinctive train names such as *The Abraham Lincoln* and *The Ann Rutledge,* became, by an ironic twist of fate, a property of a road with deep roots in the history of the Southern Confederacy—the Gulf, Mobile & Ohio. But many Illinoisians in the territory now served by that railroad (subsequently merged with the Illinois Central) still call it the Alton.

As railroad activity to the south continued to grow, so did rail construction in the north. The Chicago and North Western was a giant in Wisconsin, but shortly it would not be a lone giant. A great many other roads were being built all over the state, and later many of these were swallowed up in a larger system that ultimately had Chicago as its destination—the Chicago, Milwaukee and St. Paul Railway Company, incorporated in Illinois in 1872. The ties between the cities of Chicago and Milwaukee, and between Chicago and the Twin Cities, which would later account for the greatness of the Milwaukee,

When the Rock Island had its centennial celebration in 1952, none of its very earliest engines were in operative condition. Suitably antique looking, however, was this well-decked and polished ten-wheeler on display at the Englewood Station in Chicago.

(The Rock Island)

had more predecessor railroads than it would be possible to mention: the Milwaukee and Mississippi Railroad; the Milwaukee, Fond du Lac & Green Bay Railroad; the Milwaukee & Watertown Railroad; the Racine, Janesville & Mississippi Railway; the Menominee Branch Railroad, and sundry others.

The Chicago, Milwaukee & St. Paul added the word Pacific to its name only in the twentieth century when it began its extension to the Pacific coast in 1906, a decision that proved financially disastrous to the company from the very beginning. But the Milwaukee would always be a famous name in the Midwest because of its beautiful and distinctive *Hiawatha* trains between Chicago, Milwaukee and Minneapolis-St. Paul, and in Chicago for its well-kept-up commuter service between Union Station and the

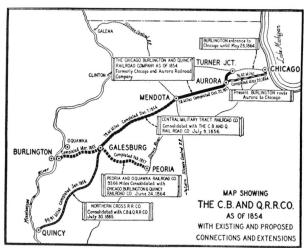

northern suburbs. When Amtrak took over the national passenger service in 1971, it was the Milwaukee route to the Twin Cities and the Northwest that survived.

The amalgamation of railroads that resulted in the Milwaukee was pretty much the story of the giant railroads east of Chicago. Actual connection of Chicago with the East was effected early, but this didn't mean that quick through

The great Burlington Lines began as the Chicago and Aurora Rail Road, whose timetable for 1854 is shown here. The original goal of the line was to contact Aurora with the Galena Road at Turner's Junction, 13 miles distant. But by 1854 the line had been extended to La Salle and the call of the Mississippi and beyond had been heard by the founders and movers of the road.

(Burlington Northern)

CHICAGO & AURORA RAIL ROAD.

TIME CARD NO. 4.

FOR THE GOVERNMENT AND INFORMATION OF EMPLOYEES ONLY.

To take effect on and after Monday, August 14th, 1854.

TRAINS WESTWARD. | **TRAINS EASTWARD.**

Freight Train	Express Mail	Passenger	Miles		Miles	Passenger	Freight	Express Mail
5.45 Leave A. M.	8.55 Leave A M	4.15 Leave P.M		..Chicago..	104	10.30 Arrive	4.35 Arrive	9.00 Arrive
				.Canal Street.				
5.58		4.20 Meet Fr't	2	..City Limits..	102		4.20 Mt Past&DP	
6.22	9.15	4.30	8	..Oak Ridge..	96	10 12	3.55 Meet B. P.	8.40
6.38	9.32	4.47	16	..Cottage Hill..	88	9.54	3.18	8.22
7.17	9.42 Meet Pass	4.57	20	Babcock's Grove	84	9.42 Meet Pass	2.58	8.12
7.30	9.50 Meet B. P.	5.03	23	..Danby..	81		2 42	8.05
7.44 Meet D. P.	9.55	5.09	25	..Wheaton..	79	9.30	2.30 Meet R. Frt	7.58
7.57	10.00	5.15	27	..Winfield..	77	9.24 Meet G Pass	2.20	7.52
8.11	10 05	5.20 Meet B Pass	30	..Junction..	74	9.15	2.10	7.45
8.55 Meet Pass	10.30	5.35	36	..Batavia..	70	8 55 Meet Fr't	1.15	7.25
9.45	11.00	6.00	43	..Aurora..	61	8.40	12.30	7.00
	11 01	6.05		.West Aurora.	61	8.35		6.50
9.55	11.08	6.10	46	..Montgomery..	58	8.30	12.00	6.46
10.05	11.12	6.15	48	..Oswego..	56	8 25	11.40	6.40
10.25	11.20 Meet Freight	6.30 Meet Pass	51	..Bristol..	53	8.15	11 20 Meet Pass	6.30 Meet Pass
10.50 Meet Fr't	11.40	6.50	57	..Plano..	47	8.00	10.50 Meet Fr't	6.15
11.15	11.53	7.00	62	..Newark..	42	7.45	10.15	6.00
11.30	12.05 P. M	7.12	65	..Somonauk..	39	7.35	9.45	5.50
12.30 P.M. mt pas	12.30 Pass Fr't	7.32	71	..Waverly..	33	7.20	9.05	5.30
1.20	12.50	7.50	78	..Earl..	26	7.00	8.15	5;10
2.20	1.10	8.20	89	..Mendota..	15	6.35	7.15	4.45
3.50 Arrive	2.00 Arrive	9.00 Arrive	104	..La Salle..		5.30 A. M. leave	6.00 A. M. leave	4.00 P. M. leave

Trains meet and pass at Stations marked by FULL FACE FIGURES.

SIGNALS.

1. A Red Flag by day, or Red Lantern by night, upon an Engine, indicates that another Engine is to follow it, out of the regular train, and must be waited for as a regular passenger train.
2. A Red Flag by day, or a Lantern by night, waved upon the track, signifies that a train must come to a full stop.
3. A Stationary Red Flag signifies that the track is not in perfect order and must be run over with great caution.
4. A Red Signal Light must be exhibited on the rear car of each train in the night time, until the train arrives at its destination.
5. One Puff of the Steam Whistle is the signal to Brake. Two Puffs of the Steam Whistle is the signal to Loose the Brakes. And three Puffs is the signal to Back.
6. One stroke of the Bell, *Stop*. Two strokes of the Bell, *Go Ahead*. And three strokes of the Bell, *Back*.

RULES FOR RUNNING TRAINS.

1. No Train will, under any circumstances, leave a Station before its time specified in time table as regulated by the standard time at the Chicago Ticket office.
2. Trains moving West will have the right to the Road over trains of same class moving East, after waiting five minutes beyond their own time at passing Stations and will leave each succeeding Station five minutes behind their regular time until the approaching train is passed.
3. Freight Trains will keep ten minutes out of the way of Passenger Trains.
4. Gravel and Construction Trains will in all cases keep ten minutes out of the way of Passenger and Freight Trains.
5. Any Train following a Passenger Train will proceed with great care, keeping at least one mile in the rear of it.
6. Trains moving East will have the right to the road over Trains of same class, after waiting thirty-five minutes at passing Station, and will leave each succeeding Station thirty-five minutes behind its regular time, until the delayed Train is passed; five minutes of the above time must be allowed for safety, and not to be used by either Train. This rule will apply only to Trains upon the C. & A. R.R.
7. The Conductor will have entire charge and control of the Train and all persons employed upon it, and is responsible for its movements while on the Road; he will be at the Station twenty minutes before the time designated to leave; will allow no one to stand on the platform of the Cars while in motion, except the Brakeman.
8. Engineers on approaching a Station or Road Crossing will sound the Whistle and ring the Bell at least 80 rods before crossing any road. Pass Stations and switches cautiously, and at a rate of speed not exceeding 12 miles per hour.
9. Engineers will allow no person to ride on their Engines, except permission is given by the Superintendent, Master Mechanic, or Road Master.
10. When two or more Engines are running in company, all but the last one must carry a Red Flag in the day and a Red Light at night; the forward ones must not leave a Station until they are all in sight. Trains meeting an Engine with a Red Flag or Light, must wait and pass them all at the same point.
11. No Extra Engine will be allowed to pass over any portion of the road unless following a Regular Train, except by permission of the Superintendent.
12. Trains having occasion to stop on the road will stop where the view is long and clear, keeping signals out in such a position as to guard against the possibility of a collision with other Trains.
13. In any case where there is room for doubt as to the right of the road, or the safety of proceeding from any cause, *adopt the safe course*, keeping signals far enough in both directions to obviate any danger.
14. In all cases, by night or by day, when repairing the track so as to obstruct or endanger the passing of a Train, a Red Flag or Lanterns as the case may be, must be placed on the track, so as to be seen by any approaching train at least one half mile each way from the place of danger.
15. The Track must be kept clear of all obstructions; no cars allowed to stand on the main track unless in charge of proper persons to see the track is clear at least twenty minutes before a train is due, and nothing allowed to be piled within four feet of the track.
16. Trains while running upon the Galena and Chicago Union Road, will be governed by the running rules of said Company. Particular attention is called to Rule 6.
17. Conductors will collect fare of all Passengers not having a pass from proper authority, unless otherwise ordered by Superintendent.

WALTER S. JOHNSON, Superintendent.

Chicago, August 10, 1854

thought of as providers to the West. The Pennsylvania was built, as the name suggests, as a railroad for the state of Pennsylvania. It wished only to connect Philadelphia and Pittsburgh. The Baltimore and Ohio's destination was clearly spelled out by the company name. The original objective of the New York Central was to traverse the "central" part of that state—from Albany to Buffalo at the most. At first there was no intention of linking these central counties of New York with New York City. This link was the brainchild of wily old Commodore Cornelius Vanderbilt, who merged the never very successful Central with his own New York and Harlaem Railroad. Most typical of all was the case of the Erie, which was built between the Hudson River at Piermont, N.Y., and the Great Lakes, following the southern tier of New York State, but built to an eccentric six-foot gauge decreed by its founders, who wanted to be sure that the Erie wouldn't link up with any other railroads.

The two railroads whose names will always be associated with the New York to Chicago traffic are the New York Central and the Pennsylvania. But neither of them had made complete connections to Chicago before the 1870s. When Commodore Vanderbilt combined the New York Central with his New York and Harlaem in

service was immediately available. Quite the opposite was true. One didn't just board a train in New York in the 1850s and 1860s and wind up in Chicago the next day. There was no single railroad making the journey, but a series of smaller roads offering transfers, some of which were trying and difficult—if not downright impossible. Consolidation of the through lines was a long time in coming.

The reason for this disorganization is not hard to understand. The great eastern roads, such as the Pennsylvania, the Baltimore and Ohio, the New York Central, and the Erie, were originally chartered to serve the transportation needs of the Eastern states, and were in no sense

1867, he must have realized that it was not Buffalo but Chicago that must be the western terminus of his line. For shortly after this time he started buying shares in the Lake Shore & Michigan Southern, a road that was never in very good financial condition, but which offered a nearly water-level route between Buffalo and Chicago. Vanderbilt was able to buy an especially large amount of Lake Shore stock after the Black Friday panic of 1869. Shortly thereafter he became president of that railroad also. Then, and for some time to come, the two railroads maintained their separate identities and passengers had to change trains, and lines, at Buffalo.

But Commodore Vanderbilt was not satisfied with this single link to Chicago. Shortly he turned his eyes toward the Michigan Central because it was an exceedingly well-run line into Chicago and had some very profitable feeder lines. Also, Vanderbilt had brought another line from Buffalo, through southern Ontario to Detroit, called the Canada Southern. Obviously it wouldn't do the Commodore any good to have the Canada Southern without a way to Chicago from Detroit. That way was the Michigan Central. To obtain this line Vanderbilt had to lay hands on the Boston interests of John Murray Forbes and James F. Joy, which he did—by intricate maneuvering—over a period of several years. Forbes and Joy, unseated by the Wall Street savvy of Vanderbilt, left the Michigan Central for their newer interests in the Burlington (but not without becoming deadly foes for the rest of their days of Vanderbilt and Vanderbilt railroad enterprises.)

In any case, the acquisition of the Michigan Central and the Lake Shore gave the New York Central not one but two main lines between Buffalo and Chicago. In later years the Central was to develop and stimulate heavy traffic on both these lines.

The Pennsylvania's conquest of Chicago was similarly by acquisition. The Pennsylvania's main line from Philadelphia to Pittsburgh was opened on July 18, 1858. Even before this main line across the difficult terrain of Pennsylvania was completed, the road's officials in Philadelphia were thinking of ways to continue westward. Indeed, there was already considerable railroad activity in the state of Ohio, especially the Ohio and Pennsylvania Railroad. By 1843, 187 miles of this railroad were open from Crestline to Allegheny City. Two other railroads were chartered to make the connection to Chicago—the Ohio and Indiana Railroad between Crestline and Fort Wayne and the Fort Wayne & Chicago Railroad for the remaining distance to Chicago. All three of these railroads were consolidated into the Pittsburgh, Fort Wayne and Chicago Railway Company and service was inaugurated between Pittsburgh and Chicago on Christmas Day, 1858.

This road prospered on its own for a number of years, but the Pennsylvania made no move to take it over, although this would have been the logical thing to do. Officials of the Pittsburgh, Fort Wayne and Chicago were so puzzled and wounded by this slight that they started looking around for another Eastern line to which they could propose matrimony. They even considered building their own line to New York. The Pennsylvania, however, was brought to its senses when it learned that Jay Gould was buying up Pittsburgh, Fort Wayne and Chicago stock. It moved quickly to acquire the railroad by means of a 999-year lease, signed June 7, 1869. Through access to Chicago, if not through service, was consummated on that date.

The Baltimore & Ohio, under the leadership and guidance of the great John W. Garrett, also saw that its destiny was Chicago, although it, too, was having to cool its heels in Pittsburgh in the years right after the Civil War. The Baltimore & Ohio was forced to do some building. At first Garrett contemplated building a line due west of Pittsburgh. But the terrain there was rugged, and both banks of the Ohio River, which would have provided easy passage to the West, had already been preempted by other railroads. So the Baltimore & Ohio struck out to the north and planned to start its big westward push from a place just south of Sandusky. From here it would be able to build virtually straight as an arrow across the flattest parts of Ohio and Indiana. When this route was completed to Chicago in the fall of 1874, the Baltimore & Ohio would have a shorter route (784 miles) between Washington, D.C., and Chicago than the Pennsylvania would ever enjoy.

After it arrived in Chicago, the Baltimore & Ohio used the terminal facilities of the Illinois Central, entering the original Randolph Street Station at lakeside. Nearby the B & O built a commodious brick freighthouse 600 feet long. The B & O continued this arrangement for 17 years until it became the major owner of the splendid new Grand Central Station at Harrison and Wells streets, sharing facilities there with several minor roads: the Chicago & Great Western, the Pere Marquette and the Soo. As a passenger carrier the Baltimore & Ohio, alas, is no

longer a part of the Chicago railroad scene, although it remains a freight carrier, and continues its commerce through the Baltimore & Ohio Chicago Terminal Railroad.

The Erie was always a distinctly poor country cousin when it came to East-West competition. It never had the big name, and never ran the great trains. Still, it was always a formidable force and nurtured its own strong trade between New York and Chicago. In some ways it is a wonder that the Erie ever got to Chicago at all. There was, first of all, the serious problem of the six-foot gauge to which it was built starting in the 1830s. The legislators of New York State were determined to have a strictly New York State railroad that could not form entangling alliances with any other railroad. In the end they were wrong. The Erie finally succeeded in merging with other railroads, but only after encountering financial catastrophe. The Erie had to endure, as part of its management, some of the worst financial buccaneers and robber barons of the Gilded Age, including Daniel Drew, Jay Gould, and Jim Fisk. Someone once said of Drew that he viewed railroads as some people do apple trees—as things to be shaken of their fruit. Not too much better could be said of Gould and Fisk.

Interestingly, the railroad that was to make the Erie's connection to Chicago was also built to the six-foot gauge. This was the Atlantic & Great Western Railroad, which began as three separate lines sponsored by local citizens' groups in three locales: Jamestown, New York; Meadville, Pennsylvania; and Franklin, Ohio. From the start it was assumed that the Atlantic and Great Western would be a mate for the Erie, although in view of the aloofness of the New York State founders, it is not at all clear why the Ohio and Pennsylvania people thought that they could court the Erie with success.

Actually, no fancy wedding ever took place. The Atlantic and Great Western fell helplessly into the Erie's lap in the process of numerous reorganizations and financial disasters. During the mid-1870s, Gould was divesting himself of the Erie, realizing that there were fatter roads to be milked elsewhere (and, in part, he was being pushed out, having been recognized for the rascal that he was). When the entire Erie system from New York to Chicago was finally put together like some giant tattered quilt, all parts of it were in sad shape financially and physically. With Gould out, a new president named Hugh Jewett at the helm, and a massive financial reorganization at last possible, the Erie was able to take up the Atlantic and Great Western, complete the western-most linkage between Marion, Ohio, and Hammond, Indiana, and effect a connection with the Chicago and Western Indiana Railroad, a terminal railroad with facilities in Chicago. It was also able in the 1870s to double track all of the road on the main stem between New York and Chicago, and, above all, to get rid of the bothersome six-foot gauge. With its various bankruptcies and upheavals, the Erie did not run its first train between New York and Chicago until 1880, long after its two major competitors had come upon the scene.

Soon after its arrival in Chicago, the Erie became a tenant of the Dearborn Station, and remained so until the end of its long-distance passenger service in 1970. The Dearborn Station effectively captured the spirit of Erie—old from

birth, crumbling, a medieval pile of stone, but still pleasant and fascinating with a real and individual personality about it. The Erie's trains lumbered along between New York and Chicago, but through a very scenic route, especially in the Delaware Valley and across the southern tier of New York. They stopped at almost every village and hamlet along the way, never making the trip in less than 20 hours even in the age of the diesel. But to those who loved going that way, the Erie was a lovely and delightful old railroad.

Another and perhaps more famous tenant of the Dearborn Station was the Santa Fe, also a late arrival on the Chicago railroad scene. The Santa Fe did not come until 1888, but when it arrived it did so with a flair, after one of the most frenzied construction drives in U.S. railroad history.

The Santa Fe was originally the brainchild of Cyrus K. Holliday, who had actually gotten his start in railroading on the Erie. Holliday had been a young and enterprising attorney in Meadville, Pennsylvania, who had helped to organize the Atlantic and Great Western in the 1850s. With a venturesome spirit and substantial capital, he later moved westward with the dream of building a railroad to follow the old Santa Fe trail from Kansas to the Southwest. A great idea it was, too, for the Santa Fe was a prosperous railroad from the very beginning, never troubled by the clutching poverty of the Erie. The Santa Fe moved westward from Kansas very briskly in the 1860s and 1870s. By the 1880s, however, it became obvious to the railroad's directors, as it had to other directors before, that a line with an eastern terminus in Kansas City was stunted in its growth. The Santa Fe would have to be content to be a feeder line unless it could have its own route to Chicago.

In 1880 the interline shipping agreements of today had not yet been worked out; Southwestern farmers and shippers who wanted to get their produce to the Great Lakes or the East Coast would first have to ship to Kansas City on the Santa Fe, and then make other arrangements for the trip to Chicago—a slow and costly process. In a way the same problem was faced by the Union Pacific, which had its eastern terminus at Council Bluffs, Iowa. Roads like the Santa Fe and the Union Pacific lived in mortal fear that some eastern road would build into their territory if they did not take a more active part in getting their shipments at least as far east as Chicago.

In the early 1880s the Santa Fe knew that it had to act. For a while it toyed with the idea of buying a feeder line to get to Chicago. One candidate was the Chicago & Alton. Later, however, it was decided that the best bet was to build a new line from Kansas City to Chicago. It was not entirely new, however, since a small line called the Chicago & St. Louis was bought which provided about one hundred miles of track west of Chicago. Even this one hundred miles would have to be rebuilt, since it was in poor condition.

Most of the way would have to be built from scratch. Thus began a classic American railroad scramble that would make the rapid Rock Island construction across Illinois look like child's play. The work began in March of 1887, and very shortly involved the use of some seven

thousand men. Construction was under the direction of two soon-to-be-distinguished engineers: Octave Chanute, later to become a famous aviation pioneer; and J. F. Wallace, who served as the Chief Engineer of the Panama Canal a few decades later.

The whole 450-mile line was completed in a little over a year, with much of the construction completed in the bitter winter of 1887–88. The genius of Octave Chanute was expressed in the erection of five long bridges, mostly constructed in vicious winter weather and involving almost two miles of bridge construction. There was the Illinois River Bridge, of 1,438 feet; the Mississippi span, of 2,963; the Missouri bridge, of 4,053; the Grand crossing, of 458; and the Des Moines bridge, of 900. The building of the big-

Cyrus K. Holliday, the Ohio lawyer who dreamed of building a railroad to follow the old Santa Fe Trail. His railroad enterprise was successful from the beginning, but the Santa Fe took a long time getting to Chicago, not arriving there until 1889.
(Kansas State Historical Society)

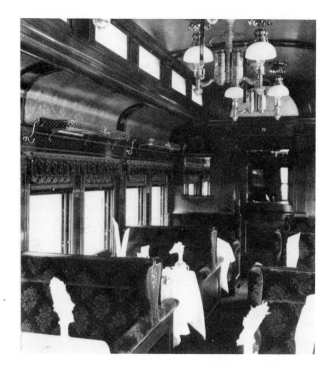

The very moment that the Santa Fe arrived in Chicago it saw itself as a transcontinental carrier of epic dimensions. To mark the event the line went out and purchased the very best of modern vestibule cars, Pullmans and dining cars for the Fred Harvey dining service, already the envy of the railroads around the country.
(Santa Fe)

Chicago continued to get most of its locomotives from the East, and they were getting handsomer and sturdier. Here is the 4-4-0 type *Crawford* built for the Chicago and North Western in 1867.
(Smithsonian Institution)

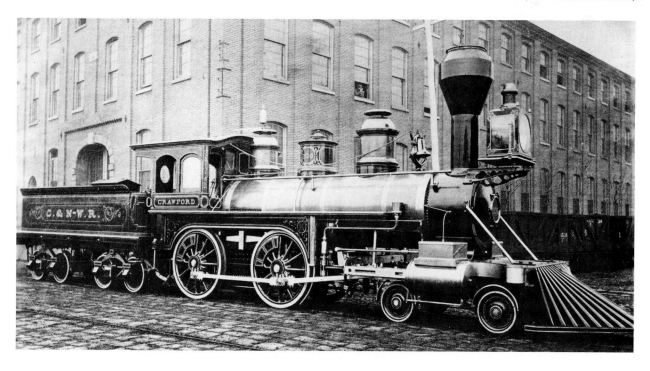

56

gest bridge of all, over the Missouri River, was hampered by ice and snow, but it was finished on schedule on February 11, 1888.

Meanwhile the Santa Fe was getting ready for a big celebration in Chicago. The railroad intended not only to get to Chicago, it also planned to arrive there in style. During the period of construction the railroad had spent $13,000,000 on real estate and construction in the city of Chicago, and now was in the process of ordering a fleet of electric-lighted vestibule trains for its passenger traffic between Chicago and the West. This was to be the beginning of a Herculean effort on the part of the Santa Fe to capture the carriage trade between Chicago and

One can only surmise what occasion prompted the photographic portrait shown here from the 1870s. The locomotive "Elkhorn" was not new, having been built in 1867, but the very neat-looking arch culvert at Rockford, Illinois, appears new. Its opening might have been the occasion of the portrait.

(Smithsonian Institution)

the Southwest—an effort and a battle the Santa Fe was to win and maintain as long as luxury-oriented passenger traffic lasted in the United States. The opulence offered by the "vestibuled cars" in 1888 burgeoned into the magnificence of the *Chief* and the *Super Chief* in the half-century between 1920 and 1970, a luxury that became fabled in American literature and films.

In Chicago the Santa Fe became a tenant of the Chicago and Western Indiana, just as the Erie had done, and was therefore an occupant of the Dearborn Station. The Santa Fe was as inappropriate for the Dearborn Station as the Erie had been appropriate. But that's the way things were in Chicago. Chicago had become the greatest junction of the American railroads. Every phenomenon known to the railroad industry was soon to be found in this fast-sprouting American metropolis. The great and the small, the strong and the weak, would all seek out Chicago as the place of hope and destiny.

By the mid-twentieth century, the railroad would be eclipsed in Chicago as the industry of industries. It would become one among many. In the late years of the nineteenth century and the early years of the twentieth, however, the railroad was not just a physical property but a creative, driving force that could impel men onward to feats of achievement like the Santa Fe's mad dash eastward from Kansas City. In those times Chicago and the railroad grew together with a frenzy and passion. While this would

Before the decade of the 1870s was over the Chicago and North Western was a giant enterprise. In 1881 it opened the famous Wells Street Station shown here—the station and yards are the present site of the Merchandise Mart.

(Chicago and North Western Railroad)

sometimes be the source of trouble as well as fame and fortune for both, the magic of the spectacular growth of Chicago as a railroad town was a display of economic achievement never matched in human history.

CHAPTER 4

Days of Growth and Glory

The years after the Civil War have often been referred to as the Gilded Age; it was a time of great ambition, dynamism and growth in all phases of American life. It was a time in which great fortunes and industrial empires grew and prospered. So they did, too, in Chicago, and Chicago was not without its own set of millionaires—men like Potter Palmer, Marshall Field, Philip Danforth Armour, and, even earlier, William Butler Ogden, whose railroad and real estate holdings made him Chicago's richest citizen in the years before 1865.

But it was not so much opulence and wealth that impressed visitors about Chicago; it was the tremendous pace of things, the almost unbelievable growth of the city in all of its dimensions. Chicago had to hustle to keep abreast of other metropolises, and this was never more apparent than the period immediately after the great Chicago Fire of 1871. Chicago had to rebuild and it had to rebuild on a grandiose scale if it was to once again join the first rank of American cities.

The rebuilding was almost immediate, and no historian has ever been able to give an adequate explanation of this indomitable expression of the human will. Potter Palmer had lost both his hotel, the Palmer House, and a fortune in State Street real estate. He began to rebuild both immediately. Marshall Field and Levi Leiter had had their dry goods business leveled; yet they opened in a temporary location in a South Side car barn while their new State Street store was being finished. William D. Kerfoot, later a great real estate tycoon, inspired his neighbors and fellow citizens by erecting a makeshift shack exactly one day after the fire, nailing to it a sign that read, "All lost except wife, children and energy."

And the rebuilding effort was more than the work of a few isolated individuals. All trade and commercial organizations were eager to get back into business. On October 10, 1871, the day after the fire, the directors of the Chamber of Commerce, which then housed the Board of Trade, met and decided to build a larger and more lavish temple of commerce than the one they had just lost—a very typical pattern of the day. True to their word, they built one which opened exactly one year later.

One major industry that was in a position to snap back especially quickly was the railroad—the industry that had made Chicago the great city that it already was. True enough, most of the city's major passenger terminals were wiped out in the fire, but the tracks were little harmed and ready to receive traffic almost immediately. People and cargo could for the time being be unloaded at the side of the track when necessary, even though it was not necessary for very long. New and better stations were needed anyway and these were immediately provided.

Chicago had already proved itself as the great railroad junction of America, and it did not have to prove itself over again. The period between 1871 and 1900 was one of even more unbelievable growth, with more and more lines

On Sunday evening, October 8, 1871, a fire started in the vicinity of Patrick O'Leary's barn on De Koven Street. It soon became, as everyone knows, the Great Chicago Fire. In this picture, the fire is shown hopelessly out of control spreading across the Chicago River, probably with the aid of ships' masts.

(University of Illinois Library)

GAZETTE EXTRA.

Terrific Fire in Chicago.
The Fire Still Raging.   Many Lives Lost.

Earlville, Monday Oct. 9th, 12 M.

A sad day is this for Chicago, the Pride of the West. A fire originated in the heart of the city, last night, which has destroyed many lives, and a large proportion of the wholesale business houses, public buildings, hotels, printing houses and others. Among the most prominent are The Court House, Sherman House, Tremont House, Board of Trade building, W. U. Tel. building, Post Office, J. V. Farwell, Crosby Opera House.

At this hour, 12 M. the orders of the C. B. & Q. R. R. Officers indicate that they do not expect to save the Union Depot. No freight is allowed to go east of Aurora, and all engines there are ordered into the city.

The Mayor of Aurora sent in the Aurora fire engines this morning, to assist in the terrible struggle.

Miss Rockwell, telegraph operator, from whom we obtain these news, and who still has communication with the Railway operator at the South Branch learns that the Fire is now working among business houses on Lake Street, and had crossed to the West Side of the River, on Monroe Street.

No trains have arrived at this station from Chicago to-day, and the understanding at Aurora is that none will leave Chicago today.

LATER, AND MORE CORRECT.   2 P. M.

The Operator learns that the Fire commenced on Saturday night, in a barn; at my request she asked how the fire originated; the reply was, "There are many rumors; one is, that a woman was milking a cow by the light of a lantern, and the cow kicked the lantern over." This might have been ironical.

The Union Depot, and the Gen. Office of the C B & Q are burned, not blown up, as first reported.

The Fire has reached Lincoln Park, THREE MILES NORTH. OF THE RIVER, AND AT This hour they say it is so bad on the North Side, that nothing but RAIN can save them! (Miss Rockwell says it has been raining hard in Galesburg for an hour) "ONE-FOURTH OF CHICAGO IS BURNED." "Fire is worse than ever." No Express goods, stock or freight are allowed to enter the city, "for," say the respective officers, "there is no knowing where this thing may end."

LATER.—5 P M.—The Company have decided to send out Pass. No. 7 this evening; Time here 6:28. Probably Cumming's train also.

CALL FOR AID.

Dispatch from Sargeant.

Aurora, Oct. 9th, 1871.

To all Agents:

There will be a train leave Galesburg at 8 o'clock to-night, with box cars to pickup PROVISIONS for the Suffering People of Chicago.

Thousands there are without FOOD.

Notify your people to bring to Depot to-night, what they wish to donate.

A. L. SARGENT,
Master of Transportation.

THIS TRAIN WILL BE IN EARL ABOUT MIDNIGHT. NO LATER NEWS YET.—6:15.

News of the fire spread quickly by means of telegraphy, the wires of which followed the railroad lines. As can be seen in this poster, disaster relief was on the way by rail from nearby communities all over Illinois.

(University of Illinois Library)

being built to every point of the compass. Chicago's function as a great rail center brought all kinds of new dimensions to the city's reputation. In 1873, with prominent citizens like Potter Palmer taking up subscriptions, the Interstate-Exposition Company was organized, the intention of which was to build an exposition hall. This gave rise to one of Chicago's most famous industries from that day to this: the convention business. By 1884 Chicago had enough hotels and other facilities that both the Republican and Democratic parties could hold their national conventions in the city. And in less than a decade city boosters were talking about a great exposition to celebrate the four hundredth anniversary of Columbus's discovery of America.

The period between the Great Fire and the Columbian Exposition was one of regular and unceasing proliferation of railway lines in and out of Chicago: the building of a few completely new roads and the reinforcement of others that were once small-scale roads serving a few local points. Above all, competition caused the development of many parallel and competing lines, some of which eventually grew to be giants of the railroad industry, others of which were later swallowed up or abandoned.

There was, for example, no easing of the great competition to the east of Chicago, where the battle of the titans, between Vanderbilt and Frederick F. Joy, continued apace. In time a

A panorama of the Chicago fire as compiled by newspaper artists of the day. The railroads suffered heavy losses in stations, offices and warehouses. In fact, the only important rail structure to survive was the Illinois Central freight house. But the iron rails were responsible for the quick recovery of the city.

(University of Illinois Library)

spate of trunk lines pushed into Chicago from the East, serving especially the Great Lakes cities of Detroit, Cleveland, Buffalo and Toledo. So many lines struck out across southern Michigan and northern Indiana that it is nothing short of miraculous that civil war didn't erupt over territorial rights. By and large, most of the activity was an effort to spite old Commodore Vanderbilt (and later those of his heirs and assigns).

Some rather important railroads arrived in Chicago as a result of this competition. One was the New York, Chicago and St. Louis Railway (later popularly known as the Nickel Plate)

WHERE THE FIRE BEGAN.

POST-OFFICE AND CUSTOM-HOUSE.

CHAMBER OF COMMERCE AND COURT-HOUSE.

LAND-OFFICE, ILLINOIS CENTRAL R.R.

CROSBY'S DISTILLERY.

REPUBLIC LIFE INSURANCE COMPANY.

MASONIC TEMPLE, DEARBORN STREET.

FIRST NATIONAL BANK.

which was in a position to threaten Vanderbilt's monopoly of the traffic between Buffalo and Chicago. The railroad was chartered in 1881 in Indiana and was built almost its entire length in one year—an almost incomprehensible achievement by today's standards. It followed the path of Vanderbilt's Lake Shore route the whole way like some annoying and malicious twin brother. It did not immediately gain admittance to Chicago, however, and had to settle for trackage arrangements that were neither advantageous nor secure. Shortly, the inevitable happened: the commodore's son, William K. Vanderbilt, new commander of the Vanderbilt empire, could not abide this upstart and bought it out in 1883. The result was that on May 2, 1883, Nickel Plate trains began running into Chicago on Lake Shore tracks. Thus it also became a tenant of the La Salle Street Station.

Vanderbilt's efforts to stifle competition were not always this effective. The arrival in Chicago of the Grand Trunk Western is a case in point. The Grand Trunk Western Railroad was an offspring of the Canadian giant called the Grand Trunk Lines, the railroad that eventually became the Canadian National in 1922. The Canadian line wanted to have its own access to Chicago, because that city had become important in the commercial affairs of all North America. For a time it was content to roll its own cars to Chicago over the tracks of the Chicago, Detroit & Canada Grand Trunk Railroad, which didn't actually go to Chicago but connected Port Huron, Michigan (the Canadian port of entry), and Detroit with the Michigan Central, which allowed a transfer of Grand Trunk cars for Chicago. This connection began in 1859, and all went well for 20 years until William K. Vanderbilt decided to put a stop to this traffic and blockaded the Grand Trunk.

For once, however, Vanderbilt had an unexpected battle on his hands. Sir Henry Tyler, the Grand Trunk's president, stormed out from Montreal with a fierce determination to build his own wholly new line to Chicago. This line was opened on February 8, 1880. Passenger trains to Chicago at first used makeshift terminal facilities, but after the opening of the Dearborn Station the Grand Trunk became a tenant there, and remained so till the end of Grand Trunk passenger service in Chicago in 1971. The Grand

The Wells Street Station of the Chicago and North Western gives an idea of the already brisk passenger traffic of the road in 1881. But in 20 years this station would be hopelessly inadequate and outmoded. The rigs in the foreground are the celebrated omnibuses of the Parmalee Company.

(Chicago and North Western Railroad)

Trunk also picked up some very brisk freight business with its new line to Chicago, and quickly became a very competitive partner in the east-west grain and livestock business. Much of this was business that Vanderbilt could have kept had he not denied the Canadians access to the Michigan Central main line into Chicago.

Another ghost from the past also came back to haunt Vanderbilt. James F. Joy, the former lawyer from Detroit who had made a success of the Michigan Central only to find it rudely snatched away by Vanderbilt interests, took an unconcealed delight in taking charge of a new railroad in the same territory—the Wabash. Joy's rail interests had mostly moved westward after he had assumed the presidency of the Burlington, but he must have chortled with delight a few years later when he could stir up a little commotion in the Vanderbilt fiefdom. At first the Wabash was not an obvious threat to the southern lakeshore territory; it moved out of Detroit, but with no glance toward Chicago. In-

deed, the main stem of the Wabash thrust out in a southwesterly direction, through Toledo and thence winding its way down along the Wabash River and lush valleys of Indiana, across the central Illinois prairie to St. Louis. It was an excellent route structure in every way.

In another decade, however, the Wabash would be knocking on Chicago's door from the East, entering competition with the New York Central, the Nickel Plate, the Grand Trunk, the Pennsylvania and the others. In May 1892 the Wabash opened up its new line from Montpelier, Michigan, to Chicago—a very decided and convenient short-line between Detroit and Chicago. Joy had retired from the Wabash management by this time, but he lived long enough to witness this affront to the New Yorkers in actual operation. In the twentieth century, the Wabash took every advantage of this short-line and set out to skim the cream off the Chicago–Detroit trade. The line continued to be a thorn in the side of the Central for many years. The Wabash took up residence in the Dearborn Station—along with the Grand Trunk.

Most of the other railroads that arrived in Chicago in the last two decades of the nineteenth century developed from small local carriers that

The first of two famous stations in Chicago called Union Station (both located at Canal and Adams). It was built in 1880 to bring together the passenger services of the Milwaukee, the Burlington, the Alton, and the Pennsylvania, and their predecessor companies. The station continued in service until 1925 when the present Union Station was opened.

(Milwaukee Road)

made their way, and their name, by going somewhere big—Chicago. In the June 1893 issue of the *Railway Guide* one finds a list of 32 railroads whose names began with the word Chicago. Most of them naturally did not start in Chicago; they started out in the country and gravitated toward the big city.

A good example of such rural origins were two railroads born in Indiana as local carriers—the Monon and the Chicago and Eastern Illinois. Both were chartered in the Hoosier State and, at first, had no thought of extending to Chicago. The C&EI, for instance, started building in 1849, but its first track was a 28-mile stretch from Evansville north to Princeton, Indiana. For many years the C&EI was known locally as the Evansville Route. It kept east of the Wabash River, a homespun local product of the Hoosier State, but by the 1880s the road had made its way over into eastern Illinois and started the

The interior of the old Union Station, showing the inadequate but beautifully ornate waiting room. This station had to carry on during the 10 long years that the present Union Station struggled to come into being.

(Burlington Northern)

dash for Chicago. By the 1890s the official name of the road offered no mention at all of the state of Indiana. Even the executive offices had long since been moved up to Chicago.

In the twentieth century, many Chicagoans esteemed the C&EI for the ultra-deluxe flyers it ran between Chicago and the sunny shores of Florida—trains like the *Dixie Flyer*, the *Dixie Limited*, the *Henry L. Flagler*. Few of these luxury-loving travelers to the Floridian resorts even knew that they were passing through the state of Indiana—or, for that matter, cared.

Another railroad which eventually arrived in Chicago from Indiana, but which refused to lose its Hoosier identity, was the Monon, the popular name for the Louisville, New Albany and Chicago Railroad, strictly a local Indiana line. Its moving spirit was a downeasterner from Maine, James Brooks, who somehow inveigled the State of Indiana into giving him a remarkable "roving charter" to build a railroad "to any

other point or points in the state." The Monon did, in fact, do a lot of building in Indiana, and arrived at Michigan City, Indiana, on Lake Michigan, as early as 1854. Strangely enough, President Brooks thought for a long time that this should be the end of the line, since he had in effect tapped the resources of the Chicago area. Furthermore, he favored the idea of Indiana passengers sailing to Chicago from Michigan City by steamboat. For a long time, therefore, the Monon failed to penetrate the Chicago railroad spaghetti bowl. But the inevitable could not be avoided, and the Monon arrived in Chicago in 1881, first over Erie tracks from Hammond,

The end of the nineteenth century saw an extraordinarily large number of railroad lines in the Chicago area, most now completely forgotten. Here is the Oak Park Station of the Chicago, Harlem and Batavia Railroad, sometimes called the "Dummy Line." The year was 1885.

(Oak Park Public Library)

then, after 1884, over its own rails to a connection with the Chicago and Western Indiana terminal tracts. The Monon has always stubbornly kept its Indiana identification, using the slogan "the Hoosier Line" in its advertisements. It did, however, extend as far south as Louisville, Kentucky.

Another railroad that can be solidly identified as having Indiana roots was the so-called "Big Four" (the Cleveland, Cincinnati, Chicago and St. Louis). It was basically an east-west railroad which linked central Indiana with major cities in both directions—Cincinnati, Cleveland, Peoria and St. Louis. Chicago was in the name, but was never a really important point on the route. The Big Four brought its passengers to Chicago over the Illinois Central from Kankakee northward, and the line's Chicago passengers arrived and departed from Central Station in Chicago for many years. In the early 1890s the Big

Four merged with the New York Central, but maintained operational independence—the Vanderbilts for once seemingly understanding of the need for regional autonomy. The Big Four had its own executives and its own office building in Indianapolis, and the name New York Central was not seen on the lobby directory board.

New lines from the north and east were venturing toward Chicago in the years after the Great Fire. One latecomer was the Chicago Great Western, which, like the Monon, was the brainchild of a displaced New Englander—Alpheus Beede Stickney. During its prime the Chicago and Great Western operated 1,500 miles of track in the states of Illinois, Iowa, Kansas, Minnesota, Nebraska and Missouri, running through some of America's richest agricultural territory. Appropriately, the road took on the nickname, "The Corn Belt Route." In spite of the identification with Chicago, it never became an important carrier of passengers to Chicago, arriving in the city only in 1892. The road became a long-time tenant of Grand Central Station, and became a weak-sister competitor in the Chicago-Twin Cities rivalry. Passenger service into Chicago ended in 1956, and the Chicago and Great Western passed into history altogether in

1967, when the line was merged with the Chicago and North Western.

Shortly after its construction in the early 1890s, Grand Central Station became host to two other railroads that reached out to the territories north of Chicago. One was the Wisconsin Central, which eventually became absorbed by the Minneapolis, St. Paul and Sault Ste. Marie Railway (Soo Line). At one point the Wisconsin Central was even the owner of the Grand Central Station, but a scant few years later was forced to sell it to the Baltimore & Ohio. Still later the Wisconsin Central became nothing but the southern spur of the Soo. The Soo was a railroad of Canadian origin, the dream of Sir William Van Horne, titan of the Canadian Pacific, who built the Soo as a short-cut route across the northern peninsula of Michigan—thus avoiding the long Canadian route north around Lake Superior. (This was also a very clever way to slip Canadian freight through the upper United States.) Later on the Soo ran a number of successful trains to the Pacific Northwest, some of them out of Chicago, but the line was never

The major commuter lines of Chicago had mostly taken on their present form and character by the late 1880s and 1890s. In those years they built some fairly large stations, such as this one the C&NW at Geneva built in 1895. This picture was taken in 1897, but the station was sufficiently substantial to the last until about 1960.

(Geneva Historical Society)

River Forest, in spite of its closeness to Chicago, was strictly a country delight when this picture was taken in 1903. Today the stop doesn't generate much business, but in the early part of the century, before the automobile, things must have been different.

(Oak Park Public Library)

highly significant in the Chicago area. And all passenger service into Chicago was abandoned in 1965.

Another long-time visitor to Grand Central Station from the North Country was the Pere Marquette, which was an amalgamation of a number of railroads in central and northern Michigan. The Pere Marquette arrived in Chicago in 1903, and over the next several decades contributed a significant part of the passenger business in Grand Central, especially in the summertime, when a large number of Chicagoans took trains to the Michigan vacationlands. This traffic was severely reduced with the coming of the automobile after World War I, however. The Pere Marquette was merged with the Chesapeake & Ohio Railroad in 1947, and the latter road continued to operate a small number of the old Pere Marquette runs into Chicago until the closing of Grand Central Station in 1969.*

To the outside observer, the late nineteenth century was more than a time for the construction of lines to Chicago; it was a time of specialization and intensification for both the railroad industry and other industries that depended on it. Any industry that could be or needed to be served by the railroads grew up with breathtaking swiftness. So, Chicago became a center for grain, lumber, iron and steel, meat packing, and merchandising of every conceivable sort. When some of the cattle trade was diverted to western cities like Omaha or Kansas City, Chicago got into meat packing in a big way, with Gustavus Swift ingeniously devising a way to send his meat products around the country in refrigerator cars. It was a time for discovering that Chicago didn't have to be simply a place where things passed through on the way from East to West (or vice versa). Chicago could devise new and independent manufactures of its own. In 1880 Chicago was only sixth in the number of manufacturing establishments in the United States, behind New York, Philadelphia, Brooklyn (which didn't become part of New York City until 1898), Baltimore and Boston. But by 1880, Chicago ranked third behind New York and Philadelphia.

Because of some fluke of history not easy to explain, Chicago never became a center for the manufacture of railroad locomotives in the nineteenth century. This industry remained in the East with such works as that of Matthias W. Baldwin of Philadelphia and Thomas Rogers of Paterson, New Jersey. The Chicago Locomotive Works of Hiram H. Scoville, at Canal and Adams on the south branch of the Chicago River, produced a number of locomotives, including six for the Galena and Chicago Union Railroad. Later in the nineteenth century, the Hicks Locomotive and Car Works was busily engaged in rebuilding locomotives, and had a large plant for manufacturing railway cars. During the days of the steam locomotive, however, Chicago did not become a major railway manufacturing center. This historical oddity was redressed in the twentieth century with the location in La Grange of the world's largest diesel locomotive manufacturing plant.

There was one major exception, of course, and one that Americans have had occasion to remember for one reason or another. This was the car-manufacturing business of George Mortimer Pullman, a man whose name would shortly be known throughout North America. For a time, Pullman did some of his manufacturing outside his home base of Chicago (he moved to Detroit for a while), and later on the manufacturing became decentralized, but altogether the Pullman Company must be thought of as a Chicago concern and the sleeping car industry grew to

*The Chesapeake & Ohio had its own rail connection to Chicago from its main eastern regions, but it was never an important carrier in the Chicago vicinity. For a while it sent passenger trains on its own lines into the Illinois Central terminal, but after 1932 these trains came into Chicago over the Big Four tracks.

George Mortimer Pullman, the man who popularized the sleeping car and made it respectable. In time the manufacture of Pullman cars centered in Chicago and resulted in the great industrial complex and model town of Pullman on the south side of the city. The Pullman "system" of both manufacturing and operating its luxury cars worked remarkably well for a time, but economic troubles of the 1890s resulted in the Pullman strike and something of a diminution of Pullman's reputation.

(Library of Congress)

nationwide prominence by the efforts of its Chicago plant.

Like so many of Chicago's great names in railroading, Pullman was not a native and he was not drawn to the city by an interest in railroads. Pullman was born in Brocton, Chautauqua County, New York, in 1831. His father was a successful but not prosperous house builder, and George followed in his footsteps, first as a cabinet maker and then as a builder. One aspect of his father's work was rather peculiar, however, and it was this specialty that later drew Pullman to Chicago. When the New York State legislature decided to widen the Erie Canal, the elder Pullman won several contracts from the state to move houses that were too near the

banks of the canal at Albion, New York. George's father died in 1853, leaving the work unfinished, and George quickly became an expert at house moving.

After the work along the Erie Canal was finished he moved to Chicago and quickly found himself involved in even more elaborate house-moving enterprises. In the early 1850s the city of Chicago was having severe problems with properties that were nearly at the same level as Lake Michigan and the Chicago River. Street drainage became a nightmare, and citizens, even those with mansions along Michigan Avenue, found it impossible to keep cellars dry. The only answer was to raise the levels of the streets, and this naturally meant raising houses as well. George M. Pullman had arrived in Chicago just in time to put into practice his expertise, and he opened an office and shop on Madison Street west of La Salle. For several years he plugged away at the business of raising houses, and before long he was the city's undisputed master in this field. In 1858 he was handed the most challenging job of all when Chicago's largest hotel, the Tremont, had to be lifted. Lifting a frame house is one thing, but raising an entire four-story building made of brick is something else. Yet Pullman did it with aplomb. Using a thousand men and four thousand jackscrews, Pullman managed to elevate the hotel without even having to evacuate the guests.

Later on Pullman raised a whole block of brick stores on Lake Street without breaking so much as a single pane of glass. By the age of 27, he was one of the city's more prominent citizens, worth $20,000. The house-raising business could not last forever; Pullman knew that he soon must discover another line of work. One winter when frozen conditions made the raising of buildings impossible, Pullman returned by train to the East. It was then (as he later told it) that he conceived the idea of building a decent railway

Pullman kept his company's executive offices close to downtown Chicago even as he was building his model manufacturing town on the south side. This is the Pullman Building at Michigan Avenue and Adams Street, the present site of the Borg Warner Building.
(University of Illinois Library)

Pullman bought a seven-square mile tract on the west shore of Lake Calumet in 1880 and erected the town and manufacturing center that brought him first fame and then grief. Behind a graceful artificial lake is the main building of the Pullman car works which stands to this day, although in a much more dreary environment.
(Library of Congress)

sleeping car. In the 1850s travel between New York and Chicago was positively deplorable. The trip took about three days, almost all of which was endured in smoky, poorly heated and ill-ventilated day coaches. One had to change trains several times and stay in hotels of dubious or unknown quality. The unsophisticated traveler who didn't know how to plan his trip found himself traveling at night on wooden seats and discovered the uncertain delights of having to stagger out of the cars with his luggage in the middle of the night, or perhaps give it over to the ministrations of some local baggage smasher.

Pullman became convinced that the public would be more than happy to pay a little extra for sleeping facilities on a train and would do almost anything to escape the worst of the uncomfortable and fragmented journey. Pullman was not the first to install sleeping facilities in a railroad car. As early as 1836 the Cumberland Valley Railroad had installed some beds in its regular day coaches. Two years later one Charles McGrew took out the first patent for a sleeping car. The first really significant designers, however, were Webster Wagner, a New York stationmaster (who in 1856 fitted out a sleeping car that won the approval of Commodore Vanderbilt for service on the New York Central), and T. T. Woodruff, a master mechanic of the Terre Haute and Alton line. In time both became prominent sleeping car manufacturers and, for a few years, were major competitors of Pullman.

Pullman's first venture into the sleeping car business was not particularly successful. In partnership with a fellow New Yorker, Pullman contracted to build and operate sleeping cars on two railroads, the Chicago and Alton and the Chicago and Galena. At first Pullman merely reconverted cars already in existence, but in 1862 he built a sleeping car from scratch for the Alton. Even this was rather primitive, and probably not as successful as those being built by Webster Wagner. Unfortunately, with the Civil War in full swing, the sleeping cars then in existence were requisitioned by the Union Army for use in troop transport.

Later in the war, and after a period of inactivity in which he spent long hours at the drawing board thinking up new ideas and devices for sleeping cars, Pullman went back to work for the Alton. This time he came up with something impressive. After many months of working with master mechanics in 1864, Pullman produced a railroad car which soon became a classic fixture of railroad lore. This car, known as the *Pioneer* (alas, a name too often repeated around Chicago), displayed a tremendous advancement in luxury and quality. Longer, wider, and higher than any car built up to that time, and costing much more to build ($20,000—five times the cost of a typical railroad car of that day), the *Pioneer* had two cast-iron trucks (each with eight wheels), and coiled springs reinforced with rubber blocks. But it was the interior that really caught the eye. Doors and window sashes were of hand-made and polished woods; there were plush carpets and gilt-edged mirrors. And there was an ingenious feature for which Pullman would long remain famous: hinged upper berths, which could be cleverly concealed behind luxurious wood paneling during the day.

Shortly after the *Pioneer* was built, Pullman had an extraordinary opportunity to publicize his efforts. After the assassination of President Lincoln in April of 1865, an elaborate funeral train was requisitioned to take the president's body from Washington to his home in Springfield. The part of the journey between Chicago and Springfield would be on the Alton. Pullman managed to have the *Pioneer* included in the funeral train and drummed up a great deal of local publicity for his extraordinary new car. Especially impressed were the officers of the Alton, who put the car into regular service on May 25, 1865. Pullman took advantage of all the publicity surrounding the *Pioneer* to approach several other roads, including the Burlington and the Michigan Central. Orders started pouring in.

By May of 1866 there were 21 Pullman cars in operation, and by year's end there were 48 cars. Everyone who rode in them testified that Pullman cars were *the* answer to the agony of long-distance train travel. No car made in Amer-

72

The center of community life in Pullman was the Arcade Building which contained the stores, the Pullman bank, a post office and other necessities of ordinary life. In the beginning it was all very impressive, and one reporter described it as an American oriental bazaar.

(Illinois Historical Survey)

ica at that time gave anything even approaching such a comfortable ride. In a twinkling railroads all over the United States were experiencing a revolution in passenger service.

In later years, after he had become a millionaire many times over, Pullman was asked the secret of his success. His invariable answer was that his success was due to the "Pullman system." He was referring to another concept in his plan for the sleeping car. Pullman sensed very early that it was not enough to merely manufacture cars and put them out on the roads. For this new product to succeed it would have to be part of a complete system of transportation. Not only would the Pullman company build its cars, it would also operate them. It would establish and maintain standards and conditions of service right down to the minutest detail. The Pullman system codified all of its services. It developed a system of smooth baggage han-

dling. It hired its own conductors to enforce company rules, such as the rule against wearing boots to bed. Later on came that great American institution, the Pullman porter, who was trained by the company to render efficient service to passengers, to make up beds and clean cars. The highest standards of cleanliness were maintained. The Pullman company hired "spotters" to ride as passengers and to take note of soiled linen or less-than-gleaming washbasins. Hygenic standards were unexcelled for that day. Each car was equipped with 100 sheets and pillow cases, 40 blankets, and many towels of various types. All bedding was removed regularly, beaten and exposed to the sun. Bedding was changed every night without fail. It was not just the Pullman car, but Pullman service that immediately caught on with the public. Those who went Pullman would not only travel in comfort, but in style as well.

Before too many years Pullman was to add a third element to his "system." Not only would there be a Pullman car and a protocol of Pullman service, there would be a unique manufacturing arm of the company geared to large-scale production. This last idea took the longest to develop in Pullman's mind and did not materialize for a number of years. It involved the planning and construction of a "model town" south of Chicago, a place not only for the construction of Pullman cars but for the housing of Pullman workers as well—a total environment for living and working. In 1880 Pullman bought a seven-square-mile tract on the west shore of Lake Calumet that had mostly been a desolate marshland. Here with the help of Solon Spenser Beman, later the architect of Grand Central Station, and landscape architect Nathan F. Barrett he built a model industrial town, the purpose of which (in Pullman's mind) was to counteract the grime of the inner-city industrial neighborhoods and to provide a clean and orderly environment for manufacturing. Pullman himself was a neat and tidy man and he saw no reason why manufacturing had to be carried on in squalid and degrading circumstances. The town of Pullman was not a town in any legal sense, but only a subdivision of Hyde Park. The Pullman Company owned the land, the building, and all the news media.

For a while the project seemed like a good idea. Even the workers admitted the town was beautiful. It had parks, playgrounds, lakes and gardens; it had churches and even a splendid library. It was in every sence what a correspondent of the New York *Sun* called in 1885 a "philanthropic monopoly."

In time, however, this brand of paternalism soured. Pullman was at heart a self-righteous moralist who knew only too well what was good for other people. He stood firmly against liquor, prostitution and trade unions. His workers paid dearly for the neat, tree-lined streets. Rents were 25 percent higher than in Chicago. Workers generally responded to Pullman's overbearing supervision with an unspoken but smoldering resentment. One worker who did speak out put it this way: "We are born in a Pullman house, fed from the Pullman shop, taught in the Pullman school, catechized in the Pullman church, and when we die we shall be buried in the Pullman cemetery and go to the Pullman hell."

This sullen chafing continued for a number of years, until in 1894 things turned positively ugly. The Panic of 1893 had resulted in a financial retrenchment for the Pullman company. Manufacturing of the "palace cars" continued unabated as did the operational side of the company. But Pullman had also gotten into the

This is a replica of Pullman's first attempt to build a sleeping car -- Chicago & Alton's No. 9 which Pullman converted from an ordinary coach in 1859 at the Alton's Bloomington's shops. He got $2,000 for the conversion. This was a far cry from the Pullmans of the next generation which established the word Pullman as synonymous with opulence and luxury.
(University of Illinois Library)

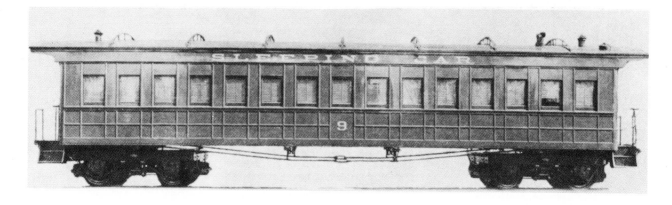

CHICAGO, Burlington AND QUINCY RAILROAD.

IS THE ONLY ROUTE RUNNING

PULLMAN 16-WHEEL

DRAWING ROOM SLEEPING CARS

IN AMERICA.

PULLMAN SIXTEEN WHEEL SLEEPING CAR.

BURLINGTON

THE ONLY ROUTE RUNNING

PULLMAN DINING CARS

FROM CHICAGO TO OMAHA!

The Press and Traveling Public pronounce it the Favorite Route for all points in

Nebraska, Wyoming, Colorado, Utah, Idaho, Montana, Nevada, Oregon, Arizona

AND CALIFORNIA.

You will find Tickets at General Office, 59 Clark St., Central Depot, Indiana Ave. and Canal St. Depots.

W. B. STRONG. Gen'l Sup't. Chicago, Ill.   JAMES WALLACE. City Pass. Agent. Chicago.   D. W. HITCHCOCK, Gen'l West'n Pass. Agt., Chicago, Ill.

CHICAGO EVENING JOURNAL PRINT.

manufacture of ordinary coaches, and orders for those fell drastically. There were layoffs, and finally Pullman cut the salaries of his workers by 25 percent, even though rents for the cottages in the town continued at the same rate.

The winter of 1893–94 was bitterly cold and bleak in the model town. The slums could have been no worse. Many children lacked the shoes to go to school and some had to stay in bed because there was no coal to heat the house. Into this gloomy picture stepped Eugene Victor Debs, a golden-tongued orator who had shortly before established the American Railway Union and with it had won the first strike by a railway union against James J. Hill's Great Northern. On May 11, 1894, Debs called the Pullman workers out on strike. By the following month the strike had spread to the railroads when they took to dismissing switchmen who refused to handle Pullman cars. The situation darkened and George Pullman earned himself the reputation (not entirely deserved) of being a hidebound traditionalist and gluttonous capitalist. Even the conservative Mark Hanna, soon to be the national leader of the Republican Party, said "A man who won't meet his men half-way is a God-damn fool."

But these were not propitious times for labor. President Grover Cleveland ordered the Army to break the Pullman strike over the protests of Chicago Mayor John P. Hopkins and Illinois Governor John Peter Altgeld (one of the most progressive American politicians of the time). Debs was arrested and later jailed, and the Pullman strike was broken.

Things were never the same thereafter for Pullman's model town. Of course business picked up again after the depression of 1893 and manu-

facturing went on, but thereafter nobody could look upon the town of Pullman in the same light. Its spirit was lost, and in time its substance as well. In 1898 the Supreme Court ordered Pullman to sell its residential holdings, and this decision eventually, if not immediately, spelled disaster for the remarkable aesthetic planning of Beman and Barrett. Pullman eventually declined into an inferior working-class neighborhood. Still later the Pullman Company itself moved away, leaving its old factory facilities to other firms. A small area of Pullman has now been revitalized after what is called "South Pullman" was named an historic site in 1969.

The Pullman Company (later Pullman Standard) continued to be an important force in the life of Chicago, even after the model community failed. Executive offices were maintained in the city, and, for a long time, so were manufacturing plants. After the long-distance rail business in the United States faded in the 1950s, Pullman discontinued making sleeping cars, but moved forward into other lines, one of which was the fulfillment of a large contract to manufacture the cars of the Chicago Rapid Transit Authority. And they did not entirely leave the luxury field. In 1979 Pullman Standard unveiled a line of semi-luxurious coaches and dining cars for use by Amtrak. This equipment was built in the company's Hammond, Indiana, plant.

The real importance of Pullman in American railway history is unrelated to the stormy history of the Chicago works, or to the mere invention of the sleeping car. Pullman, more than anyone else in America, was responsible for promoting the railroad as a safe, comfortable and even luxurious means of overland travel. After the 1870s it was not enough for the railroads to move people from place to place in a haphazard manner. Railroads had become big business—a business that appealed to the public with great flair and style. The Pullman Company (and, for a time, its competitors like Wagner and Woodruff) displayed ingenuity in providing all of the

An advertisement from the 1880s shows how the Pullman mystique had captured the railroad world. Here the Burlington is advertising 16-wheel drawing room sleeping cars as the main inducement to riding its trains between Chicago and Omaha.

(Author's Collection)

An artist's rendering of a sleeping car from the era of the stovepipe hat and the pot-bellied stove. It could be that this is a car from Pullman's early competitor Webster Wagner. In any case, some of the details are probably inaccurate and no car of this width would probably have been possible, even on the 6-foot Erie.

(University of Illinois Library)

trappings of fine homes and estates within the confines of a railway car. In the lingo of railroad men, the word "varnish" became synonymous with the passenger train, even though the passenger car did not universally borrow the varnished woods and plush interiors put into service by the Pullman Company. But Pullman was there to set the standard for all of the lesser conveyances: sumptuous decors, polished woods, private rooms, observation cars and lounges, luxurious dining, an abundance of food and drink courteous porters, and later, all manner of other helpful retainers such as barbers, ladies' maids, valets, secretaries and the like. In time the Pullman Company introduced all-steel construction, air conditioning, private rooms (and

even showers), and every imaginable convenience. As long as large-volume railway passenger travel lasted in America, these were the very hallmarks of railway luxury, the standards by which all such services were judged.

The introduction and spread of the sleeping car were also responsible for still other developments in railroad passenger service, namely the appearance of the crack long-distance train. If one wanted to ride between New York and Chicago in 1870, one would have to put up not only with sooty and tortuously uncomfortable and unheated cars but would also have to endure endless changes of trains, unreliable or unfamiliar inns, hostile baggage handlers and all the other nuisances of segmented travel.

The middle of the 1870s saw a growing and at times quite obsessive interest in a new element of rail travel that had previously been neglected: speed. The report of the New York Central and Harlem River Railroad in 1876 gave "the average speed of an ordinary passenger train as 25 miles per hour, including stops." An express train was not much faster, with an average speed of 30 miles per hour including stops. This might make for about 35 miles per hour in motion.

A few years before things had started to change, at least with a few very special routes. The New York Central was one of the innovators. James Gordon Bennett, Jr., publisher of the flamboyant *New York Herald*, goaded Commodore Vanderbilt to put some crack trains on his lines. Bennett's major interest was in promoting a fast train to Saratoga in upstate New York, then a very posh summer resort which Bennett hoped to be able to reach with his newspaper. And the goal was accomplished that very summer. The following summer Bennett was at it again, this time urging the Commodore to run a

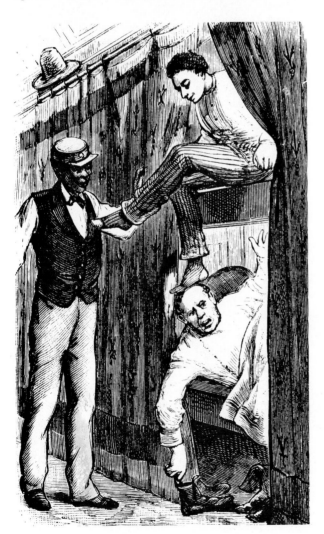

train right across the state of New York to Buffalo. If Buffalo, Bennett reasoned, why not all the way to Chicago? That's where the New York Central tracks really ended.

And so it was done. A two-car speed train, with Mr. and Mrs. Bennett aboard, left New York at 2:30 A.M. (after the Herald's morning paper was off the press) on July 4, 1875. The train stopped the following morning at Albany for breakfast (in 1875 there were no diners on the New York Central), was at Buffalo by 1 P.M., and in Chicago the next morning at 8 o'clock, a trip of almost 30 hours, quite astonishing for that long-ago time. Bennett paid the New York Central $1,000 for this little exploit and he paid the same sum for a similar run every Sunday for the next 10 weeks.

The idea did not exactly catch on like wildfire, but a precedent had been set. The Central put on a new engine, fresh out of its Syracuse shops, and said to be the fastest engine then in service in the United States. The engineer, Jim Wood, drove the engine between Albany and Buffalo, a distance of three hundred miles, at a time when no locomotive was run more than one hundred miles without being taken off for servicing. Too, this marathon train running, not only over several divisions, but over several distinct railroads (the Harlem, the New York Central and the Michigan Southern), prompted railroad officials and the general public to think in terms of long hauls and through service. It would be not too many years before the New York Central would unite its various lines, the distinctions between the earlier lines all but forgotten except perhaps in financial papers and director's reports.

So it wasn't long before the idea of a crack train between New York and Chicago caught

The American sleeping car provided for a certain amount of privacy, unlike some of its European counterparts where total strangers were often confined together for the night. Nonetheless, the open Pullman berths had their provisions for the risque, and, as shown here, they were not without strong possibilities for comic misadventure.

(University of Illinois Library)

James Gordon Bennett, Jr., the dissipated playboy owner of the *New York Herald,* was never without his surprises. Perhaps best known today for sending H. M. Stanley into darkest Africa to find Dr. Livingston, he deserves a footnote in railroad history as the instigator of the great railroad war for the traffic between New York and Chicago.

(New York Historical Society)

Sometimes the Pennsy and sometimes the Central were ahead in the race between Chicago and New York. In 1890 the Pennsy probably had the edge with its *Pennsylvania Limited,* shown here. But the New York Central would gain the upper hand in 1902 when it unleashed a train with the very compelling name *Twentieth Century Limited.*

(Penn Central)

H.L. Mencken, a notorious partisan of the Baltimore and Ohio, once remarked that a writer couldn't write anything worth reading for two or three hours after eating on the dining cars of the Pennsylvania Railroad. Undoubtedly that judgment would not have held in 1883, when the Pennsy invited its passengers to enjoy this holiday bill of fare.

(Penn Central)

1883-4. **Holiday Menu.** 1883-4

BLUE POINTS ON HALF SHELL

Terrapin Soup.
Kennebec Salmon with Green Peas.
Potatoes à la Parisienne.

Boiled Leg of Lamb, caper sauce.   Boiled Capon, cream sauce.

Ribs of Beef with brown potatoes.

Turkey, cranberry sauce   Tame Goose stuffed with apples
Roast Beef.

Sweetbreads larded with Mushrooms.
Salmi of Quail with Truffles.

Roast Partridge, bread sauce.

Chicken Salad.   Smoked Buffalo Tongue.   Paté of Snipe in Jelly

Celery.   Olives.

Baked Sweet Potatoes.   Pickled Beets.   Mashed Potatoes
French Peas.   Asparagus.   Marrow Squash.

Steamed Fruit Pudding, Cognac sauce.

Apple Pie.   Mince Pie.   Strawberry Ice Cream.   Roman Punch
Macaroons.   Confectionery   Assorted Cake.

Florida Oranges.   Apples.   Malaga Grapes.
Bent's Water Crackers.   Roquefort.   Edam.
Coffee.   Tea.

MEALS, ONE DOLLAR.

on. In the public imagination this soon became a train that would speed from New York to Chicago in 26 hours or even 24 (in the next century this was to be cut to 16 hours, and even, for a very brief time, 15½).

All of this easily and logically led to the great train, the train with a name, the train that would offer the best in service, and also act as a railroad's flagship of wealth, aggressiveness and individual style. Not surprisingly, it was the Eastern roads, roads like the New York Central and the Pennsylvania, that led the way in railroad opulence. The competition was still for the New York-to-Chicago traffic and both the "Pennsy" and Central (and later—to a lesser ex-

tent—the Baltimore and Ohio) wanted to steal each other's business. The whole game became one of outdoing one another in speed, in ostentation, in finer points of service, in fancy names. In time it became a war of publicity men.

In the 1880s and 1890s it seemed as though the Pennsylvania had the edge in the cutthroat competition. First with its *New York and Chicago Limited* and later with its *Pennsylvania Limited*, the Pennsylvania kept abreast of all the latest technological developments as well as all of the symbols of luxury. As early as 1887 the *Chicago Limited* offered electric lights as standard equipment. In 1889 the Pennsylvania experimented with heating cars by steam from the locomotive, an advance widely praised by grateful passengers. During the same period the Pennsylvania was introducing new and previously unheard-of service personnel—a barber, a stenographer, a lady's maid and an electrician (all the wrinkles not yet having been worked out with that new invention called electricity). All this in addition to the eye-popping grandeur of plush cushions, mahogany woodwork, crystal glass and spotless linens.

But the New York Central wasn't to be left behind, and soon the Central's management had the Pennsy gasping. The Central had, it seems, the slickest passenger agent of them all in the person of its general passenger agent, the pudgy, mutton-chopped George H. Daniels, a man with an eye for things that caught the public's fancy.

It took a long time for rail travel west of Chicago to become as sedate and luxurious as it was in the East. First there were vast stretches of territory to be built up (as shown here during the late 1860s), and for many years the wide-open spaces were inviting to hostile Indians, buffalo, train robbers and all the other menacing phenomena known to the watchers of Western movies.
(Illinois State Historical Library)

Daniels could think up superlatives in endless profusion, including the slogan by which he referred to the New York Central as "America's Greatest Railroad!" In 1891 Daniels put on a great crack express between New York City and Buffalo. He called it *The Empire State Express*—and it was a train on which the Central never ceased to lavish its best equipment. But Daniels' most famous and longlasting achievement was his 1902 selection of *The Twentieth Century Limited* as the name for the road's flagship on the New York-to-Chicago run. The Pennsylvania immediately countered with its own *Broadway Limited*, but this train never quite caught the public fancy like the *Twentieth Century* did, even though it was as excellent in every point of comparison.

Great luxury trains out of Chicago to the West were mostly a product of the twentieth century. As soon as the Santa Fe had built to Chicago, it was eager to get into the luxury business almost immediately. It put in an order for vestibuled cars, even though real luxury sleeping service to the West Coast did not begin until the mid-1890s.

Fred Harvey, the man who civilized the West. Harvey's first association was with the Santa Fe, for which railroad he built and ran some marvelous restaurants and hotels right out in the wild and woolly West. Even the most unruly cowboy took off his hat in a Harvey establishment, and nobody put a bullet through the walls. Chicagoans would come to know the Harvey name mostly through the fine restaurants of a later year in a number of the great stations of the city.

(Kansas State Historical Society)

Until the nineties the Western roads were generally compelled, in the absence of sleeping and dining cars, to break up passenger journeys into segments, with passengers being forced to stay in local hostelries and eat in depot restaurants. But some of the western roads took their obligations seriously and provided well for their passengers. Leading the way was the Santa Fe, which had made an agreement with an extraordinary Englishman named Fred Harvey. This en-

terprising entrepreneur took over the road's station restaurants and operated them with meticulous care. He had a high sense of propriety at a time when the West was still largely populated by rough-hewn men who might try to enter the station restaurant without coats, who spit on the rugs, swore, or even attempted to discharge bullets into the walls. One eager frontiersman even tried to ride his horse into a Harvey dining room.

Fred Harvey subsequently took over the Santa Fe's dining cars as well, although dining cars were slow to be put on the Western roads. Indeed, everything was slow to come out West. But it was through service between Chicago and the California coast that soon gave rise to trains like the *California Limited* on the Santa Fe and the *Overland Limited* on the Union Pacific (a train which arrived in Chicago over the rails of the Chicago and North Western). The West was, as they used to say, wild and woolly, and for a long time people who rode trains like the *Overland Limited* or the *California Limited* lived with the queasy feeling in the pit of their stomach that they might be attacked by wild Indians, derailed by a herd of buffalo, or perhaps held up by a masked rider of the plains.

There were always incidents happening out there in the West, right up to the end of the nineteenth century and even beyond. On October 31, 1895, the Santa Fe's *Chicago Limited* left Los Angeles at 9:00 P.M., but by 10:40 P.M. it was reported as "lost" somewhere east of San Bernardino. Imagine a nine-car train with five brand-new Pullmans on it—just lost. Well, things like that could happen out there in the Wild West, even though the Santa Fe was already running first-class trains all over the territory. What really occurred was that the train was climbing to Cajon Pass at 35 miles per hour when suddenly a huge shape loomed before the engineer. The engineer and fireman, thinking it was another train, jumped off without taking time to cut off the steam or apply the brakes. It was a foggy night, and what the engine crew couldn't see was that their obstacle was a stalled hay wagon being driven by a Mexican. The train slammed into the wagon and proceeded on its way up to the pass—finally coming to a stop on a steep grade. The poor Mexican was uninjured but the engineer broke his leg. A new crew was summoned to continue the journey, and the train went on its way, arriving at Chicago's Dearborn Station three hours late.

But if happenings of this kind were not uncommon in the West, it must not be forgotten that it was the railroad that did most of the civilizing of that vast territory. By the 1890s, the railroad had brought Eastern standards of comfort and service to the most remote parts of the frontier. And, of course, all of it passed through Chicago. Chicago had now become, as St. Louis had been in the age of Lewis and Clark, the key transfer point between East and West. If the railroad was, as has sometimes been said, "America's first big business," it was more importantly an agency of cultural exchange, and it was small wonder that Chicago quickly took on the role of economic and cultural center for the American heartland.

The lines west of Chicago grew mightily after the Civil War, although a number of them took many years to make the transcontinental connection. By the late 1860s, the Burlington already owned this impressive looking office building at 2 South Water Street. Unfortunately it was destroyed in the 1871 fire.
(Burlington Northern)

In only a few decades the Wild West enjoyed all the luxury of the East and perhaps more. One of the great trains of American record was the *Overland Limited* whose dining car of 1905 is shown here. Passengers could enjoy the badlands of Nevada with the same convenience that they enjoyed the urban corridor between New York and Boston. It arrived in Chicago over the left-handed rail of C&NW.

(Union Pacific Railroad Museum)

Through passenger service on the Illinois Central between Chicago and New Orleans did not become possible until the great Mississippi River Bridge was constructed south of Cairo, in 1889. But shortly after that it began operating name passenger trains on the north-south runs, leading to the eventual appearance of the fabulous *Panama Limited* in 1911.

(Illinois Central Gulf)

The great Columbian Exposition of 1893 brought thousands of visitors to Chicago; some will say it put Chicago on the map. Transportation to the Exposition was mostly by railroad, and the Illinois Central carried them out by the thousands as suggested here. This picture gives an idea of Chicago's already sophisticated skyline in 1893, including the famous Louis Sullivan Auditorium—in the center of the three large buildings. Columbus himself gives his blessing to the affair in the form of a dignified statue at the left.

(Illinois Central Gulf)

This ticket for Chicago Day, Oct. 9 1893, could not tell the story that on that day the Illinois Central transported 263,282 passengers from downtown to the Fair (and that in addition to another 200,000 or more in its regular commuter service)—a record in passenger train movement that may stand to this day.

(Author's Collection)

Before the turn of the century the Illinois Central had quite a few suburban stops just south of downtown. Here is their station at 22nd Street as it appeared in 1896.

(Midwestern Railway Historical Society)

When this station at 147th Street was built, the surrounding territory must have been strictly arcadian. But it has now been swallowed up by the city. The station, like so many of its kind, disappeared with electrification.

(Midwestern Railway Historical Society)

Homewood was one of the few places on the Illinois Central that got a better station with the passage of time. The substantial Spanish-style station that still stands would soon replace this small structure used by both long-distance and suburban trains. But the peaceful setting shown here would be gone, never to return.

(Illinois Central Gulf)

This timetable from 1901 shows 11 trains daily between Kankakee and Chicago. Today there are but three.

(Author's Collection)

Trains from Kankakee to Chicago

Time in effect September 29, 1901.

NOTE.—Big Four Trains leave Kankakee from C., C., C. & St. L. Ry. Station.

Miles	STATIONS	22 Daily	Big 4 37 Daily	18 Daily	32 Daily	4 Daily	26 Daily	Big 4 11 Daily	24 Ex.Sun	20 Daily	Big 4 19 Ex.Sun	2 Daily
0	Lv Kankakee	4.50 AM	5.25 AM	5 41 AM	7.30 AM	9.12 AM	11.24 AM	4.00 PM	4.50 PM	6 00 PM	7.10 PM	7.50 PM
2	Lv Bradley	f4 55 AM	x5.28 AM	f5.45 AM	7.35 AM		f11.27 AM	x4.03 PM	4.55 PM			
5	Lv Tucker	a5.03 AM			7.42 AM		a11.35 AM		5 01 PM			
9	Lv Manteno	f5.10 AM	c5.40 AM		7.52 AM		11.40 AM		5 09 PM			
16	Lv Peotone	f5.22 AM	c5.51 AM		8 08 AM		11 50 AM		5.23 PM			
22	Lv Monee	f5.35 AM	c6.02 AM		8.23 AM		12.01 PM		5.37 PM			
27	Lv Richton				8.37 AM				f5.47 PM			
28	Lv Matteson	f5 47 AM	c6.12 AM		8 40 AM		12.11 PM		5.50 PM			
33	Lv Homewood	6 00 AM	c6.20 AM		8.53 AM		12 19 PM		6.00 PM			
36	Ar Harvey	6 07 AM	c6.27 AM	6.47 AM	9.00 AM		12.25 PM	c4.50 PM	6.07 PM	z6 50 PM	c8.00 PM	
39	Ar Riverdale				9 06 AM				f6.12 PM			
42	Ar Kensington	6.20 AM	c6 37 AM	a7.00 AM	9.15 AM	a10.18 AM	12.35 PM	c5.00 PM	6.20 PM	7.00 PM		
47	Ar Grand Crossing	6.35 AM	c6.47 AM	7.11 AM	9.30 AM	a10.28 AM	12.47 PM	c5.10 PM			c8 20 PM	
48	Ar Chicago, 63d Street	6.40 AM	6.52 AM	7.16 AM	9.37 AM	10.33 AM	12.52 PM	5.14 PM	6.37 PM	7 14 PM	8.24 PM	9.09 PM
50	Ar Chicago, Hyde Park	6.44 AM	6.56 AM	7.19 AM	9.42 AM	10.36 AM	12.56 PM	5 17 PM	6.42 PM	7.17 PM	8 27 PM	9 12 PM
52	Ar Chicago, 39th Street	6.51 AM	7.01 AM	7.25 AM	9.50 AM	10 41 AM	1.01 PM	5 22 PM	6.50 PM	7.22 PM	8.32 PM	9.17 PM
54	Ar Chicago, 22d Street	6.57 AM	7.07 AM	7.32 AM	9.57 AM	10 47 AM	1.07 PM	5.27 PM	6.57 PM	7.27 PM	8.37 PM	9.22 PM
56	Ar Chicago, Cent. Sta.	7 00 AM	7.10 AM	7.35 AM	10 00 AM	10.50 AM	1.10 PM	5.30 PM	7.00 PM	7.30 PM	8.40 PM	9 25 PM

f Stops on signal. a Stops only to leave passengers. c Stops only to leave passengers from points east of Kankakee.
x Stops to receive passengers. z Stops to leave passengers from St. Louis and points beyond. (OVER)

In 1895, when this old engraving was made, Clyde was a near-in suburb on the Burlington, about 8 miles west of Union Station. Today the station and the suburban neighborhood have all disappeared, devoured by the murky urban quicksand. But the name endures in the vast Burlington freight yard nearby.

(University of Illinois Library)

92

Downers Grove was long a prominent Chicago suburb on the Burlington. Here we see the station and a typical Burlington commuter train as they were captured by the camera in the late 1890s.
(Burlington Northern)

The classical stone station at Highlands was built for the Burlington in the mid - 1870s by John and Alanson Reed, owners of Reed's Temple of Music in Chicago, whose home was nearby. The shed on the near side was a much later addition. The station is every bit as appealing to the eye today as it was a hundred years ago.
(Burlington Northern)

93

This station at Western Springs, built in 1891, is typical of the impressive structures the Burlington was building for its prosperous suburbs in that era. The picture was taken about 1910.
(Western Springs Historical Society)

Aurora was and is a major junction on the Burlington and the western end of its commuter territory. The station shown here was built in 1865 and replaced by the present station in 1922. This picture, taken on September 13, 1917, depicts a very familiar ritual and ceremony of the time—sending the boys off to France.
(Burlington Northern)

Burlington commuting as it was. Here, next to Engine No. 1309—built in the Burlington's own Aurora shops in 1879—stands the entire train crew on a run to Chicago. The picture was taken at Riverside in 1903.

(Burlington Northern)

At the far left is seen a local station on the Chicago and Western Indiana Railroad. The C&WI was the terminal company that owned the Dearborn Station, but it had its own little commuter line, nearly all of it within the city of Chicago. There were no grade separations on the C&WI, so the going must have been provided hectic encounters with wagons, streetcars, horses, and pedestrians. This picture looks up Archer Avenue (with streetcar tracks), the C&WI crossing left to right.

(University of Illinois Library)

CHAPTER 5

The Great Stations

Chicago was a city of great railroad stations, and a curious lot of them survived for many years. To be sure, there were cities elsewhere in the world with more great terminal stations—one need only think of London, which, in its heyday, could boast 10 imposing terminals from which emanated a vast number of lines reaching to every corner of the British Isles. And in America one could find terminals that were larger than any of those in Chicago, and others that could report a larger volume of traffic. Still, no city in America had more large stations than Chicago, and nowhere else were they more distinctive and charmingly eccentric. Nowhere were they more all-pervasive, more an integral part of the warp and woof of the city's being than in Chicago.

At the apogee of railroad passenger service during the first half of the twentieth century there were six major stations in Chicago, fed by a complicated network of tracks running directly into the heart of the city itself. It was always important to the railroad to get people just where they wanted to go, and in this respect Chicago was the ideal railroad town. All of the big stations were situated very close to the Loop. But besides being convenient, the stations were all markedly distinctive in architecture, all eccentric as to mood and style of operation. Each had its own charm, its own flavor, its own wayward personality. Long into the twentieth century many of them were attacked for their lack of aesthetic appeal (if not downright ugliness) or their technological backwardness, but all of them were captivating monuments to the nation's largest railroad center.

All of the stations that were standing at the middle point of the twentieth century were built between 1885 and 1925. They were arrayed in an arc around the Loop, most of them to the south and west of the central business district. You could walk from any one of them to any other one in 15 minutes, and a number of them were separated by only a few blocks. Some of them were better known to Chicagoans than others, most especially those which housed large commuter operations as well as long-distance carriers. While the steam locomotive maintained its old authority, all of them were observable and tangible ornaments of public architecture.

The oldest of the great Chicago stations is the Dearborn Street Station, still standing in 1981. Somehow the word "old" has always been connected with Dearborn. It was born old, it grew up old, and has been old ever since. It was built in 1885, and 10 years later people were already calling it the "old Dearborn Street Station." Probably its style of architecture was already rapidly passing from the scene in 1885. The architect was Cyrus L. W. Eidlitz, who designed a number of similar railway stations in the United States, the most characteristic of which was the Michigan Central Station in Detroit. (He also designed the New York Times Building at Times Square in New York City, which was opened in 1904.) Eidlitz was fond of High Victorian Gothic, and there are hints of Dracula's castle about the Dearborn Station. Some pretended to find it ugly, and, as seen in the days of steam, all sooted up, with freight yards hard by, it was hardly a pretty place by any usual aesthetic standards.

CHICAGO PASSENGER RAILROAD TERMINALS

(Railroad Lines as of 1950)

DEARBORN STREET STATION
Location:	Polk and Dearborn Streets
Opened:	1885 (Closed 1971; not demolished)
Owner:	Chicago and Western Indiana Railroad
Railroads:	Atchison, Topeka and Santa Fe
	Chicago and Eastern Illinois
	Chicago, Indianapolis and Louisville (Monon)
	Chicago and Western Indiana
	Erie
	Grand Trunk Western
	Wabash

GRAND CENTRAL STATION
Location:	Harrison and Wells Streets
Opened:	1890 (Demolished 1971)
Owner:	Baltimore & Ohio Railroad
Railroads:	Chicago Great Western (Corn Belt Route)
	Baltimore and Ohio
	Pere Marquette
	Wisconsin Central

CENTRAL STATION
Location:	Michigan Avenue at 11th Place
Opened:	1893 (Demolished 1974)
Owner:	Illinois Central Railroad
Railroads:	Cleveland, Cincinnati, Chicago and St. Louis (Big Four)
	Illinois Central
	Michigan Central

LA SALLE STREET STATION
Location:	Van Buren at La Salle Street
Opened:	1903
Owner:	Rock Island and New York Central (joint owners)
Railroads:	Chicago, Rock Island and Pacific
	New York Central
	New York, Chicago and St. Louis (Nickel Plate Road)

CHICAGO AND NORTH WESTERN STATION
Location:	Madison and Canal Streets
Opened:	1911
Owner:	Chicago and North Western Railway
Railroads:	Chicago and North Western

UNION STATION
Location:	Canal and Adams Streets
Opened:	1925
Owner:	Burlington, Pennsylvania and Milwaukee Railroads (joint owners)
Railroads:	Chicago and Alton
	Chicago, Burlington and Quincy
	Chicago, Milwaukee and St. Paul Railway (Milwaukee Road)
	Pennsylvania Railroad

The Dearborn Street Station as it appeared at the time of its opening in 1885. The station was certainly commodious and impressive by the standards of the day, but it is tiny when compared with the Chicago stations that were built in the next several decades.
(University of Illinois Library)

But, no, Dearborn was not ugly; it had its own delicious charm. What better for such a utilitarian agency as a railroad than such a Gothic monstrosity? It gave a feeling of rootedness, of things that last. There were strange pitched roofs, pinnacles and towers, a confusing diversity of windows. Above all there was a single major tower that commanded the structure—a marvelous eyesore in the complexity of its roof. It resembled a spire more than a tower. Unfortunately this weird roof did not endure. In a major fire in 1922 the top part was destroyed, and the later, strangely truncated tower was more pleasing to the eye but less distinctive. The American railroad historian Stewart Holbrook referred to the Dearborn Station in terms hardly flattering: "The whole affair," he said, "[is] hideous, quite dirty, breeding nostalgia for the days when all locomotives had diamond stacks and all conductors wore immense moustaches and fine cutaway coats." The vaulted chambers of the station reminded another great railroad buff, Lucius Beebe, of "a first class hammam" or Turkish bath. But whatever the terms applied, they were always somehow affectionate and not derisive.

The Dearborn Street Station was really on Polk Street and for a time was called the Polk Street Station. After the turn of the century there was a tendency to change the names of the stations to honor the north-south streets rather than the east-west streets. The same thing happened to the La Salle Street Station, which, for many years, and over three separate structures, was known as the Van Buren Street Station. The north-south streets ran into the Loop and be-

The Dearborn Station (in the early years often called the Polk St. Station since it really fronts on Polk Street) as it appeared in 1908. The Wabash, whose freight station is in the foreground, was one of the long-time tenants of the station.

(Chicago Historical Society)

The Dearborn Station suffered from a major fire in December 1922. But the overall appearance did not basically change except for the strange gothic tower on the roof which disappeared, leaving a truncated top. One can only conjecture on whether the altered form was an improvement.

(Chicago Historical Society)

The Dearborn Station as it appears today. Closed as a passenger station in 1971, it has thus far been preserved as an historic and architectural relic, though the inside is gutted. The future of a station of this age can only be conjectured.

(George H. Douglas)

yond, while the east-west streets were broken up and ran largely through less distinguished neighborhoods—thus the name change.

The Dearborn Street Station had a rather motley group of tenants. The station itself was owned by the Chicago and Western Indiana Railroad, which was mainly a terminal company. But the C&WI in turn was owned by its tenant railroads. The most illustrious of these tenant roads was the Santa Fe, but also housed at Dearborn were the Erie, the Wabash, the Monon, the Grand Trunk and the Chicago and Eastern Illinois.

In the later years of its public service, the Dearborn made big efforts to modernize. And it did so with rather effective results—at least on the inside. The outside never seemed to change, and the vibrations it gave off were always the same. But the carriers wanted the station to look like any other on the inside, so various plans of remodeling were carried out. The main waiting room was modernized in 1946. There was for a long time a very pleasant Fred Harvey Restaurant with rare old Chicago prints on the walls and a quite tolerable cuisine. New ticket win-

dows replaced the bank-window grills of yore. The news stands were given a kind of art deco modernity. The modernization was mostly a mistake, because it canceled all the eccentric charm of the station's façade.

Always a choice spot in the Dearborn Street Station was the lounge on the mezzanine level, which looked out over the train shed so that passengers and their guests could watch train arrivals and departures. Almost invariably, there was a colorful array of trains: the Santa Fe *Chief* or *Super Chief*; perhaps the Wabash's *Blue Bird* to St. Louis, or the *Erie Limited* to New York; the Monon's *Thoroughbred* to Louisville; the C&EI's *Meadowlark* and *Whippoorwill*, the Grand Trunk's *International Limited* or *Maple Leaf*.

To be sure, a great many of these trains had a hard time fitting into the station. The station, after all, was built for typical operating conditions of the 1880s. In the 1930s or 1940s, if you stepped off the *Super Chief* from Los Angeles, and you were on the head end, you would be under the train shed (an old truss-type shed that was only 165 feet wide). If you detrained near the center you would be protected by a butterfly shed added to give a little more length to the platform's capacity; if you got off at the rear end there would be no shed at all. In fact, if the train were long enough you might find yourself standing on no platform at all. You might start your trek to the station out among the yard goats and locomotives—or next to the freight house—then pass through the dismal and antique train shed into the affectedly modern waiting room—a

walk that would surely give the average traveler the full feel of American railroadiana.

The Dearborn Station's carriers were an assorted bunch by any standard. The Santa Fe was always preeminent in the lot. When the *Super Chief* came in there was always a full complement of red caps lining the platform, and, strange by today's standards, reporters and photographers from the *Trib* or the *Daily News*. For the *Super Chief* brought in the celebrities from the West Coast; beautiful starlets tramping through the dust of the shed. There were furs and alpaca coats aplenty, adorning famous personalities ready to transfer to the Union or La Salle Street Stations for continuation to New York on the *Broadway Limited* or the *Twentieth Century Limited*. One could stay on at Dearborn and go to New York by the *Erie Limited*, but what sophisticated traveler could abide the nearly 24-hour run of that rambling old country gentleman of a train? Only a few, perhaps.

The tower of the old Dearborn Station, looking down Polk Street toward the once largest hotel in the world, the Stevens (now Conrad Hilton). The date is May 24, 1979.

(George H. Douglas)

The Dearborn Station has been visible to thousands of Chicagoans in the Loop as they go about their chores or take a lunchtime stroll. In these days many may not know its name or purpose, but it is quite conspicuous as far north as the Chicago River.
(George H. Douglas)

As late as 1950, Dearborn had 75 trains daily; 50,000 passengers a month. Interestingly, some of these were commuter trains, although few today will recall Dearborn as having anything to do with the commuter business. The commuter enterprise was operated by the Chicago and Western Indiana, which at that time ran nine daily trains to Dolton, just barely beyond the city limits. Commuter operations stopped entirely in 1965.

Passenger operations of all kinds faded rapidly at the Dearborn Street Station after 1960. When Amtrak took over long-distance passenger service in 1971, all such operations were moved to Union Station and Dearborn Station immediately became part of the dead and pathetic past. Luckily, it has been spared the fate of the Grand Central Station—although the train shed has been razed. Citizens' groups have

striven to stave off demolition and one can only hope that the fatal moment is still far off. Title is now held by the City of Chicago, which has some extensive urban renewal plans for the neighborhood.

Grand Central Station was opened in 1890 and was located at the corner of Wells and Harrison Streets. Architecturally it was probably the most distinguished of the Chicago stations. It was a sad day in the life of the city when, in 1971, it was rudely and unceremoniously torn down. Today the spot where it stood is a vacant lot frequented by pigeons—an eyesore to motorists on the Congress Expressway who could instead be enjoying the graceful Norman lines of old Grand Central.

Grand Central Station was built by the Wisconsin Central (later part of the Soo), but most people today associate the station with the

In its later years the Dearborn Station made some effort to modernize, at least on the inside. This is how the waiting room of the station looked in the 1950s, with a good-sized crowd waiting for the *San Francisco Chief*. Somehow such modernity never really suited the Dearborn mystique.

(Santa Fe)

Baltimore & Ohio, whose *Capitol Limited*, a graceful streamliner, was long the proudest occupant of the station. From the very beginning Grand Central was the least used of all the Chicago stations. In the early days there were some suburban trains running out of Grand Central, but this ended in the 1890s. For a good number of years there was also heavy traffic in the summertime, when the Pere Marquette carried vacationers to Michigan, but this business was largely eroded by the advent of vacation travel by auto-

mobile. By the late 1940s, Grand Central served only about 30 trains a day—perhaps 13,000 passengers a week. During its last decade it was something of a ghost station.

What a splendid ghost it was, even at the end! Grand Central was designed by Spenser Solon Beman, who was also the planner and architect of the town of Pullman. Some later architects, heeding Louis Sullivan's formula that form should follow function, objected to a railroad station that was cast in the mold of a Norman fortress. But somehow the whole thing was just right; a creation of real beauty. The scale, and the relationship between the station and the graceful arched train shed, were nearly perfect. It was a dignified edifice, with none of the kind of pretense that tended to creep into stations built in the next generation.

The station was modest in size with only six tracks running into its shed. Beman planned the station in a traditional L-pattern, with a carriage court on Harrison Street, and a waiting room along Wells Street, the train shed fitting into the angle between the two. At the juncture there was also a five-story office building that was surmounted by a clock tower that rose to a height of 247 feet. The clock chimed in the early years and, at the time of its construction, was the second largest in the country. The bell weighed eleven thousand pounds. The foundations of the tower were unusually solid and massive, the material being of Connecticut brownstone, brown pressed brick, terra-cotta, Tennessee marble, granite and iron.

Those who passed through the station in the early years can never forget the graceful porte cochère, which had a frontage of 250 feet, on the Harrison Street side. This had the effect of a gracious mansion or private dwelling. Still, a large number of omnibuses, cabs and private carriages could fit under the roof to discharge passengers.

The waiting room gave the feel of extreme intimacy, but was designed to handle large crowds. It was 70 by 200 feet, two stories high. The walls were of Tennessee marble, the floors of Vermont marble. The pillars were of scaglio-

The entrance and carriage court at Grand Central Station. It must have been a very elegant drive-up in the days of horse and buggy. It seemed leisurely even in the more maddening times of the motorized taxicab.

(Herbert H. Harwood, Jr.)

Inside the train shed at Grand Central. Note the delicious architectural details of the train gate in effective contrast to a streamliner of 1970. Such refinements and niceties are seldom seen in the purely utilitarian structures of today, and they call up reminiscences of the elegance of our railway past.

(Herbert H. Harwood, Jr.)

la—an imitation Mexican onyx. There were large arched windows, each surmounted by a half-circle of colored glass. The northwest corner of the room was given over to the ticket office of brown Tennessee marble. Here, as elsewhere, the minor touches and architectural refinements were charming. Beman had thought out all the details. He hired a sculptor to carve on columns floral capitals of marsh irises, perfectly complementing the foliation of the brownstone base. To echo these adornments, Beman even used a floral pattern on his doorknobs. Every touch, right down to the grill work on the station-master's office, was thought out in marvelous detail.

The station had a fine restaurant, reached by marble steps, on the south end of the waiting room. In later years it was downgraded into a lunchroom, but the Baltimore and Ohio continued to care for it even in this reduced condition and it was always a pleasant place to eat. The restaurant, like the rest of Grand Central, always gave the feeling of some subdued but elegant ducal palace.

The train shed was something of a marvel. It was of the single arch type, of wrought-iron

The main waiting room at the Grand Central Station. The walls
were of Tennessee marble, and the pillars were of scagliola—an
imitation Mexican onyx. The floors were of Vermont marble. The
owners and the architect, Spenser Solon Beman (also the principal
architect of the town of Pullman), outdid themselves to build the
most beautiful of all the Chicago stations.

(Library of Congress)

This was the balcony level of Grand Central Station leading from the dining room. The dining room, although it was small and intimate, was always a pleasant place to eat, even in later years when it was downgraded to a lunchroom.

(Herbert H. Harwood, Jr.)

108

trusses. But it was not of the overblown type that would be built during the next decade—examples of which can be seen most spectacularly in the Reading Terminal in Philadelphia, the Union Station in St. Louis, and the South Station in Boston. The shed's relatively small size (it was 555 feet long with a span of 156 feet), contained a number of good features. It was open on the west side, and large slats in the roof admitted additional light so that the atmosphere was not the one of gloom and darkness so often associated with that type of shed. And there were other touches of genteel or nonutilitarian nature. The tracks (six of them) were enclosed by fancy iron fencing.

Above all, the station was designed to be a

Grand Central Station Concourse, looking east toward the Waiting Room. The year was 1967 and the passengers were waiting to board the B&O's famous flyer the *Capitol Limited*. Note the movie marquee over the train gate. At that time the B&O was featuring movies on its name trains.

(Herbert H. Harwood, Jr.)

warm and comfortable place, an inviting place. In addition to the warm marble and the stained glass windows, there was a massive fireplace, and, in the early days at least, there were rocking chairs in the waiting room. At one time the station had in the basement a room that was pleasantly fitted out for mothers and children. Like so many stations of the day, Grand Central had an Immigrant's Room where newly arrived citizens could be cared for and directed. The roads took this business quite seriously, too, for they provided a large bathroom where the dust of travel, and perhaps the dust of years by could be removed. Attendants stepped forth with brushes both fine and coarse, soap, towels, water and tubs (all available at company expense) to allow the foreign visitor every opportunity to spruce up before continuing his journey, perhaps to the wild and woolly Far West, possibly to some newly purchased farm in North Dakota.

Grand Central was always a warm and human place; everybody from the president of

The Grand Central train shed. Since the old 1890 shed could not accommodate the trains of a later year, an umbrella shed was used for protection of the passengers at the south end of the station. Alas, everything seen here has disappeared. The Grand Central Station was torn down in 1971—a wanton act of destruction to a monumental railroad station.

(Chicago Historical Society)

the railroad to the lowliest immigrant was comfortable there. In spite of its modest size and small traffic, it had something for everybody.

There was another "Central" station in Chicago besides Grand Central Station, and it was the next of the great stations to be built. This was Central Station, which, for all of its life, stood in lonely isolation from all of the other stations out on the lakefront. Central Station was the official name for the Illinois Central's long-distance terminal and office building in Grant Park at 12th Street. If you said "Central Station" to a Chicago cab driver, he would most likely be confused by the name. It was almost universally known in town as Illinois Central Station, perhaps to prevent the confusion with Grand Central Station.

The Illinois Central had an older terminal, built after the Great Fire of 1871—a large barnlike affair at Randolph Street. But to honor the opening of the Columbian Exposition of 1893, the Illinois Central had a new Romanesque station and company headquarters built at 12th Street. The Randolph Street station was demolished and replaced by subsequent structures for the road's suburban trains, which stand at the same location today.

110

The Baltimore & Ohio had its own eccentric route out of Chicago. Trains out of Grand Central Station passed through Englewood but trackage rights required that the B&O have its own station there. This station at 63rd Street served the Englewood area until Grand Central was closed, then it too was destroyed.

(Andrew C. Koval)

Central Station was designed by Bradford Gilbert, a prolific railroad station architect. With an ample budget at his disposal he planned a complex of four parts, all interconnected: train shed, office building, tower and waiting room. There was a certain nobility to the conception, but the station always got more than its share of good-natured scoffing for being an architectural oddity. The public never loved the arrangement of the station and train shed because a person had to climb up to the one only to have to descend to the other. Louis Sullivan, Chicago's great architectural master, wrote very amusingly of this oddity in his book *Kindergarten Chats*: "My son, here is the place—perhaps a unique spot on earth—holy in inequity, where, to go in you go out, and to go out you go in; where to go up you go down, and to go down you go up. All in all it seems to be the choicest fruit yet culled from that broad branch of the tree of knowledge, known as the public-be-damned style."

Sullivan's was a humorous comment, and one that would have tickled all visitors to Central Station who had to haul their bags up to the waiting room and then down to the tracks. But in actual practice the criticism was a bit unfair. The Central Station was not an end-station, but a kind of modified through station. The waiting room was astride the tracks, so travelers found that they did not have to walk very far to their cars. The Illinois Central was always very solicitous of its passengers, spotting their trains directly beneath the terminal and offering a full complement of station personnel and train crews to get people to their cars with little fuss and bother.

The waiting room at Central Station was pleasing and ornate, with a great arch, a mosaic floor, marble wainscoting and stuccoed ceiling. (In later years the latter was covered by a cheaply constructed false ceiling to achieve minimum headroom from the floor.) Altogether, Central Station had an air of refinement in the early days. The Illinois Central was the major north-south carrier in this part of the country, and the road always kept about it some of the Southern flavor of its owning carrier. The Illinois Central had had its start in Illinois, but its growth in Tennessee and Mississippi soon gave it strong

111

Central Station, popularly known in Chicago as Illinois Central
Station to prevent confusion with Grand Central Station, was
built in 1893 and demolished in 1974. The office buildings cluster-
ing around the station and the additional office building connected
by a covered bridge contained the Illinois Central's offices. In the
distance are the IC's coach yards, the electrified suburban lines and
Soldier's Field.

(Illinois Central Gulf)

This plaque commemorating the erection of Central Station
tells a great deal about the history of the Illinois Central Railroad.
The Illinois Central was distinctly a state land-grant railroad from
the beginning, which explains the presence on the board of directors of Governor John P. Altgeld, one of the most famous governors
in the state's history, who took his seat *ex officio*.

(Illinois Central Gulf)

112

Here are two of Illinois Central's long liners being prepared
for departure from Central Station in 1953. In that year the Illinois
Central was still in the passenger business for keeps, and its
Panama Limited was one of the great trains of North America.
(Illinois Central Gulf)

Southern roots. The meals served in the balcony
restaurant were often Southern dishes, always
served in an unhurried Dixie manner, encourag-
ing to those who like to sit and talk rather than
sit and run. Before the restaurant was downgraded, one could see pictures of New Orleans,
of Mississippi River steamboats, and of some of
the rural communities in Mississippi and Louis-
iana which the IC served so well.

Some of the same southern flavor was also
preserved in the company's offices and
throughout the station. The sturdy nineteenth
century fireplaces in the president's office and in
the ladies' retiring room preserved the quiet
dignity and charm of the old South.

Central Station served strictly long-distance
passengers, no commuters. The Illinois Central
had a suburban station at 12th Street, but it was
not connected to Central Station. As a result,
Central Station was never a large-volume operation. The station did, however, have two New
York Central tenants under a 99-year lease—the

Michigan Central and the Big Four. Needless to
say, the station never lasted 99 years. Central
Station's principal liners were always those of
the Illinois Central itself. Especially noteworthy
were the trains to New Orleans, the most
famous of which were the nighttime all-Pullman
Panama Limited, and the daytime all-coach *City
of New Orleans.* In both the steam and diesel
eras these were glorious trains, much famed for
the Creole cooking of the IC dining service and
the easy, deferential quality of train crews.

The Illinois Central had a number of other
name trains working out of Central Station over
the years. There were the *Daylight Limited* and
the *Green Diamond* on the Springfield-St. Louis
run, the *Land-o-Corn* serving the road's Iowa
spur, and a complement of trains to Florida that
the IC later handed off to the Central of Geor-
gia. The Illinois Central had a fleet of cars that
could be used on their long-distance trains, and
travelers could see the handsome equipment
standing in the passenger yards directly south of
Central Station. Those assigned to the *Panama
Limited* were the most lavish and fanciful, and
few who rode that train before 1960 will forget
the "King's Dinner" of the dining car, the Mardi
Gras theme of the Parlor Car, and all the other
delightful appointments.

Central Station nearing the end of its life as a passenger carrier in 1971. A year later, when trackage arrangements were made to take IC trains over to Union Station, the station would be closed for good.

(George H. Douglas)

The ornate ceiling of the waiting room at Central Station was covered over in the early 1950s to the dismay of lovers of the station. This World War II-era picture gives only a slight idea of the massive passenger burden that the railroads had to endure during the war years.

(Illinois Central Gulf)

Central Station was used for 79 years. In 1919 the Illinois Central expressed its intention of razing the station and building something more attractive on the site in compliance with the Lakefront Ordinance passed by the City of Chicago in that year. But this intention was never carried out and the railroad continued passenger operations until Amtrak took over its long-distance passenger business in 1971. When Amtrak took over they continued to use Central Station for another year, but finally by use of the east-west track known as the "St. Charles Air Line" achieved a complicated connection with the tracks of Union Station. When permission to enter Union Station was obtained

This picture was taken in 1971 in the modernized waiting room of Central Station. Passengers here wait to board the *Panama Limited*, whose 60-year reign at Central Station would shortly come to an end when Amtrak operations would be relocated at Union Station.

(Illinois Central Gulf)

in the spring of 1972, Central Station was closed forever.

Central Station was demolished in 1974 and with it the railroad's office building at the same location. By the time the wrecking ball arrived at Central Station, the Illinois Central had already moved its corporate headquarters to the luxurious new Illinois Center on North Michigan Avenue. But not a few company executives miss the eccentric Romanesque pile on 12th Street. It retained the flavor of the railroad to the end.

The station known as the La Salle Street Station was opened in 1903. But there were four La Salle Street Stations, all located at the same spot. There were three predecessors of the present station, the first of which went back to 1852. Another more impressive stone structure built in 1868 had been swept away in the Chicago Fire of 1871. This was replaced by a nearly identical building that lasted until work on the present structure, designed by Frost and Granger, was

Central Station was home only to long-distance passenger trains. IC suburban trains stopped at 12th Street, but the station was completely separate. This is the Florida-bound *Seminole* being prepared for departure from Central Station in 1953. The Illinois Central kept up its Florida service until the Amtrak takeover in 1971. Amtrak selected another route to Florida.

(Illinois Central Gulf)

begun in 1901. For most of the nineteenth century these stations were called the Van Buren Street Station, and even today this would be the really appropriate name, since the station has no entrance or frontage of any kind on La Salle Street. Whatever the name, the history of this station is clear-cut. Its origins go back to the time when the Rock Island made its alliance with the Michigan Southern to secure the first entrance into the heart of Chicago by an Eastern railroad.

It was always said that the La Salle Street Station was the most convenient of the Chicago stations because it is the only one actually on the Loop of the elevated line. Directly in front of the station you can board the "el" for direct connection with the rest of the city's rapid transit system. Before the demise of the North Shore inter-

urban you could even make a direct connection with rail transportation for Chicago's north coast as far as Milwaukee.

La Salle Street Station is hardly a thing of beauty. It is also a difficult building to view from any angle. The average passenger who has been through the station will doubtless have little if any recollection of the place. Not only is the entire front entrance obscured by the El, but also the neighborhood is a drab one of ware-

The La Salle Street Station as it appeared to a very imaginative artist at the time of its opening in 1903. Doubtless the station never looked quite this good, and certainly the elevated tracks were never as distant as shown here. But the station did have in those days a rather ambitious train shed and the impressive-looking carriage entrance on the west side.

(University of Illinois Library)

houses, lofts, drafting firms, wholesale outlets and the like. Doubtless the neighborhood was already on the decline when the present building was built, since pictures show all of the earlier La Salle Street stations to be much more pleasing and grandiose affairs. Certainly they were airier and more expansive.

When the present structure was built, very little effort was made to get it to look like a railroad station. If it were not for the arched entryway with its clock, the building would look like just another office building. And in fact it *is* just another office building—a structure of 11 stories that for many years housed the executive offices of the Rock Island and the regional offices of the New York Central and the Nickel Plate. Two roundels on the building's front indicate the road's two owners at the time of construction: the Lake Shore and Michigan Southern (New York Central) and the Chicago, Rock Island and Pacific. The Rock Island kept its offices at the La Salle Street Station until the late 1970s, after which it left these gloomy and crumbling quarters for more lavish diggings over on Michigan Avenue. Those fancier quarters didn't reflect the sinking fortunes of the Rock Island during this period.

Today, little remains of the station's glory from the turn of the century. One enters the station from Van Buren Station at the concourse level. The concourse is broken up and unsightly, its onetime restaurant having been replaced by a mere snack bar or hot dog stand. (But remember, the station no longer handles long-distance passengers, only commuters.) From the concourse level with its ticket booths, newsstand, and flower stall, the passenger rises to an upper level which contains at the north end a waiting room, newsstands, a bar, alcoves devoted to pinball machines and other such frivolities. This is all in a large room which is not without architectural distinction, but which is mostly obscured by the encroachments of time and the disappearance of the reasons for station elegance.

The La Salle Street Station is still a lively place, especially during rush hours. Only the Rock Island commuter trains remain, and these are operated by the Regional Transit Authority. Late in the afternoon, commuters by the thousands hurry up the escalators from the concourse level and pour out onto the platforms which are no longer protected by any kind of train shed. There was a full train shed in 1903, but this was hacked apart in 1934 and what remained has been disappearing in stages ever since. Getting wet boarding the train on a rainy day hastens commuters along the platform.

The present La Salle Street Station was preceded by two others, including this structure built after the Chicago Fire. The Van Buren St. Station (as it was then usually called) is shown as it appeared in 1883, the year that the Nickle Plate became a tenant. The station was already the home of the Rock Island and the Lake Shore and Michigan Southern (New York Central).

(Rock Island)

118

The La Salle St. Station today has the appearance of nothing more than an aging office building, which is precisely what it is. Until the middle 1970s the Rock Island continued to have its executive offices here, but they then moved to smaller but more luxurious quarters on Michigan Avenue.

(George H. Douglas)

One of the most camera-shy of stations, the La Salle St. Station defies having its portrait taken from the front. The lower floors are darkened and obscured by the presence of the elevated railroad on Van Buren Street. Nonetheless, here is the entire front of the station in 1980 as seen from the 42nd floor of the Board of Trade Building.

(George H. Douglas)

The tracks of the La Salle Street Station pass above a number of city streets, most notably Congress Parkway, which feeds the Loop from the Eisenhower Expressway. Thousands of motorists pass under the station daily.

(George H. Douglas)

A generation ago La Salle Street had some big name trains. The Nickel Plate, although only a tenant, ran regular trains to Cleveland, Buffalo and New York (by connection with the Lackawanna). The Rock Island had its fleet of trains to the southwest, to Iowa and the Rocky Mountains—its *Rockets* and its famed *Golden State Limited*, which always provided lively competition with the Santa Fe for the traffic to Southern California.

The most famous train ever to run into La Salle Street Station was, of course, the New York Central's *Twentieth Century Limited*, although several decades ago the New York Central had a score of other name trains also. But the late afternoon departure of the *Twentieth Century* was always the big moment of the day.

In the 1930s the train sometimes had three or more sections. During the 1940s and 1950s there was a daily radio interview program on the Mutual Radio network with Bob Elson in which celebrity passengers were collared as they were about to board the train to New York. And as late as the mid-1950s one could always count on the brilliant pop of news camera flashbulbs as the *Century* took its dock at precisely 9 A.M.

Leaving the La Salle Street Station on the *Twentieth Century Limited* was a glorious ex-

The time is 4:01 and the afternoon rush hour is not far away here at the entrance to the La Salle Street Station. Standing in the shadow of the elevated tracks and besmirched with the city grime, no more inelegant entrance to a large railroad terminal can be imagined. Still, the structure evokes memories of past railroad glories.

(George H. Douglas)

perience. Sitting in the rounded observation-bar car, you would move right out of the core of the city itself. As the train began to move, the Board of Trade Building, a mere block north of the station, would thrust itself immediately into view and the whole city would unfold before your eyes as in some kind of magic stereopticon. La Salle Street Station seemed to be carved out of the very heart of the city.

The Chicago and North Western Station has never been the broodhouse of a miscellaneous collection of transcontinental lines; it has always been identified with a single line—the Chicago and North Western. It is, nonetheless, one of the great Chicago stations. Its greatness and usefulness have become more apparent with the passage of time.

The present Chicago and North Western Station was opened in 1911, but it was the last of eleven terminals built by the railroad to serve all of its passenger business, both commuter and long-distance. The best remembered of the earlier stations was the immediate predecessor of the present station at the corner of Wells and

The waiting room at La Salle Street Station is on the second floor, at train level. The mellow arches and the rich architectural detail of the old station are insulted by the presence of pinball machines, soft-drink dispensers and paperback racks, all contrived to capture the attention of passengers whose wait is never more than a few minutes.

(George H. Douglas)

A lone midday passenger strides across the concourse to the train gate at the La Salle Street Station, 1979. The long-distance trains have gone, but one may still conjure up memories of the elegant departure of the *Twentieth Century Limited* only a few years ago.

(George H. Douglas)

Late in the afternoon a modern fleet of RTA commuter trains awaits departure from the La Salle Street Station. The date is June 1, 1979. Of course, thousands of commuters still think of this as the Rock Island, and who is to deny them?

(George H. Douglas)

Rock Island (RTA) commuters at a leisurely pace (for train time is 10 minutes off) step toward their coaches at the La Salle Street Station. The broken-up train shed offers non-existent protection. The two station functionaries at the left seem amazed that anyone is photographing their ancient terminal at this late point in time.

(George H. Douglas)

Kinzie Streets north of the Chicago River. The "old" Chicago and North Western Station was on the site of the present-day Merchandise Mart, a part of the city that was railroad territory from the early days—as land acquired for the Galena Company by William Butler Ogden.

The old Chicago and North Western Station on Wells was an impressive-looking Victorian affair fitted out with a central clock tower and numerous turrets and cupolas. But so rapid was the increase in the North Western's passenger business in the 1880s and 1890s that the building was soon bursting at the seams. An annex was shortly added for commuter traffic, but even this was of little help. By the beginning of the twentieth century the company was forced to plan a new and even more commodious terminal to accommodate its rapidly expanding passenger business. The earlier stations had all been north of the river, but now the C&NW acquired additional land in an area where it had

always had holdings—to the west of the river, dipping as far south as Madison Street. The new terminal would be at the corner of Madison and Canal Streets. The terminal with its train shed was actually to extend several blocks north from Madison Street, with Washington and Randolph Streets passing underneath.

The station was an expensively lavish affair, but still unpretentious and utilitarian. The beginning of the twentieth century saw a revolution in railroad station design, and the 1911 station was a clear-cut break with the past. Gone were all semblances of the Victorian past, of

The Chicago and North Western Station at Canal and Madison Streets. When the station was opened in 1911, handsome and elegant carriages used to draw up in front of the columned entrance on Madison Street. But the configuration of the station has been changed and the Madison Street entrance is boarded up. A commuter station now, but a grand one, which most commuters enter from the Canal Street side.

(Chicago and North Western)

The Chicago and North Western Station from the southwest. To the east the station is almost totally obscured by skyscrapers, so that few train riders ever get a look at the station and at the long train shed shown here.

(George H. Douglas)

Gothic romance, all hints of the woodburning locomotive and conductors with stovepipe hats. Railroads were now big business and the railroad station must be a grand public building. The Chicago and North Western Station, like the Union Station of the next decade, became a hymn of praise to Roman styles. Neither house nor barn nor fortress, the railroad station must now be an impressive public edifice such as one might design for a state capitol or a great banking house.

The Chicago and North Western Station was designed by Frost and Granger, who also did the much-less-imposing La Salle Street Station. Like Grand Central and Pennsylvania stations in New York and Union Station in Chicago, the C&NW Station was intended as an object of splendor, and to this day its impressive designs and vast interior spaces take away the breath of first-time visitors. The station proper was 328 feet wide and 218 feet long, constructed of gray Maine granite. There was a lordly main entrance on Madison Street (no longer used), where carriages could deposit departing passengers. At this entrance there were six enormous Doric columns crowned by a clock 12 feet in diameter. Passengers entered the building through a vast ground-floor lobby, around the periphery of which were ticket offices, a baggage room, and a station master's office. From here they ascended by a grand stairway to the Main Waiting Room, a place of noble proportions indeed. This room, on track level, was 202 feet long and 117 feet wide, and had been designed as a Roman atrium with a tremendous barrel-vault roof. It was large enough and dignified enough to be awe-inspiring. The pilasters up to the spring of the vaulted ceiling were of light pink Tennessee marble and the columns were of Greek Appolino marble of a

The waiting room of the Chicago and North Western Station as it has appeared in recent years since the disappearance of the long distance trains. The elegant Roman barrel-vault roof, the green marble columns, and the elaborate architectural detail, combine to make this one of Chicago's most impressive stations. Probably it is the most elegant all-commuter train station in the world.

(Chicago and North Western)

delicate green hue. The seats were originally of choice mahogany.

North of the main Waiting Room on the same level was an elegant concourse, 60 feet wide and 320 feet long, a room with its own careful attention to architectural detail and, for the comfort of the passengers, heated in winter

to prevent their suffering while standing before the train gate. From here the passengers could pass through the train gates to the tracks, covered not by an old-fashioned train shed—with its cold, smoky atmosphere—but the newer Bush type of shed which allowed the smoke to discharge itself innocuously above an ingeniously constructed slat in the roof.

The station had every imaginable convenience that could be thought of in 1911: rest rooms, ladies' retiring room, immigrant's room, barbershop, drugstore, restaurant, tea room, telegraph office, newsstands, telephone booths, baggage-check room, information bureau, lost

Here is the train concourse of North Western Station in 1967. Once reserved primarily for long-distance passengers (commuters mainly used a concourse below this for access to their trains), all parts of the station are now the province of commuting passengers, most of whom pass through the station without realizing how well they are served in the post-railroad era.

(Chicago and North Western)

The Chicago and North Western Station and its train shed are seemingly carved out of the very heart of the city with tall buildings shadowing them entirely to the east (left). In an area of such high land values all such stations face a guarded and dubious future. Shown here crossing over the C&NW tracks is the Chicago city elevated line on Lake Street.

(Chicago and North Western)

and found, and emergency room. Management and architect had planned everything in great detail. The station must be both lavish and complete. Above all, it had to serve the needs of both long-distance and commuter passengers.

North Western Station has naturally changed its personality a great deal over the years. Long-distance passenger service is no more, and only a memory are the North Western's great 400 series trains and the justly famous trains—like the *Overland Limited*—fed to the C&NW from the West. Nothing remains but the commuter trains. So the Immigrant's Room and the Ladies' Withdrawing Room no longer exist. Ladies don't withdraw from anything anymore but step right out. North Western Station is strictly a station for commuters—probably the snazziest and the best all-commuter terminal in the United States.

The whole interior of the station has been redesigned to make the station a commuter spa.

In the early days the commuters were encouraged to stay away from the vast, Romanesque waiting room. They had a special concourse that connected directly with the Washington Street trolley line so that they could ascend to the train platforms without having to pass through station or concourse. Now the entire station belongs to the commuters.

The gracious front entrance on Madison Street is boarded up, and the station is now entered almost exclusively from the east. The largest numbers of commuters arrive from the Loop across the Madison Street Bridge, after

In the days when it still offered long-distance passenger travel, the Chicago and North Western maintained a women's retiring room where the ladies could rest in undisturbed comfort before boarding the trains. As late as 1947 (the time of this picture), the retiring room was completely redecorated. Today, of course, women do not prefer to "retire" to protected comforts of their own, but in any case the hurly-burly of the commuter's life would justify no such room.

(Chicago and North Western)

which they enter the Riverside Plaza Building (formerly the Daily News Building). This puts them on the level of the station waiting room, which they enter through a covered bridge across Canal Street. A fair number of others buy their papers at street level on Canal Street and ascend to the concourse by escalators. A comparative few enter the station from the west.

But inside the station, everything is geared to the commuter now—and what a place it is. There are newsstands, candy counters, snack bars, a cheese store, a paperback book store and an oyster bar. The ticket office is no longer downstairs but has been moved into the waiting room. The once ornate washrooms have been downgraded, and a giant news kiosk marks the spot where the elegant staircase used to lead up from Madison Street. Out in the concourse there is a little flower stand where one may buy a bouquet.

The Chicago and North Western Station is still a place of some elegance, although no longer a stately palace. These days, it is geared for action. But it really has no counterpart anywhere in the United States. Nobody can imagine such a place being offered to railroad commuters in the middle of the twentieth century. Once it is gone, nobody will ever think to build a place of such high style to serve only commuters. It is a building of both utility and beauty, and both functions shine out to all who hurry through it to catch the 5:17 to Elmhurst—even though they may not stop long enough to think about it.

The largest and most recently built of the great Chicago stations is Union Station, located at the corner of Canal and Adams streets. The station, opened in 1925, was erected on land owned by the original Union Station Company, which had constructed an earlier Union Station in 1880. Union Station is, and always has been, a grandiose affair. It took 12 years to build, cost $75,000,000, and stands to this day (albeit in somewhat reduced scale and substance) as one of the most extravagant railroad stations in the world.

The Union Station might have been even more ornate than it is. When it became apparent around 1910 that the old Union Station was no longer adequate for its traffic, there was a great deal of discussion concerning what was needed in the way of a new Union Station. A number of Chicago citizens, urged on by men like

Chicago's great architect and city planner Daniel H. Burnham, believed that what was essential was a "real" Union Station that would gather all the city's passenger services under a single roof (or no more than three roofs). "Uncle Dan'l" Burnham thought it could be done, and that the unsightly trackage of the Illinois Central on the shore of Lake Michigan could be eliminated and the long-distance trains using Central Station could come in at Canal and Adams (something that eventually happened, but not until 1972).

Creeping out from underneath the train shed at North Western Station, with the slanted afternoon sun glancing through the slats in the roof, is the C&NW's racetrack special to Arlington Park. It is a fair first day of June in 1979, and the train is well patronized. (George H. Douglas)

The renowned Union Station of Chicago as it appeared when it first opened in 1925, city double-decker bus and all. The station, which replaced an older Union Station from the 1880s, is more than ever the principal railroad station for the city since it is used by Amtrak for all of its inter-city passenger trains.

(Milwaukee Road)

Similarly, if the proposed unification took place, such oldies as the La Salle Street Station and Dearborn Station could also give up the ghost.

But it was not to be. It is not that the project was impossible, or that no single station could have handled a load that great, but that the various trackage arrangement and relocation problems proved insuperable. Even so, Union Station was quite an undertaking. The railroads it served were all big carriers in 1910. Burnham himself was supposed to be the architect. He was an excellent choice, since he was probably the most successful commercial architect in the United States at that time. Unfortunately, he did not live to see the work begin. His plans had to be carried out by his company, which made some aesthetic compromises.

Work was begun in 1914 and required a great many real estate adjustments and transactions. The station company had to rebuild and perpetually maintain 12 viaducts from Lake Street to Roosevelt Road, relocate a number of freight houses, and pay for the building of bridges across the Chicago River at Adams and Monroe streets—all to satisfy the enabling ordinance adopted by the city in 1914.

The construction dragged on. Work was slowed by protracted strikes and labor difficulties in the first few years, and World War I brought about a two-year delay beginning in 1917. The station was not officially opened to the public until April 18, 1925, the old Union Station immediately adjacent being heavily used till that date. Even then, construction connected with Union Station was not completely finished. In 1931 the Union Station Company sold to the United States Government the property over its tracks between Van Buren and Harrison Streets for construction of what was to become the largest post office in the world. This necessitated the relocation of the power house at Harrison and Canal streets to a spot several blocks south.

But when it was opened, Union Station was an awe-inspiring station. The structure was essentially of two parts. There was, first, a large headhouse on the west side of Canal Street between Adams and Jackson; and, second, a Concourse Building on the east side of Canal. The headhouse contained a large waiting room and the usual collection of smaller waiting rooms, restaurants, barbershops, toilets and other facilities. The Concourse Building across the street, connected to the headhouse by an underground passage which contained ticket offices and baggage facilities, provided access to two separate groups of stub tracks, one mainly servicing the Milwaukee Road which approached from the north, and the other servicing roads like the Pennsylvania, the Alton and the Burlington, which approached from the south. (There were also facilities for through tracks, but the Union Station was always essentially a two-sided stub station.)

The station was architecturally impressive. In its original plans it bore a rather strong resemblance to McKim, Mead and White's famous Penn-

This picture, from the early 1920s, shows the Union Station under construction. The headhouse, on the West side of Canal Street, is practically complete. The concourse building in the foreground still has a way to go. The skyscraper on the far left is the Burlington Building, which for many years contained the executive offices of that railroad, one of the Union Station's principal owners.

(Burlington Northern)

132

sylvania Station in New York. It continued to
have this resemblance, especially in the interior.
The exterior had been compromised somewhat
from the original conception, since the headhouse was modified to accommodate an office
building. During those long years between conception and completion, real estate values in
Chicago had risen tremendously, and the company decided to sacrifice some exterior aesthetic
qualities to get an office building on the top

(originally a 21-story complex was planned, but
the final result was only 8 floors).

All parts of the interior are striking. The
Waiting Room in the main building was inspired
by the Roman baths of Carcacalla and Diocle-
tian, with everything on a vast scale of round
and vault architecture. The large rectangular
space of the main waiting room was almost
overpowering in its monumental scale, and seldom failed to impress visitors to the station. It

Chicago's great commercial architect and urban planner Daniel H. Burnham was one of those who pushed for a real "union station"—a station that unified all of the long-distance rail services of the city, and perhaps get train tracks away from the lake front, which Burnham had hoped to improve. But the program was too complex. Sadly, too, Burnham died in 1912 and never got to see the opening of the new Union Station that was completed on the drafting boards of his company.

(Library of Congress)

Construction work underway on the new Union Station at Thanksgiving time in 1924. This picture looks northward on Canal Street from Jackson Boulevard. The old Union Station can be seen shrouded in the background with flag flying briskly.

(Chicago Historical Society)

Spanking new are both of the Union Station buildings around the time of the grand opening of the station on April 18, 1925. The Concourse Building (foreground) was torn down in 1969 to make room for a skyscraper. The strictly railroad functions of the building continue below ground however, although the architectural glories of the Concourse Building are sorely missed.

(Milwaukee Road)

The Union Main Waiting Room as it appeared shortly after the station was opened. Today the same space is cluttered with news kiosks, signs, soft-drink machines and other eyesores, all of which detract from the Roman inspiration of the station. Nonetheless, after over a half century of use, the station can be awe-inspiring to the visitor.

(Milwaukee Road)

An architect's sketch of the completely enclosed taxi concourse at Union Station. The taxi approach was among the more ingenious contributions of the building's plan, but one wonders if the architect really believed that taxicabs would proceed in this kind of orderly dignity.

(Milwaukee Road)

The ladies' waiting room at Union Station. If this drawing is any indication, it must have been a cold and austere place. In any case, it did not survive the test of time.

(Milwaukee Road)

Ladies'Waiting Room

lay under a vaulted skylight of glass set in steel ribs 112 feet above the floor. Around the walls were 20 large Corinthian columns that rose to the springing level of the vault. These columns, of course, were steel enclosed in plaster, but the walls both here and in the entrance lobbies were of Roman travertine in colors that blended with the soft green tones of the barrel-vaulted ceiling.

The Concourse Building, demolished in 1969 to make room for a new skyscraper (although its function continues to be carried on below ground), was equally impressive in its own way. It was closely modeled on the concourse of the Pennsylvania Station in New York. The roof consisted of three parallel longitudinal vaults of glass and tile carried on a fluent system of steel

arch ribs supported on built-up columns of latticework. This steelwork gave a strong modern and utilitarian flavor that nonetheless harmonized with the classic Roman detail throughout. One cannot help but think that the Roman emperors might have found the place to their liking.

The station had every modern convenience in 1925, and most of them serve remarkably well after a half century. It was the first modern building in which a system of streets for trucks, passenger vehicles and cabs were entirely enclosed within its walls. To this day cab access is a wonder. There were all of the usual facilities, from newsstands to beauty parlors and barber shops. Baggage and ticket facilities were ingeniously and conveniently placed. The station had its own police force, and in all likelihood, the complex could have handled twice as many passengers a day than it did at any time in its history. There was a lunchroom and an elegant walnut-paneled Fred Harvey Dining Room (the latter long since defunct).

The ticket office at Union Station in the 1920s. The old-fashioned metal grill ticket windows have disappeared and the area has been entirely remodeled. The area is the present site of the Amtrak passenger lounge.

(Milwaukee Road)

The interior of the Concourse Building in the 1920s. The latticed metal columns seem to have derived their character from a similar treatment in New York's Pennsylvania Station. In fact, riders of the Pennsylvania Railroad between New York and Chicago often commented on the many similarities in the stations.
(University of Illinois Library)

Union Station's great years of service were, of course, the years of World War II, when millions of people flooded through the station annually. Servicemen constituted a large portion of the railroad ridership, and the Concourse Building provided a lounge especially for their use.

(Milwaukee Road)

This colonade serves as the main pedestrian entrance to Union Station on Canal Street. It is still impressive, although no longer widely used. The colonnade and the exterior generally are beginning to show the stresses of time.

(George H. Douglas)

The train shed which completely protected the passengers was of a new type called an umbrella shed which completely protected the passengers from the elements. There was a curved and pitched roof of glass tile. Most passengers arriving at Union Station, however, thought that they were completely underground, and more and more, this came to be true, as air rights to the south were sold to construct the vast post office, and to the north to build the Daily News Building (now the Riverside Plaza Building) in 1929 and the Gateway Plaza Building in the 1960s. But even in the days of steam they could get the steam out by means of an elaborate ventilating system—a very impressive engineering feat.

In the great days of long-distance passenger service, Union Station was host to a number of great trains. There was the *Broadway Limited*, of course, and the *Burlington Zephyr*s. And Union Station always had a competitive set-up. An information clerk had to be circumspect and

Looking down into the Union Station's Main Waiting Room from the Canal Street entrance, 1980. The columns, the brass railings, the hard wooden seats, the immense candelabra along the walls are all relics of a dignified past now forgotten by most.

(George H. Douglas)

In 1978 a crowd of suburban passengers line up to buy tickets at at Union Station. This ticket counter is located just east of the main waiting room and in the passageway to the now completely subterranean train concourse.

(George H. Douglas)

By the 1970s few of the old dignities were left in Union Station. Here we see the traditional waiting room being treated to a bewildering confusion of conflicting elements—newsstands, a large emporium for knickknacks and gewgaws, a Traveler's Aid Society raffle car, and a fancy new restaurant that never worked and which closed down (far left). The walls are desperately in need of a cleaning.

(George H. Douglas)

diplomatic when asked which was the best train to Minneapolis or Seattle, Washington. One could just as well get to those cities by the *Olympian Hiawatha* or the Burlington-Great Northern's *Empire Building*.

Union Station continues to be a very exciting place, and more than ever it is a "union station." In 1971 the National Railroad Passenger Corporation took over long-distance passenger service in the United States and within a year or so succeeded in consolidating all its Chicago trains into Union Station. All other Chicago stations are now strictly commuter stations. Amtrak put in its own modern lounge, ticket counter and baggage-handling facilities, and they have plenty of trains, many of whose names are familiar from the past, like the *Broadway Limited* and the *Panama Limited*. And Amtrak has added a fleet of Turboliners.

Some of Union Station's original elegance is gone. Certainly the demolition of the Concourse was a great blow. But underneath, where the Concourse used to be, is a pretty spirited place.

A seemingly endless profusion of short-order restaurants, newsstands, bars, shoeshine stands and flower shops serve Milwaukee and Burlington commuters as well as long-distance passengers. Yes, Fred Harvey is gone, and nothing in the world has ever been the same since, but when they built Union Station they thought big and grand. Union Station is still big and grand.

One often thinks of what might have happened if Daniel Burnham had gotten his wish and all of the railroads in Chicago had been gathered under a single roof. Certainly this is thinkable in terms of the standards of today. And it is easy to forget that the last two stations built in Chicago were truly of gigantic proportions by any standard. It is probably impossible for a mortal, living after the middle of the twentieth century, to realize how many people could

The new concourse at basement level that has served Union Station's long-distance and commuter passengers since 1969. Shops of all kinds cater to the hurried and harried traveler, and of course there are the usual watering spots where one can be reinforced against the dangers of rail travel in our great age of insecurity.

(George H. Douglas)

The layout of the new Union Station concourse is actually rather simple, but to the first-time traveler it appears to be a labyrinth of bewildering confusion. Here Mom and kids enjoy their ice cream cones while Pop tries to make sense out of the signs. The luggage cart (of which Union Station has hundreds) has largely (but not completely) replaced the redcap.

(George H. Douglas)

be handled by a facility like Union Station or the Chicago and North Western Station. Even with the passenger deluge of World War II, neither station was taxed to its limits. It is hard to guess what those limits might be. In a great traction strike in 1915, Chicago and North Western Station, which at the time handled about 50,000 commuters a day, expanded its service to handle, on one day, 194,300 passengers (in 288 trains between 6 A.M. and midnight). And probably the station could have handled twice that!

If there was a prolonged movement to consolidate the railroad terminals of Chicago, it was not because the stations were really inconvenient to one another. In fact, in no other city in the world did the railroad terminals seem so perfectly linked. For a long time this was due to the inspiration and careful planning of one Franklin Parmalee, a man now almost forgotten, although his name meant a great deal to anyone who passed through Chicago before the 1950s.

Franklin Parmalee built and maintained a system of coaches and omnibuses that linked each Chicago station with all the rest. In this en-

terprise, Parmalee got in on the very ground floor. He was one of the transportation fathers of the city. Parmalee was born in New York State in 1816 and arrived in Chicago in 1853, just when it showed signs of becoming a railroad town. He had already had some experience in the stagecoach business. Now he formed a company to transport passengers from the docks to hotels or to the railroad station. Two years later he received from the city a charter to build the first street railway in Chicago between Lake Street Bridge and Archer Road.

As it turned out, Parmalee eventually gave up the street railway business, but he built and sustained one of the most remarkable transfer companies of all time. Chicago was a city of terminal railroad stations and of railway lines that

The south interlocking tower of Union Station. The station has two such towers, the other on the north end of the station governing the Milwaukee Road approaches to the station. As seen here the maze of tracks disappear under the Central Post Office, the largest post office building in the world when it was opened in 1932.

(George H. Douglas)

sought connections. What the city needed above all else was a reputable outfit to join all these stations. In the beginning, of course, there were horse-drawn rigs attended by uniformed agents who knew the city well; furthermore, they knew everything there was to know about train schedules. These agents were all rail experts and they were known to be honest. They never hustled a fare. They never took a Union Station passenger over to Van Buren Street if the best train for his purpose was right there in Union Station.

Parmalee agents were not only knowledgeable and honest, but stylish as well. They dressed in livery with brass buttons, and for a long time wore a helmet as a hat. For a while they even wore swallow-tail coats. Passengers instinctively trusted them, and nobody would ever fear handing over a bag or a parcel to a Parmalee man.

In its great years Parmalee was a big operation. At one time the company had as many as 1,200 horses and owned a stud farm at which they bred their own animals. Such a large herd was not without its difficulties, and in the Great Fire of 1871 Parmalee suffered a tremendous loss of his animals. Several years after that a horse epidemic nearly wiped out the company, but Parmalee managed to struggle along during the emergency with oxen.

The Concourse Building was the last part of the Union Station to be finished, and the first to come down. Here, in 1969, the Concourse Building meets up with the wrecking crews to make way for a new Chicago skyscraper, Marsh and McLennon Plaza.

(Milwaukee Road)

Franklin Parmalee, whose transportation company was unique in all the world, smoothly and efficiently handled the surface transportation between the great Chicago terminals. Parmalee started his operation back in the 1850s when the rail lines were first converging, and at one time his company had as many as 1,200 horses on the city streets. After Parmalee died in 1904, his omnibuses became motorized limousines, and his company struggled valiantly through the World War II period.

(University of Illinois Library)

A typical coach of the Parmalee Company in the horse-drawn era. The Parmalee drivers were known to be absolutely trustworthy and honest, and they were rich encyclopedias of railroad information. Above all, unlike taxi drivers of today, they were polite.
(Chicago and North Western Railroad)

Here is a group of immigrants ready to transfer from one Chicago station to another. The brass-buttoned conductor could be counted on to get them to the right station at the right time. And he would not take a penny above the posted fare.
(Chicago and North Western Railroad)

Form 90 N. Y. | NEW YORK, N. Y.-N. Y. CENT.
CMStPandP, Tr, NYC
Via CHICAGO

AGENT'S   **STUB**

NOT GOOD
FOR
PASSAGE

Destination
NEW YORK, N. Y.

Chic., Milw., St. Paul and Pac. R. R. Co. | If One-half ★ Punch Here

12-18-45-26000-29999

ISSUED BY	FINAL LIMIT DATE PUNCHED	
CHICAGO, MILWAUKEE, ST. PAUL and PACIFIC R. R. CO.	Jan Feb Mar Apr / May Jun Jul Aug / Sep Oct Nov Dec	

Non-Transferable Ticket

Sold Subject to Tariff Regulations

When officially stamped

GOOD FOR

ONE PASSAGE

to destination shown hereon which must be reached not later than midnight of date punched in margin.

In selling this ticket and checking baggage hereon, the selling carrier acts only as agent and is not responsible beyond its own line, except as such responsibility may be imposed by law with respect to baggage.

Pass. Traffic Mgr.
CHICAGO, ILL.

NEW YORK CENTRAL RAILROAD | Baggage ★ Punch Here

CHICAGO
TO
NEW YORK, N. Y.

Form 90 N. Y. | If One-half ★ Punch Here
Via CMStPandP, Tr, NYC

PARMELEE TRANSPORTATION CO. | If One-half ★ Punch Here
C., M., ST. P. and P. R. R. CO. DEPOT
TO
N. Y. C. R. R. DEPOT

Form 90 N. Y. | Not Good If Detached
Destination
NEW YORK, N. Y.
Issued by Chic., Milw., St. Paul and Pac. R. R. Co. | Baggage ★ Punch Here
Via CMStPandP, Tr, NYC

Chicago, Milwaukee, St. Paul and Pac. R. R. Co. | Baggage ★ Punch Here
MILWAUKEE
To CHICAGO
Form 90 N. Y. | Not Good If Detached
Destination
NEW YORK, N. Y.
Issued by Chic., Milw., St. Paul and Pac. R. R. Co. | If One-half ★ Punch Here
Via CMStPandP, Tr, NYC

After the turn of the century, the Parmalee Company started converting to motorized omnibuses, and the last of the horse-drawn rigs disappeared in 1921. Parmalee died in 1904, but his company continued on for another half century until it was taken over by a firm which provided limousine service to the city's airports—the same kind of service, but on a smaller scale, that Parmalee had provided for the railroad stations.

So much an integral part of the city's transportation system was the Parmalee Transfer Company that, in the old days, a passenger could buy a through interline rail ticket with a Parmalee coupon on it. In 1940, say, you could buy a ticket in Philadelphia on the Pennsylvania to Chicago with a Parmalee transfer ticket to the Dearborn Station for connection with the Santa Fe for continued travel to Los Angeles. On arriving at Union Station you could be whisked, without fuss and bother, to Dearborn Station by a long, low-slung Parmalee limousine, your bags efficiently handled without need for tip, and without the interference of a surly cab driver. It was just a service—a nicety. And the cabs were always there, endlessly cruising the streets of the Loop, always knowing when they were needed.

Some people think that rail travelers weren't pampered in the old days. But they were.

This railroad interline ticket shows the Parmalee transfer being directly incorporated in a through ticket for a passenger desiring to go between Milwaukee and New York. The New York-bound passenger would arrive on the Milwaukee at Union Station and then would be whisked to his New York Central train at La Salle Street Station by a Parmalee bus or limousine. This transfer was provided for in the second stub from the bottom.
(Author's Collection)

CHAPTER 6

City of the Big Shoulders

The railroad has been called America's first big business. Even with the decline of the railroad industry since the middle of the twentieth century, the railroad business is impressive in the immensity of its services and in the dominance and force of its presence on the landscape. Nowhere in America is the might and pervasiveness of the railroad more evident than in Chicago.

Chicago is the perfect dramatic showcase for the American railroad industry. Even after the disappearance of the more vocally expressive steam locomotive, the industry remains the most obvious characteristic of Chicago's urban geography.

However one approaches Chicago, even by air, the railroad is there. Enter by any one of the great expressways that have been built in the last several decades and the railroad will be at your side every step of the way. More people arrive in Chicago by car than by train nowadays, but you can't drive your car into the innards of the city without being overwhelmed by the vast number of freight yards, industrial sidings, interlocking towers, freight houses, terminals, belt lines, crossings, junctions, main line and secondary trackages, overpasses and underpasses, locomotive and car maintenance facilities and shops, to say nothing of the modern commuter railroad lines that are still used and which spread out

from the city's center like the fingers of a hand. All of the basic railroad phenomena meet you at every point of the compass as you enter or leave Chicago.

Because the railroad is a universal carrier, it is altogether fitting that Chicago has never been dominated by a single manufacturing industry. Everything under the sun comes in and out of Chicago, and in the yards and sidings one can find sulfur from Texas, lettuce and grapefruit from California, lumber from the Pacific Northwest, locally made television sets and mixmasters bound for New York, and Midwestern grain shipments bound for Russia or the Orient.

In its classical pattern of a generation ago, the day and night ebb and flow of freight traffic was supported by the world's largest collection of freight-handling facilities. In the Chicago terminal district there were 160 freight yards, 275 freight stations, over 7,000 miles of track. This was the base for an operation of about 600 freight trains a day, with an average of about 17,000 daily carloads—more than the combined traffic of the next two largest American metropolitan railroad centers. In the depression year of 1937, one railroad alone, the Illinois Central, moved through Chicago 72,000 carloads of coal, 40,000 carloads of grain, 39,000 carloads of automobiles, 14,000 carloads of lettuce, 7,000 carloads of bananas, and 4,000 carloads of watermelons.

The predominance of Chicago in the railroad industry was always due to the city's original importance as a junction, to the fact that here railroads from all parts of the country came together—rails from north, east, south and west join and all of their arteries and capillaries blend and bleed into one another.

Even today, with the railroad industry somewhat shrunken from its once-glorious estate, the railroad is an ever-present part of the Chicago scene. You can take no road or highway in or out of the city without having the railroad constantly beside you, its hundreds of junctions and crossing points a constant reminder of the might and magnitude of the American railroad.

(Illinois Central Gulf)

The freight yards in Chicago are gigantic, which hardly needs saying. Here a freight train leaves Santa Fe's Corwith Yard with cargo bound for everywhere west.

(Santa Fe)

The development of Chicago as a vast junction of railroad lines goes back to the very beginning of railroad development in 1848, when the Galena and Chicago Union Railroad first offered rail service between Chicago and Oak Park. Things really got cracking in 1852, that banner year when the Aurora branch was opened and when a whole bunch of other railroads all entered the city. Chicago's destiny as the hub of railroad transportation was further reinforced after the Civil War with the quick trend toward railroad mergers and with the opening of the first transcontinental railroad on May 10, 1869. With the linking of the Union Pacific and the Chicago, Iowa and Nebraska at Council Bluffs, Iowa, Chicago was permanently fixed as America's great junction, the place where the great railroads from every direction inevitably met.

With hundreds of railroad lines coming into Chicago, it gradually took on the character of a city of railroad crossings. In early and more boisterous times, the crossing junctions were occa-

sions for all sorts of difficulties, legal battles, sometimes even brawls and drunken donnybrooks at the actual construction sites. The thousands of crossings and junction points made Chicago a slow place to get through for freight and passenger trains alike, although some of the slowness was ameliorated in the twentieth century as many of the crossings were eliminated by means of under- and overpasses and operations were facilitated by automated signal equipment.

For a long time the most famous (perhaps infamous would be a better word) of the Chicago crossings was the frightful mass of spaghetti at Canal and 14th streets. Another was the well-remembered Grand Crossing on the far south side. Both of these monstrosities were notorious for their long delays and frequent accidents. Both were eventually disentangled by making separations at grade of the multiple railroad lines and city streets. But others, such as the great crossing at Archer Avenue and 21st Street, remain. There the tracks of the Chicago and Western Indiana, the Pennsylvania, the Santa Fe and the Illinois Central form a bewildering confusion of frogs and switches. Even the crack passenger trains out of Union Station or Dearborn had no choice but to stop at these crossings, although in

Crossings, crossings everywhere, that's Chicago. Here, within the very shadow of Chicago's magnificent modern skyline, we are looking northward along the tracks of the Rock Island toward their rendezvous with the La Salle Street Station. Crossing the Rock Island here is the St. Charles Air Line, long an important Chicago link, one which today permits Amtrak passenger trains coming into the town on the lakeside tracks of the Illinois Central to make a connection with the Union Station trackage.

(George H. Douglas)

One of Chicago's busiest and best-known crossings over the years, the 21st Street Crossing—shown here in the 1940s. The tracks of the Chicago and Western Indiana from Dearborn Station are crossed here by the mainline tracks of the Pennsylvania. Framed in the background is a Santa Fe switcher, on tracks that are leaving the C&WI at this point. At the extreme right are the tracks of the Alton (now Gulf, Mobile & Ohio).

(Santa Fe)

Chicago has more interlocking towers than any city in the country—how could it be otherwise? Here is the 91st Street tower on the Rock Island, a major junction on that line.

(George H. Douglas)

our more technically advanced age they have been rendered harmless (or nearly so) by sophisticated signaling and interlocking systems.

But even more obvious to the casual visitor was the immensity of the freight-handling system in Chicago. Chicago, above everything else, was a city of freight transfer. From early times one could see at every hand the long freight yards jutting off from the main line tracks, and one could view the hundreds of spurs and industrial sidings which handled the business of even very small freight customers.

The growth of the city as a freight-handling center was helter-skelter and largely unplanned. Until the early twentieth century the railroads pretty much laid down their yards wherever they could on city property they owned or acquired. But as the city grew and land values increased, it became more and more difficult for railroads to construct yards at the city's core that were large enough for their purposes. At the same time, the proliferation of a great many little yards here and there became nightmarish, making it sometimes impossible for a railroad to keep track of its cars and continue everything moving in the right direction. These difficulties eventually forced the railroads to build, some 10 to 20 miles from the city's center, very large classification yards where their freight traffic could be more systematically ordered and where, by means of belt connections, transfer of freight to other railroads could be made more smoothly.

Everything in the Chicago freight yards is on a grand scale.
Santa Fe's Corwith Yard has a 32-track automatic retarder yard
with a capacity of 1,800 cars, 3 modern freight houses, a
1,362-foot car repair shed, an inbound-outbound transfer yard
with a capacity of 1,350 cars, a hold yard for 520 cars, a 110-car
local yard, diesel shop, piggyback facility, and terminal yard office.

(Santa Fe)

In the foreground of this picture of Santa Fe's Corwith Yard is one of the facility's three mobile cranes for use in piggyback operations. These cranes serve a five-track unit of the yard with a capacity of 140 cars.

(Santa Fe)

It would be hard to find a picture anywhere that more perfectly captures the spirit of railroading in Chicago. During the days of World War II, Office of War Information photographer Jack Delano photographed a typical switching operation at the Santa Fe's Corwith Yard, here shown blanketed with a fresh fall of snow, always expected in this great city by the lake.

(Jack Delano Collection, Library of Congress)

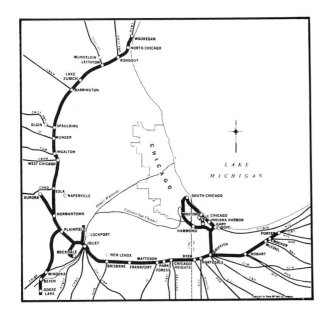

Besides the Class I railroads running into Chicago, there are a number of really important switching, terminal and transfer railroads, without whose services the large number of freight exchanges would not be possible. This is a map of the Elgin, Joliet, and Eastern Railroad, giving some idea of the many possible points of transfer on that line.

(Author's Collection)

Freight transfer is a regular and orderly business in Chicago. Here in 1943, the C&NW Yardmaster at Proviso (left) confers with crew members of the Indiana Harbor Belt Line, whose train will pick up cars for Blue Island.

(Jack Delano Collection, Library of Congress)

MAJOR FREIGHT YARDS IN CHICAGO
(Class I Railroads—About 1950)

Railroad	Yard	Location
Atcheson, Topeka & Santa Fe	Corwith	Along Southwest (now Stevenson) Expressway; about 8 miles SW of Loop
Baltimore & Ohio	Barr	In Riverdale; 18 miles S of Loop
Chesapeake & Ohio	Rockwell Street Yard	East of Kedzie, around 75th Street; 8 miles SW of Loop
Chicago, Burlington & Quincy	Clyde	In Cicero, next to Ogden Avenue; 5 miles W of Loop
Chicago & Eastern Illinois	Dolton	In Dolton; about 18 miles S of Loop
Chicago & Great Western	Chicago Transfer	About 9 miles W of Loop along Congress (now Eisenhower) Expressway
Chicago, Milwaukee, St. Paul & Pacific	Bensenville	Bensenville and Franklin Park; 16 miles NW of Loop
Chicago & North Western	Proviso	14 miles W of Loop; Melrose Park, Berkeley, Northlake—S of Lake St.
Chicago, Rock Island & Pacific	Burr Oak	In Blue Island; 16 miles SW of Loop at 127th Street
Erie	Hammond	Hammond, Indiana; 20 miles SE of Loop
Grand Trunk Western	Elsdon	51st Street, several blocks west of Kedzie; about 8 miles SW of Loop
Gulf, Mobile & Ohio (Alton)	Glenn	Forest View; about 10 miles SW of Loop
Illinois Central	Markham	About 16 miles S of Loop at 127th Street
Minneapolis, St. Paul & Sault Sainte Marie (Soo Line)	Schiller Park	Schiller Park, about 17 miles NW of Loop, near Irving Park Road
Monon	Hammond	Hammond, Indiana, about 20 miles SE of Loop
New York, Chicago & St. Louis (Nickel Plate)	Calumet	SE of Pullman Junction; 11 miles S of Loop
New York Central	Gibson	East Chicago, Indiana; about 21 miles SE of Loop
Pennsylvania	No major yard	Several smaller yards Chicago, Calumet City, and Hammond, IN.
Wabash	Landers	Western Avenue & 75th Street; about 11 miles SW of Loop

These were, indeed, gigantic yards. The biggest was probably the North Western's Proviso Yard, some 14 miles west of downtown on the Galena Division. But the Illinois Central's Markham yard and the Milwaukee's Bensenville Yard were giants on pretty much the same scale. The latest of the great yards is the Santa Fe's modern showpiece, the Corwith Yard, viewable from the Adlai E. Stevenson Expressway.

Of course, the railroads had to continue to provide freight service near the heart of the city, not only by means of their own freight houses and stations. Before the trucking industry took away most of the less-than-carload freight business, the major lines had to have their own freight houses conveniently located for

One of the few city freight houses of architectural distinction was the Pennsylvania Railroad freight house south of Union Station on the south branch of the Chicago River. Unfortunately there has been a great decline in the need for inner city freight houses, and the Pennsylvania freight house has met up with the wrecker's ball. (Northwestern University Library)

customers who wanted to ship and pick up packages and merchandise. Very often in the early days these were hideous and rickety affairs, but in the aftermath of the Burnham Plan, with pressure being put on the railroads to consolidate trackage and terminal facilities of all sorts, some pretty grandiose freight houses were built in Chicago. The most remarkable grew out of the Union Station project. This was the giant Pennsylvania Railroad freight house on West Polk Street, along the west bank of the Chicago River. The Pennsylvania freight house was designed by architects Price and McLanahan, and is in every way remarkable in design and aesthetic appeal for such a purely utilitarian structure. It was built between 1915 and 1918, during the early years of the Union Station construction. This building—combined with the erection, in the next decade, of the world's largest mail-handling facility (south of Union Station)—resulted in a unified freight-handling district that made Chicago the envy of every other city in the world. Alas, as soon as the city planners were satisfied with these moves toward larger and more centralized freight terminals, the railroads started to lose business to the trucking interests, and the inner city rail freight terminals started disappearing, although a few still stand.

The Rock Island freight house south of La Salle Street Station still stands in 1980, but as this picture shows, it has that ghostly appearance of some historic relic.

(George H. Douglas)

Another remarkable part of the Chicago freight picture was the vast network of underground rail tunnels which for a long time linked the trunk lines with nearly every building on the Loop. The "Great Freight Tunnel" it was called, and its existence was unknown to the average Chicagoan. But it was nonetheless known the world over to railroadmen and shippers. Other cities may have had their subways and other systems of mass transit in their downtown areas, but only Chicago had a real underground freight network. While it lasted, the system managed to keep thousands of delivery trucks off city streets.

This unique feature of Chicago's economic landscape had a curious beginning. It was not actually started as a freight tunnel at all. Rather, it was started in 1898 as a four-foot bore by the Illinois Telephone and Telegraph Company. The Illinois Telephone and Telegraph was a competitor of the Chicago Telephone Company (which became Illinois Bell Telephone Company in 1921). To compete with its rival it planned to put most of its lines and circuits underground to eliminate telephone poles in the city, thus avoid-

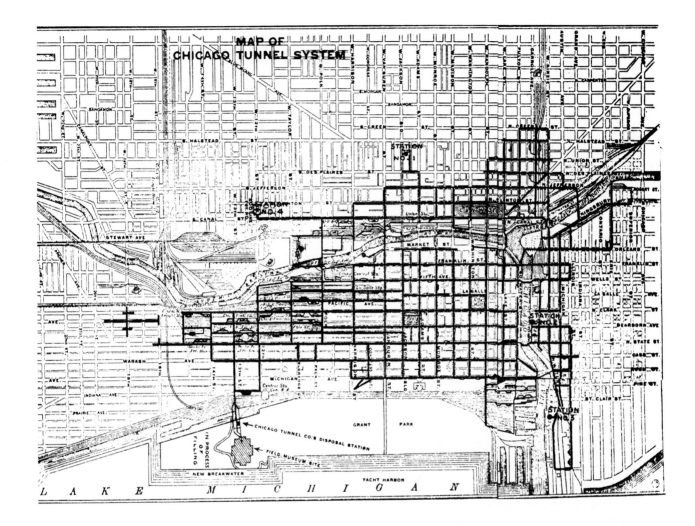

For many years an integral part of Chicago's system of freight transfer was the underground tunnel which allowed freight to be brought right up to the basements of many Loop buildings, thus keeping trucks off the city streets. The idea was a great one, but it ran into financial difficulties during the depression and operations ceased. This map shows the system when it was at its peak.

(University of Illinois Library)

ing their many weather-related difficulties. But the Illinois Telephone and Telegraph Company was not a very effective competitor. It shortly went downhill and was out of business entirely by 1917. As early as 1903 the tunnel had been bought by the Illinois Tunnel Company, which was immediately granted a franchise by the City Council to build a railroad in it. The tunnel was seven-and-a-half feet high and six feet wide at its widest part. It was only five feet wide at the bottom and had a flat-bottomed oval shape. It was intended as a narrow gauge railroad, but was totally electrified, which made it distinctive from some other city freight railroads, including one in London which used steam locomotives—

however insufferable that must have been to its operating crews.

Ultimately there were 64 miles of tunnels, and the system possessed 90 electric locomotives and over 500 diminutive "pony" freight cars. Power for the locomotives was supplied by overhead wires containing 240 volts of direct current. The trains ran on a track set at a two-foot gauge and jounced along at a top speed of about 30-35 miles per hour. Overall train movement was controlled by telephone dispatches, but there was no signal system, so train crews had to be on the lookout at every turn where an intersecting tunnel was encountered. At the peak of its traffic, trains in the tunnel moved 70,000 cars of freight a year, or about 235 per working day.

The tunnels were connected to the surface by elevator cages that moved up and down to a number of principal freight stations. Some of the freight stations were those of the major railroads, who used the tunnel to provide themselves with a very convenient local delivery sys-

This picture shows what was obviously a major transfer point and loading spot on the Chicago tunnel railroad. Trains were electric and were especially constructed for narrow gauge and low overhead.

(University of Illinois Library)

tem that they could not have enjoyed at street level. In addition to the main freight stations where goods were sorted and classified, there were over a hundred way stations, some of which were nothing more than basement doors to business establishments, warehouses or department stores.

This underground network, so perfectly logical and natural for a city like Chicago, was not to last. With the coming of the depression, the freight railway tunnel was doomed as a business venture. It became increasingly easier to move things by truck. By the early 1930s, too, the railroads were starting to abandon their in-city freight terminals. Before long only a few of them had terminals actually on the tunnel, breaking the chain that made the tunnel economical. In the middle 1930s, when the tunnel had its big contract to carry mails canceled, it started to die a lingering death.

This decline was regrettable, for the system was a good one and could have been put on a

The technology of the refrigerator car has greatly improved since the 1870s of course, but the general principle remains the same. Here are several modern refrigerator cars at Swift's Chicago plant in the 1970s.

(Swift & Co.)

The Chicago Central stockyards are closed and their function has been decentralized. But for the better part of a century they were one of the city's best-known institutions. And they were strategically placed from the beginning to be served by rail trunk lines. This picture is from the 1940s.

(Illinois Historical Survey)

Agricultural products of all sorts have always been a major part of Chicago's livelihood. And the Middle West enjoys the world's richest and most productive grain harvests. Here, ready to be shipped out to all points of the compass, is a grain train, some of it destined perhaps for places as far away as Russia or China.
(Chicago Board of Trade)

Chicago has also been distinctive as a manufacturing town, and the diversity of its products is unimaginable. Strangely one area where Chicago did not excel (at least in early days) was locomotive manufacture. For a while Hiram Scoville's locomotive works turned out a number of original locomotives, and the Hicks Locomotives Works, shown here, in the 1890s, did a great deal of car building and locomotive rebuilding. But in the 19th century, Chicago had to bow to Philadelphia and Paterson, N.J.
(Illinois Historical Survey)

managers, store clerks, red caps, station managers, computer programmers, public relations men, laundresses, car painters, truck drivers, car tonks, gandy dancers, railroad police, and hundreds of other occupations adding up to thousands of workers.

In Chicago one never had a hard time finding what historian Freeman H. Hubbard used to call "Railroad Avenue," the neighborhood or neighborhoods where railroad work was being carried on. Down by the yards and the roundhouses were the inevitable diners and greasy spoons where railroad crews hung out while waiting to be called to work. There it was that one could hear spoken languages that sounded only vaguely like English, since from the beginning railroad workers developed their own specialized argot—words like hoghead for engineer, crummy for caboose, shack for brakeman, highball for fast run, gandy dancer for section hand, varnish for passenger train. When railroad men gathered in the greasy spoons, even the food became railroadized. An outsider might be startled to hear some fireman or switchman calling to the man behind the counter for headlights (eggs), or red lead (catsup) or flatcars (pancakes). Railroad Avenue was always rich in such down-to-earth, colorful expressions.

Chicago always needed to make provision for workmen who were both permanent and transient. There were the inevitable train crews waiting to be called in and out. But there were

If Chicago never glittered as a center of locomotive manufacture, it has made up for it in the diesel era. Shown here in 1972 is the construction of a diesel locomotive in the La Grange plant of General Motors' Electro-Motive Division, the largest plant of its kind in the world.

(General Motors Corp.)

Industrial plants never have any difficulty locating near a railroad line in Chicago. Here is the giant Austin Avenue complex of the Zenith Radio Corporation, served by the Milwaukee Road. This 1,350,000-square foot plant is one of the nation's largest producers of color television sets.

(Zenith Radio Corporation)

The Morton Salt Distribution Center is conveniently served by Chicago and North Western Railway, and is regularly viewed by that line's commuters on their way in and out of town.

(Morton Salt)

This is the main Chicago plant and corporate offices of R. R. Donnelley & Sons, the world's largest printing company. Donnelley is located on the main line of the Illinois Central Railroad in the blocks south of 16th Street.

(R.R. Donnelley & Sons)

There is no better look to be had at the industrial heartland of America than through the windows of a passenger train on the old New York Central main line (now Conrail). The communities hugging Lake Michigan—communities like Calumet, Whiting, Gary, Hammond, East Chicago—are devoted to heavy-muscle industry of the kind that is basic to the survival of a developed nation. Here we see one of Chicagoland's great utilities installations, a good number of which are still powered by coal.

(George H. Douglas)

170

Whatever one thinks of in the way of basic industry can be found along the periphery of Lake Michigan. Some of these industries, like refining, can be noxious and polluting, but this immense collection of industrial giants is so awe-inspiring to the casual viewer that few wish to complain about this elemental part of our nation's economy.

(George H. Douglas)

One of the big coal users in the Chicago area is the vast Inland Steel complex shown here in all of its grim blackness on the peaceful shore of Lake Michigan. The Inland works is almost exclusively powered by coal, which arrives over the tracks of numerous Chicago railroads.

(Inland Steel Corporation)

The steel industry is strictly heavy industry in all its aspects, and thus it remains a good customer of rail freight services. Here, in June 1977, the first shipment of iron ore pellets from Inland's Minorca Mine near Virginia, Minnesota, for the furnaces in Chicago.

(Inland Steel Corporation)

Of railroad employment in Chicago, a great portion naturally is devoted to the cleaning, servicing and maintaining of railroad equipment. Shown here is a servicing facility of the Santa Fe, with a 2,000-HP diesel locomotive being prepared to turn westward for a trip out of Chicago. The turntable looks rather rickety, but the truth is it is 100 feet long and can turn a locomotive of 300 tons with ease.

(Santa Fe)

Here is yet another part of the industrial map of Chicago. On the north line of the Chicago and North Western Railroad one finds a profusion of chemical and pharmaceutical plants in the vicinity of Waukegan and North Chicago. Here, being served by C&NW siding, is the North Chicago plant of the Abbott Laboratories, one of the country's largest pharmaceutical companies.

(George H. Douglas)

Nothing in Chicago is done on a small scale. Consider the size of this roundhouse, which actually goes back to the nineteenth century! This is the Burlington's roundhouse, an Aurora which, over the years, did mighty service in storing and maintaining the line's locomotives.

(Burlington Northern)

also conferences for sales personnel and traffic men. The Chicago and North Western used to hold its examination for locomotive engineers at North Western Station. Young lads from Wisconsin or Minnesota came into town for a few days of brisk interrogation, and perhaps a fling at some gaudy midway or perfumed disorderly house. There were boarding houses aplenty with signs inviting railroad men at 50 cents a night. There always had to be several thousand transient beds available for the railroad in the city of Chicago; everything from a fleabag to a king's bed were available nightly. When the Y.M.C.A. built its largest hotel dormitory in Chicago, it pierced the sky down near the railroad yards only a few blocks from Dearborn Station.

Some of the railroad avenues were picturesque to say the least—the sorts of places that gave rise to ballad and song. One can't help but remember places like West Madison Street, where a number of the railroads had their hiring offices. In the years before the First World War so much of railroad employment was temporary and transient. The railroad hiring office was the target of the itinerant worker who was looking to be taken on at the extra board. In those earlier times these workers were familiarly known as

boomers, and the majority of them were knowledgeable and reliable railroad men.

But the railroads always had to be careful whom they hired, since only a jot removed from the boomer in appearance and temperament were some less reliable elements who also gravitated toward the seedier parts of railroad avenue. In Chicago, West Madison Street was long the mecca for these colorful hangers-on—the hoboes and tramps of visual fame who were a real part of American life, probably into the 1920s. Today we draw hardly any distinction between these shifting groups, but at one time the distinctions were all clear-cut. A boomer was in every sense a real worker with aggressive instincts; he sought constant employment. But he was rootless, and would go where the work was. A hobo was also a migrant worker, but quite a bit less assiduous in seeking regular employment. He was much more addicted to wanderlust and free-

Every sort of structure known to railroadiana is found in Chicago—from wooden tool shed and switchman's shanty to executive office building. Here is the Chicago and North Western's coal dock in the 40th Street Yard.

(Bob Lorenz)

Chicago has been called a city of neighborhoods—all of them named, all distinctive. One Chicago neighborhood whose name will always be identified with the railroad is Englewood, shown here in 1922. The picture looks north on Halsted Street from 63rd Place.

(University of Illinois Library)

dom from the cage-life of conventional society. A tramp was the next step below. A tramp merely traveled without any interest in work unless forced into it. By common agreement of all concerned the lowest rung on the ladder was the bum, usually an alcoholic derelict, not in good enough shape to travel or work.

Whatever the distinctions among these now almost-vanished species, they were all well represented down on West Madison Street in the years when that district was the location of railroad hiring offices. Some were there to be hired; some might try to get hired if an urgent need arose; and some were there simply because it was the place to be, the place where the brethren gathered.

West Madison was certainly never the worst of America's skid rows and doubtless the railroad ambience gave it something of an elevated atmosphere. It was never as depressing a spot as the Bowery in New York, perhaps, which always seemed to be but a place of broken men, of

stooped and tattered alcoholics and derelicts. On West Madison Street there were those who were broken and on the bottom of the heap, but in the hobo and the tramp, as opposed to the alcoholic bum, there was always a hint of someplace to go, the promise that tomorrow one could pick up and move on. This was no dead end, but a long railway platform for quick departure, and some prospect of a new fortune at distant remove.

Still, West Madison Street, and the other less prominent railroad avenues in Chicago, were characteristic of a rougher, cruder and more boisterous America, one we associate today with dusty frontier towns, with the districts

For many years a number of the railroads had their Chicago hiring offices on West Madison Street, and this area became a gathering point for boomers, tramps, hobos and other characters of a disreputable nature. The railroad flavor has departed, but in 1980 West Madison Street continues to be a haven for loafers and drifters, a place of gin mills and seedy hotels.

(George H. Douglas)

The circus travels by rail and accordingly Chicago has always been a focal point of circus activity. Here is a Ringling Brothers and Barnum and Bailey piggyback in Chicago in 1978.

(George H. Douglas)

of any communities where miners, lumberjacks, and itinerant field hands gathered and sought each other's company. As late as the depression years West Madison Street was the place where all the manifestations of the railroad demimonde were on display as in a movie setting—the boarding houses, diners, cheap-john stores, burlesque houses, medicine-show quacks, tattoo parlors, flophouses, brothels. To some it was all a sign of urban blight, to others a sign of the colorful ambience of a world not yet anemic and over-refined.

Railroad Avenue, as Freeman Hubbard observed, was not a place, but a way of life. And even if it was only a place, it could certainly not have been defined by the atmosphere of West Madison Street. The majority of railroad workers were not itinerant types at all, but dedicated professionals who loved the railroad. These professionals lived by the thousands in Chicago, ofttimes gathering together in fraternal

Here in a ritual as sacred as any in railroading, a brakeman puts up his marker in Chicago and North Western's Proviso Yard. The time is 1943 and this train is about to depart Chicago for Clinton—right on the dot.

(Jack Delano Collection, Library of Congress)

orders, lodges, brotherhoods, and benevolent societies. Chicago was and is a town of railroad workers on all levels. Since the days of Eugene Victor Debs, if not before, it was a strong union town, and for many years served as headquarters for unions representing workers engaged in railroad activities of every hue and description.

In 1935, the Bureau of Labor Statistics of the U.S. Department of Labor recorded that four independent unions of railway workers were headquartered in Chicago. These were the American Federation of Railroad Workers, the Brotherhood of Railroad Signalmen, the Ameri-

178

can Train Dispatchers' Association and the National Brotherhood of Dining Car Employees. In addition to these, the Railway Employees Department of the A. F. of L. had its headquarters in the American Fore Building at 844 Rush Street. This department united nine railway craft unions of considerable importance in their day: the International Brotherhood of Blacksmiths, Drop Forgers and Helpers; the International Brotherhood of Boilermakers; the Brotherhood of Railway Carmen; the International Brotherhood of Electrical Workers; the International Brotherhood of Stationary Firemen and Oilers; the International Association of Machinists; the Brotherhood of Maintenance of Way Employees; the International Association of Sheet Metal Workers; and the Switchman's Union of North America.

Chicago was also and remains today a headquarters town for the railroads themselves. Among the railroad employees of the city are presidents of the road, telegraph operators, public relations men, experts on finance, bond salesmen, and dealers and traders of all sorts. Chicago continues to be the place for the executive offices of numerous Midwestern and Western roads as it has been since earliest times. The Chicago and North Western has been headquartered in Chicago since the days when William

Chicago has always been witness to the strenuous efforts of track crews and gandy dancers—the city requires hundreds of them even in these more mechanized times. Here a crew goes at it in the very shadow of Michigan Avenue, hopefully dodging the heavy traffic of the Illinois Central's electrified commuter service.
(Illinois Central Gulf)

Butler Ogden and John B. Turner had the little cupola up above the first depot. Even when the Vanderbilt interests controlled the C&NW from New York, the president of the road was always in Chicago. The Chicago and North Western has had its offices adjacent to its station in the Daily News (now Riverside Plaza) Building on Madison Street for many years.

The Illinois Central has also always been headquartered in Chicago, even when it was a puppet of E. H. Harriman in the early years of the twentieth century and essentially run from the steep caverns of Wall Street. For most of its history the Illinois Central executives enjoyed the grandeur of their Romanesque pile next to Central Station. Since the early 1970s, however, they have been in the modern but uninspiring skyscraper called Illinois Center on North Michigan Avenue.

The job of the tower man is a big one in Chicago, and there are more interlocking towers here than in any city in America. A Union Station towerman is preparing for an intricate crossover; all without a peek-out window since he can read the whole situation on the illuminated diagram board overhead.

(Jack Delano Collection, Library of Congress)

The Burlington had its headquarters in Chicago for many years in buildings of its own. The best remembered of these was at 547 West Jackson Boulevard, diagonally across from Union Station, which remained their corporate headquarters until their merger with the Great Northern and the Northern Pacific.

The Milwaukee Road continues to keep its long-time headquarters in Union Station. In the late 1970s the Rock Island picked up its empty cash boxes from the dilapidated rookery of their La Salle Street Station office building and moved

180

This distinguished assemblage constitutes part of the membership of the Quincy Club, a Chicago rail organization that was composed of waiters, cooks and porters, mostly employed by the Burlington and the Milwaukee. The club is now defunct, but at one time had its own building on the south side of Chicago—shown here in the late 1940s. Chicago was host to many railway societies, fraternal organizations, unions, and groups of railroad workers of all sorts.
(Cleodia H. Lyles)

to more elegant surroundings on Michigan Avenue, with seemingly little effect on their dwindling fortunes. But both roads seem firmly tied to Chicago. So, too, are the Monon and the C&EI.

A number of terminal companies, belt lines, and transfer companies have their headquarters in the Railway Exchange Building at 80 East Jackson Boulevard, a building designed by

Daniel H. Burnham and once the location of his offices. But the best-known tenant of this building has been the Santa Fe, which has been strongly holding forth in its Chicago base since it made its belated invasion of the city in the late 1880s.

Altogether, Chicago remains solidly and briskly a railroad town. Every railway vocation, every railway pastime is represented. If the steam locomotive no longer lets off gusts of steam beneath the old train sheds south of the Loop, if the diesels silently and undramatically go about their business out in the yards, the railroad man is still to be found everywhere. One can't walk a block in the Loop without encountering some unmarked representative of America's first big business. For in Chicago, it still *is* big business.

Chicago has employed railroad men by the thousand in every known classification. Sometimes the railroad men aren't even men. Here are two canine employees of the Illinois Central Railroad. In the old days it was a big job keeping intruders and trouble makers off railroad property and the function of the railroad policeman was an important one. The dogs look particularly eager to sniff out unreliable personages, and, with luck, maybe even take a bite out of them.

(Illinois Central Gulf)

Chicago has had every kind of railroad worker from trackside laborer to president of the road. Here, as it appeared at the time of its opening in 1913, are the offices of the Chicago, Burlington and Quincy Railroad at 547 West Jackson Boulevard (corner of Clinton). Burlington regional offices are still in the building, but after the formation of the Burlington Northern, the company top brass moved to Minnesota.

(University of Illinois Library)

SWITCHING, TRANSFER, AND TERMINAL RAILROADS IN CHICAGO

Switching, Belt, Transfer, and Freight Railroads

Baltimore and Ohio Chicago Terminal
Belt Railway of Chicago
Chicago Heights Terminal Transfer Railroad
Chicago Junction
Chicago River & Indiana
Elgin, Joliet & Eastern
Indiana Harbor Belt

Industrial Switching Railroads

Chicago & Calumet River
Chicago & Illinois Western
Chicago Short Line
Chicago, West Pullman & Southern
Illinois Northern
Manufacturers' Junction
Pullman

Terminal Railroads

Baltimore & Ohio Chicago Terminal
Chicago & Western Indiana

Even where the railroad has disappeared from its long-accustomed places, its original presence casts a shadow. Here is Wolf Point, long a center of the C&NW's great Wells Street passenger terminal between 1880 and 1913. The C&NW sold the air rights to this very valuable piece of real estate on which is located the world-famous Merchandise Mart and Merchandise Mart Apparel Center (left).

(Merchandise Mart)

CHAPTER 7

A Festival of Trains

During the Golden Age of railroading in the United States, no country in the world was our equal in the profusion of beautifully equipped and imaginatively named long-distance trains. It may be that we could not match the old-world elegance of the trains of the *Compagnie des Wagons Lits*, or the aristocratic booking lists of the great trains of the European continent such as the *Orient Express* (some of which were better known for their mysteriousness than their actual luxury), but no country or continent could match us in our large number of excellent trains—each with its distinctive traits and eccentric personality. As America's big junction, Chicago was the regular host to more name trains than any other city in the land—if not the world.

There were, of course, great American trains that had no connection with Chicago. Chicago saw neither hide nor hair of the *Orange Blossom Special*, the *Congressional Limited*, the *Sunset Limited*, the *Knickerbocker* or the *Bar Harbor Express*. Nonetheless, Chicago was *the* place to see trains in America during the apogee of railroad service. To Chicago they came from north and south, east and west. During the Second World War the Pennsylvania Railroad had a dozen daily name trains between New York and Chicago alone! When one begins to count the number of pedigreed trains on the heavily traveled intermediate runs in and out of Chicago, the totals become nothing short of startling.

The name train, the "high varnish" of legend, was purely and simply the product of railroad affluence and of the fierce competition among the rival lines. Before the Civil War, and while the roads traveled their own meandering ways through sparsely settled countryside, there was no need for name trains, or for luxury equipment for that matter. But in the 1880s, when the railroads started fighting tooth and nail with one another for the existing passenger business along often competing lines, enterprising passenger agents made their appearance with all kinds of delights and gimmicks, the most important of which was the distinctive train. Distinction became a matter of more than name alone. During the glory years the rail passenger was pampered by cars of the most sumptuous design, and personnel trained and prepared to deliver service worthy of a king. With the advent of the overnight sleeping train, and with Pullman designers working in top form, there were plush seats and walnut wainscoting, private compartments, fresh-cut flowers in the dining car, and ferns for planters in the observation car. There were buffets, bars well stocked with drinks and comestibles of all sorts; abundant hot and cold water, separate tub baths for ladies and gentlemen and later on showers for the large private drawing room or master room. Functionaries of all sorts met any imaginable need: train secretaries, valets, barbers, ladies' maids, a matron to attend the children, and any other miscellaneous convenience that could be thought up by a management willing to

---

The two greatest trains in the East provided the world's most exciting railroad competition. Here the *Broadway Limited* (left) and the *Twentieth Century Limited* are shown leaving Englewood on their long trek to New York in 1937. The meeting of the two trains at Englewood (if both were on schedule) was the only place that their paths ever crossed, so the competition was always hot and dramatic at the parting of the ways.

(A.W. Johnson)

please—embossed stationery, monogrammed bed and table linen, radios, imaginative cuisine.

The name train came on the scene rather slowly in America in the 1880s and 1890s. The railroad time cards of the early years show various trains being singled out as "Express" trains or occasionally "Fast Mail," which title carried the hint that getting the mail there on time was more important than getting passengers there on time. But with the passage of time a kind of freewheeling imagination took hold and each railroad began to find names of a more distinctive character—names that would set its own trains off from those of rival lines. Sometimes these names were not official in the beginning or were carried over from some popular local tradition. Such, for example, was the case of the Illinois Central's *Cannonball Express*, which took Casey Jones to his death at Vaughn, Mississippi, on April 30, 1900. The *Cannonball* was the Illinois Central's crack train between Chicago and New Orleans and it was shown on the timetables of the day as No. 1 (No. 2 northbound), but the *Cannonball* name was not *officially* attached to it—a generation or two later it might have been. Railroad managements were not given to flights of imagination in the early days, although they didn't seem to object to locomotives having individual names.

The wild flights of fancy that brought about unique train names—and all of the finery that went with them—were mostly the result of commercial rivalry between railroads. And one of the reasons that Chicago saw the appearance of so many name trains is that it had more than its share of competitive runs. There was the famous competition for the New York-to-Chicago traffic

between the New York Central and the Pennsylvania (with a few lesser lines trying ineffectively to horn in). And there was the Chicago-to-St. Louis competition, which for a number of years engaged as many as five railroads in acrimonious warfare. Farther north there was the fight to capture the public's affection on the run between Chicago and the Twin Cities. Less intense, perhaps because of the vast territory involved, was the competition for the California traffic—both Los Angeles and San Francisco. In the last years of the golden age of railroading this rivalry involved some very glamorous and expensive duels in the purchase of streamlined equipment.

Undoubtedly the most fabled and legendary competition in American railroading was the 60-year battle between the New York Central and the Pennsylvania involving their respective flagships, the *Twentieth Century Limited* and the *Broadway Limited*. There were no greater American trains than these, for the very competition kept them at the top of their form. The railroad managements bought for them the best equipment available and saw to it that the service and amenities were consistently of the highest.

For most of the years of their existence, the *Twentieth Century Limited* was the winner in terms of revenue and passengers carried. This was probably due to its highly imaginative name and the early public relations campaign, which was the product of that most dynamic of all passenger agents, George H. Daniels. It is not at all clear, however, that overall the New York Central had the better of it on the Chicago to New York run. Over the years many other trains were also involved, including those of the Penn-

sylvania, which packed in the passengers on a great many glamour trains that served not only New York but Philadelphia as well.

But the *Broadway Limited* and the *Twentieth Century Limited* were the trains that inspired the imagination. They were twin flagships in daily confrontation with one another. Tweedledum and Tweedledee some might have said. They were inaugurated in the same year—1902. And together they advanced in all aspects of service and panache. No idea could be introduced by the management of one road without being immediately copied by the other. When one railroad advertised "20 hours between Chicago and New York," the other had to do likewise. The times were cut year by year until a rather unrealistic 15½ hours was posted under the Robert R. Young management of the New York Central in 1954. The Pennsylvania went along too, but the more plausible 16 hours was shortly restored to both roads two years later.

Both trains became streamlined on the same day (June 15, 1938), for by this late year, neither management could have tolerated the other's getting the jump on it in any quarter for as much as one day. When they were redesigned that

The competition between the *Broadway* and the *Twentieth Century Limited* was always keen and unrelenting. Both trains were inaugurated in 1902; both began streamlined service together on the same day, June 15, 1938. Here the *Twentieth Century*, always the leader in the competition because of its imaginative name, leaves La Salle Street Station on its inaugural streamlined run, under steam.

(Penn Central)

year to replace the glories of "Pullman standard," they were redesigned right down to the dining service, glassware and stationery by industrial designers Henry Dreyfuss (for the *Century*) and Raymond Loewy (for the *Broadway*). Loewy's *Broadway Limited* of 1938 was perhaps the most elegant train ever designed in the United States (there might have been flashier), although this was never admitted by the devotees of the *Century*, who were not in the least put off by the antiseptic art deco style of the first streamlined *Century*. The *Century* continued to hold its sway with the help of George H. Daniel's old moniker, "The Greatest Train in the World." It continued to remain in the public's affections until 1957, when the New York Central management bowed to austerity and added day coaches to the *Century*'s consist.

Haughty patrons flocked over to the still all-room *Broadway*.

During the glory years, neither management would concede a thing. The *Century* had obtained the lion's share of the business back in Pullman standard times, and sometimes had to run the train in as many as six sections. But the *Broadway* had its strengths, the most important of which was that it could attract the business and social elite not only of New York but also of Philadelphia (in streamlined times it left Philadelphia only an hour and 20 minutes after it left New York). Whatever train might have won in the minds of this or that segment of the public, each liner was a shining banner to the management of its road. It is said that for many years the president of the New York Central wanted to have notice of the arrival of the *Century* in New York on his desk when he started work in the morning (the *Century* was due in at 9 A.M. sharp). When he was away from his office he often

insisted on having those arrival statistics forwarded to him by telegraph. The story is told that Alfred E. Smith, president of the Central in the early 1920s, went on an African safari. The daily achievements of the *Century* were brought to him in the heart of the jungle by a naked native, carrying the news on the end of a pointed pole. Railway passenger service could only decline from that high point.

Chicago was the only place in the world where one could see the *Century* and the *Broadway* together. When they were on identical departure schedules, which they occasionally

The Broadway Limited may not have been the spectacular money maker that the *Twentieth Century Limited* was, but it was always a beautiful train. Indeed, the streamlined *Broadway*, shown here leaving Chicago on June 15, 1938, was perhaps the most beautiful train ever to run on American soil. The whole train, right down to the minute details, came from the drafting boards of famous industrial designer Raymond Lowey.

(Penn Central)

The competition between the *Pennsy* and the *Central* was not limited to the *Broadway* and the *Twentieth Century*. Both roads had a whole fleet of trains between Chicago and New York. Snaking out of Union Station at precisely 3:31 p.m. on a spring day in 1949 is another famous Pennsylvania name train, *The General*. Arriving at the same moment from the Pacific Northwest is the *Empire Builder*.

(Bob Lorenz)

were, and when both were on time, they could be seen standing together at the Englewood Station, a spot and a scene which provided inspiration to numerous railroad photographers over the years. For the record there are many pictures of both trains at Englewood in steam and diesel times, always seemingly ready to beat the gun against one another. If, as was often the case, both trains left their respective terminals at 4 P.M. (the *Century* from La Salle Street, the *Broadway* from Union Station), and if departures were on the dot and no mischief intervened—for example, the *Broadway*'s being held up by a raised drawbridge over the south branch of the Chicago River—both trains might be seen at precisely 4:15 at the Englewood Station, waiting for the highball to send them on their separate routings eastward, never again (for that trip) to be within sight of one another.

Chicago was always the place to see and photograph some of the most memorable trains of North America. Englewood was one of the choice spots for that, and one can only regret

that that once-famous station has fallen on evil days and now faces oblivion. For at Englewood could also be seen the long liners not only of the Pennsy and the Central, but also the Rock Island, the Wabash, the Nickel Plate, and the Chicago and Eastern Illinois. On the other hand, most of the Chicago terminals were difficult of access to rail fans, especially places like Union Station, where both the north and south ends were subterranean for a number of blocks, obscuring arriving and departing trains from view.

Of course the dogged Chicago rail fan could see the inbound and outbound traffic from Union Station atop the bridge at Roosevelt

Yet another Pennsy prestige run was the *Admiral,* shown here leaving Englewood on March 14, 1948. The curious-looking, hatchet-faced locomotive was a Baldwin-built T-1 Class duplex. These were pretty impressive-looking monsters, but they had a poor performance record and the Pennsylvania got rid of them as soon as possible in favor of diesels.

(A.W. Johnson)

The bookings for the *Twentieth Century Limited* were so heavy in the early years that the Central would have to run as many as six or seven sections of the train. Here, in 1929, five sections wait for the green at La Salle Street Station, and shortly all of them will be hurtling through the night toward New York.

(Fred G. Korth)

A 1948 ad for the Pennsylvania, showing that the New York-Chicago competition was still hot at that time. The ad announces 15 trains daily, perhaps something of an exaggeration, since not all were really through trains. Still, there were probably as many as 10 through express trains, leaving at all the convenient hours.

(Author's Collection)

FOR BUSINESS . . . FOR VACATION

15 fine trains daily *between*

CHICAGO-NEW YORK

Led by the all-room **BROADWAY LIMITED** with its complete range of private rooms . . . as well as the popular all-coach streamliner **THE TRAIL BLAZER,** offering luxury travel at coach fares.

★

SCHEDULE IMPROVEMENTS OF INTEREST

Broadway Limited, peerless fleet leader now leaves and arrives Chicago one hour earlier to conform with Daylight Saving Time.

Pennsylvania Limited now leaves Chicago at 6 P.M. Its new schedule brings it into New York at 11:25 A.M.

Gotham Limited again provides through sleeping car service to Washington with departure at 11:15 P.M.

Liberty Limited westbound has been changed to conform to Daylight Saving Time. It leaves Washington at 4:30 P.M.

(All times Shown Standard Time)

For complete schedules see Table 1

★

plus **8** Convenient Schedules daily between CHICAGO - BALTIMORE WASHINGTON

Led by LIBERTY LIMITED with its wide range of sleeping accommodations and new Pennsylvania Railroad reserved reclining seat coaches.

PENNSYLVANIA RAILROAD

Road, which also provided a look at trains into and out of La Salle, Grand Central and Dearborn Stations. As with Englewood, a great many of the Chicago railroads provided stops for their name trains in the suburban Chicago area or in nearby towns—for example, the Illinois Central at 63rd Street and Homewood; the Milwaukee at Western Avenue or Glenview; the Rock Island and Santa Fe at Joliet. The opportunities for seeing the name trains, standing as well as running, were always profuse.

The Chicago–New York competition between the Pennsy and the Central was not entirely exhausted by the two great flagships. Both rail-

roads had a fleet of secondary trains that could hardly be sneezed at either in quality or speed. A 1948 advertisement by the Pennsylvania boasted of 15 trains between Chicago and New York— something of an exaggeration — since the Pennsylvania craftily included a number of connecting trains. Still, in that year the Pennsylvania had on its time cards a solid bunch of name trains that obviously were only a jot behind the *Broadway* in time scheduling and quality of equipment: the *Trail Blazer* (the all-coach counterpart of the all-Pullman *Broadway*), the *General*, the *Admiral*, the *Pennsylvania Limited*, the *Manhattan Limited*, the *Rainbow* and the *Gotham Limited*. On its schedules that same year the New York Central offered, in addition to the *Century*, the *Fifth Avenue Special*, the *Commodore Vanderbilt*, the *Pacemaker* (all coach streamliner), the *Water Level*, the *Mohawk*, and the *Lake Shore Limited*.

The Pennsylvania and the New York Central had a near monopoly on the Chicago–New

The Central's No. 2 train, beloved of many of the road's patrons, was the *Commodore Vanderbilt*, shown here leaving Chicago in 1936. This streamlined steam engine with "bathtub" metal covering and white striping was introduced on the line in 1934, just when the western roads were discovering the diesel. The Pennsy and the Central had plenty of coal and wanted to give steam streamlining a chance, but the days of this kind of fairytale creature were already numbered.

(Bob Lorenz)

The New York Central also brought into Chicago a number of trains of New England origin. Here, from Boston, over the Central-owned rails of the Boston and Albany, is the *New England States*, shown arriving at La Salle Street Station in 1952. It is 8:25 A.M. and the passengers will have the whole business day ahead of them in Chicago.

(Conrail)

The B&O was never a strong competitor in the New York to Chicago run, but it usually beat out the Pennsy for the trade between Chicago and Washington-Baltimore. Here on the left is the B&O's *Capitol Limited*, waiting for departure from Grand Central Station in 1962. Also waiting for a late-afternoon departure is the C&O's *Pere Marquette*.

(B&O Museum)

The Erie had its own rambling route between New York and Chicago; there were many who liked the Erie's brand of down-home railroading. The trains stopped everywhere along the way, even the so-called crack trains. Here the Erie's *Lake Cities Express* passes 21st Street on its way to New York in 1948.

(Erie-Lackawanna)

York traffic, but this is not to say that other competition was non-existent. None of the competitors were ever able to match the time schedules of trains like the *Broadway* or the *Twentieth Century*, but some of them were eccentric or charming enough to have their own devotees. The Baltimore and Ohio was a good example. On the Chicago to Washington route the B&O was able to give the Pennsylvania a run for its money. There was many a partisan of the B&O's *Capitol Limited* who would not have been caught dead riding the Pennsylvania's *Liberty Limited* out of Washington when they could be dining on the B&O's more individualistic cuisine and enjoying its more gracious Southern hospitality. But the B&O could never capture the New York trade, even though it made complicated connections there through its subsidiaries, the Reading and the Jersey Central.

In the Golden Age of railroading, though, all things were possible. One suspects that there were some ardent B&O fans who would have gladly suffered the long, roundabout route from New York by ferryboat to Jersey City and thence to Chicago's Grand Central Station via Baltimore. The ride was well worth it.

There were other alternative routes for Chicago–New York run passengers. One direct but leisurely route was that provided for years by the Erie. This trip never took less than 20 hours, and the Erie was never in the front ranks of long-distance passenger carriers, but the scenery along the southern tier of New York and down the Delaware River valley could be breathtaking. The Erie's principal trains, the *Erie Limited* and the *Lake Cities*, were reasonably well kept up. Lucius Beebe called the Erie a "country gentleman" of a railroad and the line's passenger trains kept to the last their bucolic air, meandering along past Victorian gingerbread stations and settings worthy of a painting by John Constable or George Inness.

Another complicated and not very competitive Chicago–New York run was that provided for years by a connection between the Lackawanna and the Nickel Plate. This provided a series of very nice trains that were carried between New York and Buffalo on the Lackawanna and between Buffalo and Chicago on the Nickel Plate, although the arrangement called mainly for the mere pooling of some Pullman cars. Both the Erie and the Lackawanna-Nickel Plate variants were local carriers, and one supposes that there were not many who bought through tickets between the great cities on the Atlantic and Lake Michigan. But how convenient it was in days gone by to be able to ride a Pullman sleeper between Chicago and Binghamton, New York, or Scranton, Pennsylvania. These were local railroads and they did it right.

One famous name train that for many years never came anywhere near Chicago was the Lackawanna's *Phoebe Snow*. But by a curious irony of rail history, the *Phoebe Snow* made a brief appearance in Chicago in the days just before the Amtrak takeover of long-distance pas-

senger service. In the 1950s the Erie and Lackawanna merged, and the New York–Chicago service was combined on both roads. Accordingly, in the mid-1960s, the Erie-Lackawanna revived its turn-of-the-century name train for the New York-to-Chicago run. It only lasted a few years, but it was a pleasing footnote to think that one of railroad's genuine curios should turn up in Chicago, if only for a year or two.

Besides the New York competition, there was the long-standing interest in attracting and keeping the passenger traffic between Chicago and the Twin Cities. The main competitors were the Milwaukee, the Burlington, and the Chicago and North Western. In earlier years, these roads had some keen but probably largely ineffective competition from the Soo and the Chicago

Another long but strongly individualistic route between New York and Chicago was the Nickel Plate/Lackawanna—the Nickel Plate hosting the run between Chicago and Buffalo and the Lackawanna taking it the rest of the way. This is the *Nickel Plate Limited* leaving Chicago (at Hammond, Indiana) in 1956.
(Erie-Lackawanna)

The flagship of the Milwaukee Road was the *Pioneer Limited*, long one of the great trains in the American guidebook. The polished stainless steel observation car shows that there was no financial drain on the railroads when this picture was taken at Pacific Junction, 5½ miles from Union Station, in 1929.

(Milwaukee Road)

Great Western. Here, of course, we come to some of our indigenous Midwestern giants, carriers who from the very beginning chose Chicago as their home port and base of operations.

The Chicago–Twin Cities competition was always of special importance to the Milwaukee, for the Milwaukee's extension to the West Coast never really prospered like that of the Burlington's twin parents, the Great Northern and the Northern Pacific. Nor did the Milwaukee have the Burlington's superb route through Iowa to Omaha and beyond. The Milwaukee was thus always very jealous of the run between Chicago and the Twin Cities, most especially the heavily trafficked Chicago–Milwaukee part, of which it would yield nothing to anybody.

The Milwaukee can honestly boast one of the oldest and longest-lasting big-name trains in America—the *Pioneer Limited*. This one had its origins in 1872, although the name of the Milwaukee's Train No. 1 was not fixed until 1898, when *Pioneer Limited* was chosen in a public relations contest. But the Milwaukee was the first railroad to run through trains between Chicago and St. Paul, and it remained proud of this distinction throughout its history as a passenger carrier. Indeed, for a long time the Chicago, Milwaukee & St. Paul railroad was widely known locally as "the St. Paul Road," and it was not until 1927 that the company decided to advertise itself as "The Milwaukee Road."

The *Pioneer Limited* was filled with distinctions. It was the first train to the north country to carry sleeping cars; it was the first in its neighborhood with the Westinghouse air brake and the first to be steam heated and electrically lighted. As early as 1882 the *Pioneer Limited* was carrying parlor cars, dining cars and sleeping cars between Chicago and the Twin Cities, all of the equipment being the very best available at that time. The train was remodeled many times during the years, most notably in 1898 when the name was chosen, and was put in the livery of the yellow-orange colors similar to those for which the Milwaukee became famous in the twentieth century. The train was advanced to all-steel equipment in 1914 and it became a streamlined all-room Pullman train in 1948.

For long years it was clearly the Chicago–Twin Cities run that meant the most to the Milwaukee management, even though they had their West Coast extension to think about and had introduced such other well-appointed trains as the *Olympian* and the *Columbian*. But with the passage of time the Milwaukee saw that it would have to put more emphasis on its daytime runs and do more to cultivate the fine short-distance route it had between Chicago and nearby Milwaukee. Chicago–Milwaukee is what the Amtrak people would call a great natural corridor, and, while the Milwaukee management was not exactly slow to discover this, the early vastness of their system sometimes obscured that fact. A new group of trains came into existence

in the 1930s, especially tailored for the daytime runs between Chicago, Milwaukee and St. Paul–Minneapolis. These trains were called *Hiawathas*, and the first of them, with streamlined equipment, was placed in service on May 29, 1935. The 410 miles between Chicago and St. Paul were covered in 390 minutes.

Apparently, Indian names had long excited the imagination of Milwaukee executives, for over the years they had on their timecards such train titles as *Arrow*, *Tomahawk*, *Sioux*, and *Chippewa*. (Also, the Milwaukee had more than a few Pullman cars sporting Indian names, many gleaned from the Nebraska, Dakota, Minnesota, and Wisconsin territory through which it ran.) The various *Hiawathas* (for in time there was a *Morning Hiawatha*, an *Afternoon Hiawatha*, a *Midwest Hiawatha*, and an *Olympian Hiawatha*, with service all the way to the West

The 1948 version of the Milwaukee's *Olympian Hiawatha* begins its journey to Seattle/Tacoma behind a 4,000-HP Fairbanks-Morse diesel locomotive. The train has just left Union Station and is about to cross Canal Street.

(Milwaukee Road)

In the early years the Milwaukee was often popularly called "the St. Paul Road." In time, however, the Chicago, Milwaukee, St. Paul and Pacific Railroad found that its ace in the hole was its service through Milwaukee. So, in the 1930s, to exploit the corridor, it introduced a series of trains using the imaginative name *Hiawatha*, borrowed from Longfellow's famous poem. Here a steam-powered *Hiawatha* soots up the suburban countryside at Edgebrook in 1941.

(Bob Lorenz)

Coast), were named for the Mohawk chief immortalized by Longfellow, a legendary Indian character not at all identified with the Milwaukee's territory, but obviously appropriate for his suggestion of swiftness:

> *He could shoot an arrow from him,*
> *And run forward with such fleetness*
> *That the arrow fell behind him.*

The Hiawathas, while they lasted, were as beautiful to look at as they were fleet of foot—a suitable tribute to Longfellow's great hero. They were always elegant trains and were highly visible in the Chicago suburbs, where fans could observe them (wearing their distinctive orange coloring) as they transited suburban towns like Morton Grove, Edgebrook and Deerfield. Here they were perfect examples of streamlined steam-train perfection, smoking up the countryside with a faint reminiscence of the smoke signals and beating drums of the American past.

As for rail competition between Chicago and the Twin Cities, two lesser lines also played an important part in the action in earlier years: the Soo, with such trains as the *Mountaineer* and the *Viking*, and the Chicago Great Western, with liners like the *Great Western Limited*, the

Blue Bird, and the *Legionnaire.* These trains, needless to say, had vast importance in their own prime territories, but they never managed to skim the top off the Chicago-St. Paul traffic.

The great competitors of the Milwaukee were the Burlington and the Chicago and North Western. Over the years the Burlington always had the best of the name trains because it had not only its own obligations to fulfill but also, after 1901, those of its joint owners, the Great Northern and the Northern Pacific. As such, it carried the trains of both those roads between the Twin Cities and Chicago. Thus it was that such trains of the Pacific Northwest as the *Empire Builder,* the *North Coast Limited,* the *Western Star,* and the *Mainstreeter* made their way to Chicago.

The Burlington's pride from its early days was not its Twin Cities route, but its own main line that struck out due west for Lincoln, Omaha

and Denver. Eventually, connections with the Western Pacific for through service to San Francisco resulted in several of the most delightful and scenic long-distance runs in North America on the *Exposition Flyer* and the *California Zephyr.*

Most important to the Twin Cities competition, however, was another famous event in railroad history with which the name Burlington will always be identified. For it was the Burlington that started the rush toward the streamlined train when on November 11, 1934, it put into service the nation's first diesel-powered streamlined train, the *Pioneer Zephyr.* Long before it

When Amtrak took over national passenger service it dropped the name Hiawatha, but it did its best to keep up hotshot passenger service between Chicago and Milwaukee. Here the afternoon turboliner to Milwaukee leaves Chicago in the summer of 1980.
(George H. Douglas)

One of the great developments in American rail passenger service was the introduction of the diesel on the Burlington in 1934. Piloted by Engineer Jack Ford, the first run of the Burlington *Zephyr* passes through Aurora on May 26, 1934, having run nonstop from Denver in record-breaking time.

(Burlington Northern)

went into regular service, this liner received an unusually large amount of publicity—first when it was conceived and named by classically-minded Ralph Budd, president of the Burlington, next when it came out of the Budd Locomotive works in Philadelphia in April of 1934. It captured still more publicity when it was seen by millions of visitors at the Century of Progress Exposition in Chicago in the summer of 1934, and finally, as it flashed along the tracks past eager spectators on one of its many trial runs. Probably the most famous of its great early trial runs was the dash between Denver and Chicago on May 26, 1934, although the Burlington's various *Zephyr* trains were in the newspapers throughout the 1930s breaking speed records here and there. The original *Pioneer Zephyr* represented a milestone in Chicago rail history

and is on permanent display at Chicago's Museum of Science and Industry.

The Burlington management couldn't be kept from eventually throwing the *Zephyr*s into the fray against the Milwaukee, and on April 21, 1935, it placed in service a train to the Twin Cities called the *Twin Zepnyr*—of which there were eventually several. The Burlington always did well with its trains called *Zephyr*, even in later years when ordinary looking diesels took over the run, and they continued to buy fresh new equipment for their trains as long as they remained in the passenger business.

The last of the important competitors on the Chicago–Twin Cities run was the Chicago and North Western. The North Western actually got off to a fairly early start in the competition—almost as early as the Milwaukee. But the

Shortly the Burlington was to introduce a number of *Zephyr* trains. The name would continue to be a magnet, even after the distinctive styling of the early Zephyrs was abandoned. Shown here is the *Mark Twain Zephyr* as it appeared about 1940.

(Burlington Northern)

It was the western railroads, with vast open spaces to traverse, that discovered the diesel. But it wasn't until after World War II that the railroads found that these engines were economical as well as flashy. Here are two early diesel competitors in 1934, the Burlington's Budd-made *Zephyr* and the Union Pacific's Electro-Motive *City of Salina*, making a public relations rendezvous at Omaha.

(Burlington Northern)

Dining-Car Service

DINING CAR CRESTON

DINNER

Split Pea Soup, 20c.

Queen Olives, Individual Bottles, 15c.   Assorted Pickles, 10c.

Celery, 15c.

Raw Oysters, half dozen, 25c.

Boiled Salmon, Egg Sauce, 35c.

Boiled Ham and Cabbage, 50c.   Roast Wild Duck, 50c.

Roast Turkey, Cranberry Sauce, 45c.

Prime Roast Beef, 45c.

Rib Ends of Beef, with Brown Potatoes, 35c.

Baked Chicken Pie, 35c.   Baked Pork and Beans, 25c.

Boiled or Mashed Potatoes, 10c.

Braised Sweet Potatoes, 10c.

Sweet Corn, 10c.   Cauliflower, 10c.   Stewed Tomatoes, 10c.

Lobster Salad, 25c.

Apple Pie, 10c.   Pumpkin Pie, 10c.

Cabinet Pudding, 15c.   Plum Pudding, Brandy Sauce, 15c.

Assorted Cake, 15c.   Ice Cream, 15c.

Assorted Fruit in Season, 15c.

Preserved Fruit, Individual Package, 20c.

Roquefort or Club House Cheese, 15c.

Bent's Water Crackers, 10c.

Coffee or Tea, per pot, 25c.   Coffee or Tea, per cup, 10c.

NO SERVICE LESS THAN 25 CENTS TO EACH PERSON.

Any inattention to duty on this car please report to L. N. Hopkins, Commissary,
C. B. & Q. R. R., Chicago.

DENVER ARTESIAN WATER USED ON THESE TABLES.

The dining car "Creston" dates from pre-streamlined Pullman Standard days. Many of the Burlington's Pullman car names were selected to honor towns and cities along the route out West. Creston is located in Iowa on the main stem between Chicago and Omaha. The prices in this menu may provoke disbelief today, but in 1915 they might well have been taxing to the average purse.
(Author's Collection)

first trains were a long way from being luxurious, and it was not until the 1880s, when the North Western became a "Vanderbilt railroad," that it put together its first and most enduring great train. This was the *North Western Limited*. In 1896, after being done over by the shops of the Wagner Palace Car Company, the *North Western Limited* was unveiled as probably the most luxurious train ever to run over their lines. It was described at that time by a reporter on the Minneapolis *Journal*:

The world has been ransacked for costly woods; designers, carvers, upholsterers, and metal workers have apparently been given carte blanche in working out their ideas, with no limit placed on the cost of their materials. Silken tapestries of Oriental richness, European refinement, and pleasing variety adorn the walls of the various rooms. Each compartment has its special scheme of color, upholstering, and decoration. Circassian walnut, San Domingo mahogany, English oak, vermillion wood, bird's-eye maple, and

Even though it had put some money on the diesel, the Burlington did not give up right away on steam streamlined locomotives. On the Chicago-Denver run in 1939 we find the Pacific-type "Aeolus" pulling the Burlington's *Aristocrat*. President Ralph Budd of the Burlington was as fond of classical nomenclature as the executives of some of the competing railroads were of Indian names.
(Burlington Northern)

Truly luxury equipment may not have occupied a great deal of space in the North Western's passenger yards, but in Pullman Standard Times the company was never without an adequate complement of first-class equipment such as this dining car shown in the line's Chicago-servicing facilities.

(Chicago and North Western)

Flagship for many years of the Chicago and North Western's fleet was the *Northwestern Limited*, here as it appeared in the late 1930s. The C&NW was never able to grab off much of the carriage trade to the Pacific Northwest, but from very early days it would yield to none of its competitors on the run between Chicago and the twin cities. Introduced in the 1880s, the *North Western Limited* quickly became a legendary train of high varnish.

(Chicago and North Western)

rosewood, richly inlaid and highly polished, delight the eye.

Most of the North Western's name trains—one thinks of names like the *Corn King*, the *IronRange Express*, the *Viking*—were hardly trains deluxe, however much they have meant to some local patrons. But the *North Western Limited* was, and remained for all of its life, a source of pride to company management. The road's other big-name train, running exclusively over the C&NW's own left-handed rail, was its *Columbine* to Omaha and Denver.

In due course the North Western became the carrier of several of America's finest trains, which fell to it from connecting lines. The most famous of these was the *Overland Limited*, which Lucius Beebe has termed America's most legendary train, perhaps our only real answer to the *Orient Express*. But there were also the *Los Angeles Limited*, the *City of San Francisco*, and the *Portland Rose*, all of which began or ended their runs far from the left-handed rails of the Chicago and North Western Railroad.

Today it is hard for people who use North Western Station in Chicago to remember that it was not so long ago that one could see the *Overland Limited* crouching under the shed at the station on Madison Street. And it is hard for people out in Oak Park or Geneva to remember that not many years ago the *Overland Limited* with its open-ended observation platform might make an unscheduled stop in those suburban towns, or even more recently that the streamlined *City of San Francisco* could be seen flashing through the western suburbs at 80 miles per hour—but it is all very true, and not so long ago.

The *King Corn* was another popular name train on the North Western. It arrives here in Chicago, in the mid-1930s, behind a giant Class H 4-8-4 locomotive. The train has just passed under the Lake Street L tracks, seconds before securing her berth at the Madison Street terminal. The fact that station porters are waiting here, well beyond the covering of the train shed, suggests that *King Corn* was arriving with an impressive complement of cars.
(Chicago and North Western)

This is the North Western's Chicago passenger servicing yard as it appeared in 1947. All of the trains shown here were used for long-distance service. The C&NW was still using steam on its commuter runs at this time.

(Chicago and North Western)

In the twilight years of long-distance passenger service on the C&NW the road introduced a series of trains called the *400s*. The name derived from the running time between Chicago and the twin cities, which was about 400 minutes, give or take a few minutes one way or the other. Here is a nifty *400* observation lounge in the early 1950s at Chicago's North Western Station. Aging suburban equipment may be seen at both the right and left.

(Chicago and North Western)

"THE OVERLAND LIMITED"

IS THE FASTEST TRAIN
ON THE BEST TRACK IN THE WEST
WITH THROUGH CAR SERVICE

VIA

Chicago, Union Pacific & North=Western Line

ONLY TRAIN WEST OF MISSOURI RIVER CARRYING BUFFET, SMOKING AND LIBRARY CARS.

MAGNIFICENTLY EQUIPPED WITH PULLMAN PALACE DOUBLE DRAWING ROOM SLEEPERS, PULLMAN DINING CARS, FREE RECLINING CHAIR CARS, PINTSCH LIGHTS, ETC.

THE "OVERLAND LIMITED" ON THE UNION PACIFIC.

The Union Pacific Bridge is a magnificent structure of eleven spans, 75 feet above the water, each span 250 feet long, and is the only double-track steel bridge across the Missouri River.

UNION PACIFIC BRIDGE BETWEEN OMAHA AND COUNCIL BLUFFS.

The Pullman Dining Cars

On the Union Pacific are operated on the a la carte plan (pay for what you order). Excellent meals are served at very low rates.

DINING CAR ON UNION PACIFIC

The Overland Limited was the most gracious and legendary train west of Chicago. It arrived in Chicago over the left-handed rail of the Chicago and North Western. It naturally became a common practice of both the Union Pacific and the Chicago and North Western to take joint ads to attract patronage to their joint venture on the Chicago-San Franciso run.

(Author's Collection)

At the height of its glory, the *Overland Limited* is shown leaving Oakland Mole for the long trek to Chicago in 1905. This was gracious traveling indeed when one considers that a mere 35 years before travel to California from the East was by ship around the Horn or by dusty overland stagecoach.

(Union Pacific Railroad Museum)

The *Overland Limited*, a scant 20 minutes away from Chicago on its two-day trip from San Francisco, makes an unaccustomed stop at Oak Park in C&NW suburban territory at 8:20 a.m. on July 13, 1934.

(A.W. Johnson)

By 1912 the *Overland Limited* was sporting an observation car with open platform for those who didn't mind having their hair blown around. Of course by this time the hazards of Indian arrows or malicious buffalo had mostly (but not completely) disappeared.
(Union Pacific Railroad Museum)

The C&NW and Union Pacific made every attempt to cash in on the Chicago-Southern California trade. In the beginning the competition provided by trains like the *Los Angeles Limited* was brisk and effective. Perhaps the Santa Fe always had the edge, and in the end they came away with the prize. Shown here is a lady boarding the *Los Angeles Limited,* probably around 1905, when the run was inaugurated.

(Union Pacific Railroad Museum)

The Grand Trunk provided a "Canadian connection" for Chicago until the Amtrak takeover eliminated it. Shown here in 1948 is the GT *Maple Leaf* on its way to Montreal, out of Dearborn Station and crossing Pennsy tracks at 21st Street. These very distinctive looking locomotives were first put in service in 1936 and became a hallmark of motive power on the Canadian National and Grand Trunk; they were built in the Montreal Locomotive Works.

(Canadian National)

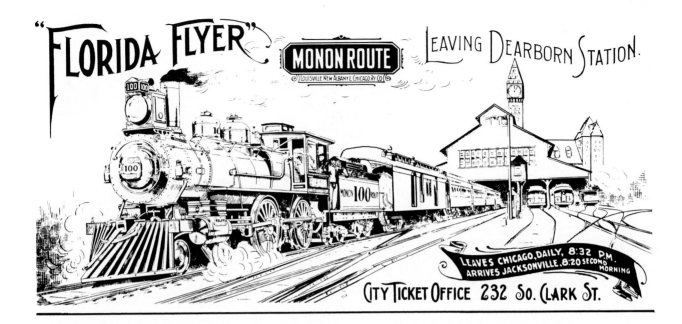

"FLORIDA FLYER" MONON ROUTE LEAVING DEARBORN STATION.

LOUISVILLE NEW ALBANY & CHICAGO RY CO

LEAVES CHICAGO, DAILY, 8:32 P.M. ARRIVES JACKSONVILLE, 8:20 SECOND MORNING

CITY TICKET OFFICE 232 So. CLARK ST.

Undoubtedly the hottest (if not the most important) of the railroad competitions in the Chicago area was one that was sparking in the 1920s on the run between Chicago and St. Louis. Here, for a while, the Wabash, with its *Blue Bird* and *Banner Blue*; the Illinois Central, with its *Green Diamond* and *Daylight*; the Chicago and Eastern Illinois, with its *St. Louis Zipper* and *Cardinal*; the Chicago and Alton, with its *Alton Limited* and *Abraham Lincoln*; and the Gulf, Mobile & Ohio, with its *Gulf Coast Special* made the Chicago-to-St. Louis route vigorously contested by day and night. There was nothing like this density of competition anywhere in American railroading. There were five railroads, and back in the 1920s there seemed to be enough passengers for all of them without cutting each other's throats.

The same thing might be said, to a lesser extent, about the long-standing competition on the run eastward between Chicago and Indianapolis, which for a number of years supported the Monon, the Big Four (New York Central) and the Pennsylvania.

A much less intense competition, but nonetheless productive of some of the greatest trains of record, was that between the Santa Fe and several joint carriers for the passenger business between Chicago and the sun states, most espe-

There were a number of less-distinguished lines that offered service from Chicago, and early in the twentieth century a number of them were more than just minor passenger carriers. For many years the Monon route offered not only its familiar service to the Hoosier State, but a full link with Florida and the Deep South. The Monon remained a tenant of Dearborn Station until the end of its Chicago service in the 1960s.

(Author's Collection)

cially Los Angeles and Southern California. The Santa Fe was a Johnny-come-lately to Chicago, having spent its early years striking out from Kansas City along the difficult terrain of the Santa Fe Trail. When it finally reached Chicago, it quickly made up for lost time. By the fall of 1892 it had introduced the first of a long string of celebrated name trains on the Chicago–Los Angeles run. This train was the *California Limited*, which made it to Los Angeles with a six-car consist behind a diminutive ten-wheeler. Still, the cars were gas lighted throughout, and served the superb cuisine of Fred Harvey for which the Santa Fe had already become famous, and provided nearly every other amenity offered by rail travel in that now-distant day. California was just beginning to sell itself as America's sun-filled paradise. A flower boy boarded the train near the California state border and presented every lady passenger with a boutonniere of

The most outstanding tenant of the Dearborn Station was always the Santa Fe, which made its belated arrival in Chicago in 1889. Over the years one of the best-known Santa Fe flyers was the *Chief,*, shown here positively brightening up a drab rail-yard scene at Dearborn Station in the early 1950s. There were still plenty of steam locomotives around in that now distant time.

(Santa Fe)

choice flowers, and every male passenger with a souvenir alligator wallet.

The *California Limited* was to be on the Santa Fe's timetables for many years, but by 1911 it was partly eclipsed by another and even more glamorous train, the *De Luxe*, which in another 15 years was superseded by that most magnificent of all Santa Fe trains, the *Chief*. Like the railroads of the northern plains, the Santa Fe had decided to cash in on the Indian theme for their trains, and in the years to follow would exploit to the full many Indian motifs, designs and flavorings.

However, what skyrocketed the *Chief* into national fame was the publicity it received almost immediately as the carrier of Hollywood notables who became its loyal and devoted patrons—Greta Garbo, Charlie Chaplin, Douglas Fairbanks, and others. The presence of these notables was immediately exploited by the

road's public relations officers, who saw to it that both photographer's bulbs and champagne corks popped on the occasions of departure from Chicago's old Dearborn Station. Similar fanfare awaited the train's arrival in Los Angeles. The *Chief* became almost immediately a veritable Hollywood on wheels.

The *Chief* was to continue, even after the Santa Fe unleashed a streamlined *Super Chief* behind Electro-motive diesel power in 1936. The latter, which made the trip to California in 39¾ hours, quickly became the flagship of a whole fleet of Santa Fe trains to Southern California: the *Chief*, the *California Limited* (which had not been forgotten), the all-coach *El Capitan*, and the *Scout*. But the *Super Chief* became a train of such legend and sybaritic luxury that it became the prime recipient of Hollywood fanfare and publicity.

Over the next several decades, but most especially during the years of World War II, when air travel was stifled, the *Super Chief* became the kingpin of luxury transcontinental travel in America when it linked up with the *Broadway Limited* and the *Twentieth Century Limited*. The ambience of these rolling hotels and palaces of intrigue was perhaps described to perfection

By 1960 steam equipment has vanished from Dearborn Station, but the Santa Fe is still supplying most of the color. Here the *Texas Chief* prepares for departure, wholly outside the protection of the inadequate Dearborn shed. The vista-dome equipment to the right is also Santa Fe.

(Santa Fe)

The Santa Fe became quickiy dieselized of course, but as late as the early 1950s had some very impressive steam locomotives for use in passenger service. Here #3460 pulls the *El Capitan,* all coach streamliner and companion train of the *Chief* and *Super Chief* on the Chicago-Los Angeles run.

(Santa Fe)

From the early days, when its dining service was run by Fred Harvey, the Santa Fe outdid itself in the culinary arts. Here, although perhaps posed by professional models for the public relations department, we nonetheless see a true picture of some of the best in American railway dining in the 1950s.

(Santa Fe)

This is the main lounge of the Pleasure Dome car on the Santa Fe's *Super Chief.* The Indian-motif wall decor must have been obtained at great expense, but the furniture somehow seems uninspired for a name train—a sometime occurrence in streamlined interiors.

(Santa Fe)

in Frederick Wakeman's novel, *The Hucksters*, pressed into film immortalizing Clark Gable as the shining lothario of the Pullman drawing room.

The great Santa Fe mystique never captured the imagination of *all* the travelers to the great Southwest. The Santa Fe had the only through route, but there was very lively competition from two other joint routes, the Chicago & North Western/Union Pacific and the Rock Island/Southern Pacific. The Union Pacific's spur into Southern California was never the mainstay of its existence, but for a number of years it offered as a competitor to the *City of San Francisco* its beautiful streamlined *City of Los Angeles*.

During the 1940s, transcontinental travel by rail, with Chicago as the only accepted stopping-over spot for travelers in the know, became so enshrined in legend and so ingrained as a social habit among the traveling elite, that a campaign by Robert R. Young of the New York Central to bypass Chicago and run through trains coast-to-coast never materialized. For a few years in the late 1940s, a scattering of iso-

The Santa Fe *Super Chief* was always a big attraction to Hollywood nabobs before they took to the skies for transcontinental travel. And here to cater to such luminaries is the Turquoise Room, one of the few private dining rooms in regular service on an American railroad.

(Santa Fe)

lated cars made the trek from New York to Los Angeles, but this was half a loaf, for it was really nothing more than a switching operation in Chicago during which coast-to-coast passengers had to sit in the Chicago passenger yards while waiting to be hooked onto another train.

It may not have been inevitable that the Chicago-born Rock Island would ever become a nationwide carrier of note, but the Rock Island entered the competition in a fierce way in 1937, when it revived a train it had used from the very beginning, and made a real play for West Coast clientele. The name was "Rocket," a name which recalled the little 4-4-0 Rogers-built engine that had pulled the first Rock Island train from Chicago to Joliet in 1852. The connection between the Rock Island and the Southern Pacific was of

The Santa Fe's passenger coach yard south of Dearborn Station as it appeared in 1934. In that faraway time and deep in the heart of the Depression the Santa Fe was still almost completely dependent on traditional Pullman Standard equipment—no sign of streamlining yet.

(Santa Fe)

Robert R. Young, perhaps the last of the railroad magnets, offered a nifty scheme to allow through passengers to ride right through Chicago. For a while there were a few through cars (not trains), but the scheme never really took hold. Today, as a hundred years ago, Chicago is the end of the line and a new beginning for everybody who passes through it.

(University of Illinois Library)

There is no such thing as traveling through Chicago from coast-to-coast, as was made clear in this widely published ad from the mid-1940s. The Chesapeake & Ohio and its aggressive chairman, Robert R. Young, wanted to do something about that and proposed a new through service that would allow people to sail through Chicago.

(B&O Museum)

A Hog Can Cross America Without Changing Trains—But YOU Can't!

The Chesapeake & Ohio and the Nickel Plate Road again propose to give humans a break!

It's hard to believe, but it's true.

If you want to ship a hog from coast to coast, he can make the entire trip without changing cars. You can't. It is impossible for you to pass through Chicago, St. Louis, or New Orleans without breaking your trip!

There is an invisible barrier down the middle of the United States which you cannot cross without inconvenience, lost time, and trouble.

560,000 Victims in 1945!

If you want to board a sleeper on one coast and ride through to the other, you must make double Pullman reservations, pack and transfer your baggage, often change stations, and wait around for connections.

It's the same sad story if you make a relatively short trip. You can't cross that mysterious line! To go from Fort Wayne to Milwaukee or from Cleveland to Des Moines, you must also stop and change trains.

Last year alone, more than 560,000 people were forced to make annoying, time-wasting stopovers at the phantom Chinese wall which splits America in half!

End the Secrecy!

Why should travel be less convenient for people than it is for pigs? Why should Americans be denied the benefits of through train service? No one has yet been able to explain it.

Canada has this service . . . with a choice of two routes. Canada isn't split down the middle. Why should we be? No reasonable answer has yet been given. Passengers still have to stop off at Chicago, St. Louis, and New Orleans—although they can ride right through other important rail centers.

It's time to pry the lid off this mystery. It's time for action to end this inconvenience to the public . . . NOW!

Many railroads could cooperate to provide this needed through service. To date, the Chesapeake & Ohio and the Nickel Plate ALONE have made a public offer to do so.

How about it!

Once more we would like to go on record with this specific proposal:

The Chesapeake & Ohio, whose western passenger terminus is Cincinnati, stands ready now to join with any combination of other railroads to set up connecting transcontinental and intermediate service through Chicago and St. Louis, on practical schedules and routes.

The Nickel Plate Road, which runs to Chicago and St. Louis, also stands ready now to join with any combination of roads to set up the same kind of connecting service through these two cities.

Through railroad service can't be blocked forever. The public wants it. It's bound to come. Again, we invite the support of the public, of railroad people and railroad investors—for this vitally needed improvement in rail transportation!

Chesapeake & Ohio Railway • Nickel Plate Road

Terminal Tower, Cleveland 1, Ohio

The Rock Island was never one of the resplendent carriers, but it did have a fine roster of trains to all of its western territories. Here in 1941, before the Rock had taken to the diesel, Engine 4051 leaves Englewood for Southern California with the *Golden State Limited.*

(Bob Lorenz)

much earlier origin, to be sure, since the two roads had inaugurated their *Golden State Limited* on November 2, 1902, doubtless as a strong attempt to pry loose some of the trade and good will won by the Santa Fe's *California Limited.*

The Rock Island offered a number of other name trains over the main stem of its line over the years, and Rock Island fans of an earlier generation will remember the *Rocky Mountain Limited*, the *Californian* and the *Apache*. But it was a stroke of Depression-born genius of Rock Island president John Dow Farrington to resurrect the "Rocket" name for the line's premier passenger fleet, which eventually caused the road's publicity department to dub the Rock Island "the Route of the Rockets." The road sent

some deluxe "Rockets" out of Chicago, starting in 1937, dieselized from the very beginning, and bearing names like the *Rocky Mountain Rocket*, the *Corn Belt Rocket*, and even (for the Rock Island did not stint on intermediate-distance trains in those days) a *Peoria Rocket*. After World War II, the Rock Island and the Southern Pacific embarked on a venture to give the Rocket name its widest exposure of all, with a new California train that might even hope to put the *Super Chief* in the shade. In 1946 both roads unveiled plans for a deluxe train to be called the *Golden Rocket*. Indeed, the train was ordered, built, and finished down to the last detail. Thousands of dollars were spent on advertising in the national media, right up to the point where the imaginative name was becoming a household word. Photographs of the great new train, both exterior and interior, were made by the hundreds, as were posters, circulars and advertisements. Alas, the *Golden Rocket* never carried a passenger. In the fall of 1947 the Southern Pacific management got cold feet and withdrew its part of the order to the Pullman Company and,

The name "Rocket" went back to very early Rock Island history. In an effort to glamorize service and attract patrons the name was reborn in 1937, and the Rock Island inaugurated a number of distinctive "rocket" trains, including the *Rocky Mountain Rocket* and *Corn Belt Rocket*. For a long time the Rock Island provided well for its intermediate-distance passengers, as with its *Peoria Rocket* shown passing through Oak Forest in the Chicago suburbs in 1949.

(Bob Lorenz)

With long-distance traffic still very much alive on the Rock Island in 1960, the road's best known name-train, the *Golden State*, passes by Englewood station on its way to California. Needless to say this site was always one of the favorite places for train spotters in the Chicago area, with many great trains converging from all points of the compass.

(Rock Island Lines)

The candy train on the Illinois Central was the *Panama Limited*, which had its inaugural run in 1911. From the very beginning, the IC went all out for this train; every restyling and modernization was done with spit and polish. Shown here leaving Chicago about 1920, the gleaming engine shows that the locomotive had received an extra measure of polishing before taking the track to New Orleans.

(Illinois Central Gulf)

by implication, its approval of the joint train. The Rock Island was stuck with its order, however, and had to reassign its cars to the *Golden State*. This was one of the many sad misfortunes in the history of the Rock Island, always so close yet so far from grandeur.

The withdrawal of the *Golden Rocket* in 1947 might have been something of an omen, since the age of competition for rail passengers was nearing an end. In a mere 10 years the New York Central would add coaches to the *Twentieth Century*, effectively ending its long Chicago–New York competition with the Pennsy. Maybe it was wrong to view the Chicago railroad scene as one wholly inflamed by competition. There were a few name trains produced during the golden age of railroading that were not motivated by parallel lines and traffic density. A few lines continued their service pretty much in lonely isolation, still running some major trains across the continent. One thinks of that great carrier of the American heartland, the Illinois Central, which, except in its Chicago–St. Louis route, never really suffered from the intrigues of competing carriers. The Illinois Central had its Chicago–New Orleans route all to itself (the wayward New Orleans run of the Gulf, Mobile & Ohio was not worth talking about).

And, yes, the Illinois Central produced some superior trains. In the earliest years, on the Chicago–New Orleans route, deluxe trains were

a little slow in coming. Technically there could be no through trains to New Orleans until 1889, when the IC completed a giant bridge over the Mississippi River south of Cairo. Shortly thereafter they began their *Chicago & New Orleans Limited*, popularly known as the *Cannonball*. Not too many years later, with the completion of the Panama Canal and in honor of the Illinois Central's growing freight trade with the various banana republics of Central America, they inaugurated a new premier train called the *Panama Limited*. This train went into service on February 4, 1911. In every way, it was to become one of the finest American trains. It was redesigned and upgraded several times, and the Illinois Central kept it up as long as they stayed in the passenger business. During the depths of the Depression the train disappeared from the timetable for a year or two, but demands for it were so high and so spirited that the Illinois Central was forced to bring it back in 1934.

Perhaps the most wonderful and memorable *Panama* of all was the streamlined version of the train which was inaugurated in 1942, the last major deluxe train placed in service before World War II restrictions were imposed. The train was fitted out with a new yellow-brown-orange livery, and was an all-Pullman train to the Gulf, carrying parlor cars between Chicago and Carbondale. Like a number of trains of this period, it was treated to a total design, right down to the linens and pencil holders in the dining car. The prevailing motif was of the Vieux Carré of New Orleans, with some admixtures of Mexican and Central American styles. Like the *Twentieth Century Limited* and the *Super Chief*, the *Panama* was an extra-fare train, but the extra fare was well worth it. The Illinois Central dining service was always superlative, but after the last streamlining they outdid themselves, and the Creole cooking of the kitchens was legendary, as was the "King's Dinner" of a slightly later period.

Every detail had been thought of in the last of the great *Panama Limited's*. Special diesel units, bearing its name permanently affixed on

An all-new streamlined and dieselized *Panama Limited* was put in service in 1942. In fact the equipment was the last major passenger train to appear before World War II restrictions went into effect. Every inch of the train was designed using a New Orleans Vieux-Carre motif. Engines were assigned specifically for the run as the monogrammed insignia shows here.

(Illinois Central Gulf)

their sides, were assigned solely to that train. The bar in the lounge car was a faithful reproduction of a New Orleans courtyard, complete right down to the potted ivy. The Parlor cars—kept on for the short daytime and evening part of the run through Illinois—were fitted out in a gay Mardi Gras motif. The *Panama Limited* was advertised as a 16½ hour run between Chicago and New Orleans, and while the Illinois Central management maintained its faith in the train up to the late 1960s, it was. When Wayne Johnson was President of the Illinois Central Railroad,

the train was scheduled to arrive in Chicago on the northbound run at 9 A.M., and there were no excuses for it arriving at 9:10. Its progress was monitored every inch of the way by company top brass.

The *Panama Limited* still exists, for it was taken over from the Illinois Central by Amtrak in 1971. But the old spirit died in the 1960s, and there is probably no way that that kind of spirit can be revived. The *Panama* is still a nice train. At least the equipment is new. Parlor cars are a thing of the past, however, and sometimes even the sleeping cars are taken off. The train has a dining car, but the cooking is done in microwave

Until its streamlined equipment started to give out in the late 1960s, all of the IC's long-distance trains were luxurious and well-kept. Leaving Chicago in 1962 is the all-coach reserved day train to New Orleans, the *City of New Orleans*.

(Illinois Central Gulf)

The Panama Limited was not the first IC train to be streamlined because the train was given an all-new Pullman Standard consist in 1934. But the IC did not delay going over to the diesel, and in 1936 purchased for the *Green Diamond* (on its Chicago-Springfield-St. Louis run) this electro-motive diesel with turret cab. The train—an all-daytime run—is shown here near Chicago in 1940.

(Bob Lorenz)

ovens, which mostly serve the tastes of hamburger eaters.

It is still fun to ride the *Panama Limited* and many of the other long-distance trains out of Chicago. But all of the old glory has gone.

CHAPTER 8

Showcase for the Interurban

Interurbans have nearly disappeared from the American scene, although in the early part of the twentieth century they played a vital role in the transportation network. The interurban railroad was a thing of mixed parentage, a cross-breed—child, one might say, of a city trolley car line and a conventional railroad. The name interurban doesn't tell too much because the phenomenon it described was so varied. Some interurbans were merely city street-car lines that strayed beyond the city limits. Sometimes they didn't rise much above the level of makeshift Toonerville Trolleys ambling out among the tall grasses of the countryside. Others were vast, well-built systems of transportation with modern cars and equipment that were sometimes hard to distinguish from the passenger equipment of Class I railroads.

During the heyday of the interurbans, Chicago had three of the very best lines in the country. Only one survives today, but the history of Chicago's lines is such that it is fair to admit that Chicago was the showcase of interurban development at its highest level. All three lines were traffic carriers operating in densely populated urban and suburban territory. All of them possessed well-built modern equipment that sometimes bordered on the luxurious. They vigorously competed with the regular railroads for suburban commuter traffic and sometimes had the railroads beat. All of them performed major transportation functions in the Chicago area, and most of their partisans would probably agree that none of them should have been permitted to die.

Electric city streetcars made their appearance at the end of the nineteenth century. It is somewhat hard to pinpoint the time when lines began extending beyond the city limits, but the first interurban seems to have been one which began operating between Minneapolis and St. Paul in 1891. Perhaps the first bona fide interurban was the 15-mile East Side Railway between Portland and Oregon City, Oregon, in 1893.

Wherever the interurban phenomenon began, it didn't immediately catch on like wildfire. After 1896, however, certain technological developments, specifically the introduction of distribution systems that stepped down voltage in substations to low-voltage direct current, and also the introduction of multiple-car control systems, made possible the extension of long lines with actual "trains" running over them. The word "interurban" was coined by Senator Charles L. Henry of Indiana, who built that state's first line (11 miles long) in 1897, and pushed the idea until he had built a 400-mile system, later known as the Union Traction Company, which served much of central Indiana.

Interurbans were bound to catch on during the early years of the twentieth century, since the automobile had not yet made its appearance as a form of cheap and practical transportation. Above all, they filled in the gaps in the offerings of the steam railroads, which simply couldn't connect every little town and hamlet in a rapidly expanding country. On the other hand, the interurbans immediately demonstrated their superiority over the horse and buggy. They were quick; they stopped almost anywhere (and didn't usually need stations); and altogether they offered a really great way to get to town.

The first two decades of the twentieth century saw an almost unbelievable spread of interurbans in the United States. By 1917, there were over 18,000 miles of interurban lines and nearly 10,000 cars being operated in the United States, with the Midwest seemingly being the stronghold of the movement. Nearly 40 percent of the nation's interurbans were in the states of Illinois, Indiana, Ohio, Michigan and Wisconsin. In time Indiana and Ohio had nearly complete systems, and centrally located Indianapolis became a kind of traction center of the Midwest, containing an impressive traction terminal for 12 entering lines that handled 7 million passengers in 1914.

Illinois never had anything like a complete system, but there were lines of all kinds proposed and built. Anyone who desired better transportation could build a line from here to there, and

often did. Dr. C. L. Van Doren, a physician from Urbana (and father of two well-known American writers, Mark and Carl Van Doren), built the Urbana and Kankakee Railroad, a line that was bound to fail at the first chug of an automobile engine. Conversely, Illinois had some mighty systems, even downstate. Illinois even had its own "traction senator" to compete with Senator Henry from Indiana. He was Senator William B. McKinley, who put together

Chicago's three great interurbans began in a rather inauspicious way. Here, in 1895, is the first car of the Bluff City Electric Company in Waukegan, the forerunner of the North Shore Line. Electricity still seems to be a euphemism in 1895, but Waukegan is in the period of its greatest growth, with horses providing plenty of electricity in this bustling crowd.

(Waukegan Historical Society)

Before too many years the Bluff City Electric Company outgrew the city of Waukegan and began its run down the North Shore toward Chicago. This ticket office, looking like an old stage coach office, shows that by 1910 the line was a respectable interurban and was offering hot competition to the Chicago and North Western's Milwaukee Division.

(Waukegan Historical Society)

what was the Midwest's largest single interurban, the Illinois Traffic System. It began as a 6-mile line between Danville and Westville, Illinois, in 1901. McKinley pushed his system right across the state, eventually linking important downstate cities like Champaign, Decatur, Bloomington, Peoria, and Springfield with each other and with St. Louis on the other side of the Mississippi River. In its prime, the Illinois Traction boasted parlor-observation cars, dining cars and even sleeping cars—unexpected luxuries in a trolley car.

The interurbans had the advantage of combining long-distance train service with the convenience of city streetcar lines. The cars of Senator McKinley's Illinois Traction, for example, could amble through the downtown streets of Peoria or Springfield, and then jut right out into the cornfields on the way to the next big town, picking up farmers or other local riders wherever they happened to pop up. For con-

venience it would be hard to imagine anything better in the pre-automobile era.

There were other contributions of the interurban that were later adopted by the automobile. The period before World War I was ideal for the trolley "excursion." There were excursions to take people to baseball parks, picnic grounds, race tracks, chautauquas, scenic mountain resorts, zoos, to every form of amusement known to human experience. Southern California's Pacific Electric System was probably the most assiduous in attracting this kind of business, and in the years of its glory it was said to be the only way one could really see the sights of Southern California.

Unfortunately, the interurbans were to be mostly short-lived. The agency of their demise was near at hand even at the time of their birth. The automobile would soon make it possible for a man to get himself into town to visit the drugstore or transport his family out to the amusement park without having to wait for the streetcar. He could drive there in his own automobile at his own convenience. The interurbans struggled bravely through the 1920s, but when times became really rough in the Depression, most of them vanished. To a large extent they had been weakly capitalized from the beginning. Too, the lines were hastily put down, usually with little or no ballast, and with little attention paid to engineering standards. Few were built to allow conversion to heavy duty service of any kind, and few could permit opera-

Samuel Insull, the utilities tycoon who built Chicago interurbans from weak local lines into the most modern interurbans in the country. The interurbans staggered on for a good number of years after Insull's financial collapse in the early 1930s, but they sorely missed the touch of that master financier.

(Library of Congress)

tion of high-speed passenger trains that might have permitted them to compete effectively with the automobile.

Yet there were places where the interurbans might have been able to vie with the automobile. Certainly the densely populated and congested city belts were ripe for the kinds of services the interurban offered, so that if they were well constructed and financed, they might make a go of it. The Chicago metropolitan area was such a place, and, as a result, Chicago had three interurban railroads that for a long time offered very effective competition to the automobile and provided high-class rapid transit service to an urban megalopolis that was in urgent need of it. An interurban makes the most sense where high-speed track can beat out the automobile between towns; where the automobile driver must stop and go and wait in long lines of impatient vehicles. Chicago and its suburbs had conditions that were ripe for this kind of convenience.

Most people living today associate the Chicago interurban lines with the fabulous but now shadowy financial career of the remarkable British-born utilities tycoon, Samuel Insull. Insull did not start the lines, for they all had independent beginnings around the turn of the century, but he came on the scene very shortly thereafter and was responsible for the capitalization that made the Chicago lines strong and prosperous. If any reassessment of poor old Sam Insull's career be made, it is impossible to escape the conclusion that Insull's ultimate effect on the Chicago traction lines was both salubrious and honest. The truth is, Insull built the most modern and technically advanced system of interurbans in the country.

Samuel Insull was born in London in 1859, and began his long business career at the age of

After the Insull takover of the Chicago interurbans, the North Shore line was able to make an effective connection with the Chicago elevated lines, which had already become an Insull property. Accordingly, North Shore trains were able to sail right through to the Loop rather than terminate at the city line in Evanston. This is a North Shore train on Wabash Avenue "EL" tracks on June 23, 1962.

(William D. Middleton)

14 as an office boy with a salary of five shillings a week (only a third of the wage paid by Ebenezer Scrooge to Bob Cratchit). He came to the United States at the age of 21 and soon became a private secretary to Thomas Edison. Edison taught Insull what he knew about the electric utilities business, but the truth is, Edison was never much of a businessman. In a few years Insull knew a great deal more than his mentor and was ready to go off on his own. Edison had first sent Insull to Schenectady, New York, to learn all that he could about running an electric manufacturing plant, and later made him a vice president of General Electric, the electrical manufacturing company that Edison had started. Shortly thereafter, Insull accepted the presidency of the small Chicago Edison Company, which he built up and eventually took over. The Chicago Edison Company was only

A North Shore train at the Mundelein Station in the dark of winter, Jan. 20, 1958. The bleakness of the weather perfectly expresses the fortunes of the line at this time.

(William D. Middleton)

the beginning for Insull. During the next few decades he fashioned the largest and most powerful network of utilities in the Middle West. By 1907 Insull had merged his Chicago Edison Company with the rival Commonwealth Electric Company, creating a new conglomerate called the Commonwealth Edison Company. By 1912 Insull had formed his first electrical utility holding company, Middle West Utilities. By means of this holding company Insull was to build a financial empire that was pyramided and weakly capitalized, and therefore capable of the quickest possible expansion, but also of potential disaster.

Insull was far from being the grasping and conniving capitalist that he was sometimes portrayed as being. He was a man of keen intelligence and definite statesmanlike attributes. At a time when the robber barons still reigned in America, Insull was a man with strong civic pride and a decidedly advanced business philosophy. He possessed an interest in ecology and urban development very untypical for his time. His civic contributions to Chicago were

During the 1930s the North Shore spent its advertising dollar proving that theirs was not a local streetcar line but a superfast intercity railway. Notice the emphasis not on the North Shore suburban communities, but on the Chicago-Milwaukee connection.
(Author's Collection)

A now nearly forgotten sight in the Chicago Loop. Looking like some ghostly interstellar intruder, a North Shore Electroliner, Train No. 804, passes the Lake Street tower on the Chicago El, June 23, 1963. The end of the line was a mere 7 months away, and after this the el tracks would no longer play host to these visitors from afar.
(William D. Middleton)

236

CHICAGO NORTH SHORE & MILWAUKEE RY.

N CHICAGO (Howard St.)
TO
NORTHFIELD

Good For Passage of One
3 Months In Addition To Date
Stamped On Back.

SUBJECT TO TARIFF
REGULATIONS

Form R. T. 10   40653

CHICAGO NORTH SHORE & MILWAUKEE RY.

S NORTHFIELD
TO
CHICAGO (Howard St.)

Good For Passage of One
3 Months In Addition To Date
Stamped On Back.

SUBJECT TO TARIFF
REGULATIONS

Form R. T. 10   40653

With only a year to go, the North Shore is still doing yeoman service on its long-haul runs. On June 21, 1962, Train No. 414 is boarding a respectable number of passengers at Racine, Wisconsin, for the trip to Chicago.

(William D. Middleton)

The least prominent of Chicago's three interurbans was the Chicago, Aurora and Elgin, whose lone Car No. 451 is shown here near Lakewood on August 21, 1955. The line gained entrance into Chicago via the Metropolitan West Side Elevated Company as early as 1905.

(William D. Middleton)

Waukegan, because eliminating grade crossings, curves, street traffic and the like could not be done without adventures of capital that would even make Samuel Insull blanch. So, in the mid-twenties, the North Shore began a wholly new line a few miles to the west in the less populous Skokie Valley. When the Skokie Valley Route opened in 1926, the North Shore now had a line that was the equal of any high-speed electric railway in the world. The whole route north to Milwaukee from the Chicago city limits took on the characteristics of the older route between Waukegan and Milwaukee which was already a speedway. The North Shore was immediately in a position to compete with the steam railroads for through traffic. To make good on this challenge, the Insull management started to invest in equipment to match the quality of their new roadbed. Like Senator McKinley in central Illinois, they saw the virtue of buying luxurious stock that included parlor cars, dining cars, observation lounges and all the rest. And that was not all. Unwilling to play second fiddle to the major steam railroads between Chicago and Milwaukee, the North Shore introduced its own limited express trains, with names like *Interstate*, the *Eastern Limited* and the *Badger*. These trains made the run from Chicago to Milwaukee in a little over two hours, indicating that here was no Toonerville Trolley, but a superfast modern railroad.

The second of the Chicago interurbans, with services to the western suburbs, was the Aurora, Elgin & Chicago Railroad, which was begun by a Cleveland syndicate shortly after 1900. By 1902 this line had established service to Aurora and Batavia, and in 1903 a branch was opened from Wheaton to Elgin. The line employed the third-rail system of power instead of the overhead wire, and from the very beginning the intention was to secure a modern high-speed transit system from Chicago to the suburbs. The Aurora, Elgin and Chicago did not

Ready to depart from Wheaton is the Chicago Express on the Chicago, Aurora and Elgin. Alone of all the Chicago-area interurbans, this line was powered by third-rail, which always provided some hazard in built-up areas, especially since it is not possible to keep people from straying onto the tracks.

(William D. Middleton)

later have to spend millions rebuilding and upgrading its line, since from the very beginning it employed 80-pound rail, secured the track with rock ballast, constructed its bridges of concrete and steel, and planned no curves that could not take speeds of 70 miles per hour. Another early achievement of the Aurora line was that it gained access into the Loop very early. This was arranged in 1905 through a connection with the Metropolitan West Side Elevated Company.

In spite of its fast schedules and early entrance into Chicago, the Aurora always had the slim profit margin that was characteristic of the interurbans. It had to be reorganized in 1922, and the name changed at the time to the Chicago, Aurora and Elgin, which it kept to the end of its days. There were many capital improvements after the 1922 reorganization, but the system still remained vulnerable to the blandishments of huge infusions of cash that could

be offered by Samuel Insull's Midland Utilities Company. A few years later it too was swallowed up in the Insull empire.

The third of Chicago's interurbans brought service to Michigan City, Gary and South Bend, Indiana, shortly after the turn of the century. This company was called the Chicago & Indiana Air Line Railway at its incorporation in 1901, and originally its prospects for routes and equipment were modest. But when the name of the company was changed to the Chicago, Lake Shore and South Bend in 1904, it was clear to the promoters that a linking of the South Shore and Indiana communities with Chicago could have grand possibilities if things were done right.

The job was done up brown by early standards. The line achieved notoriety around the country for its use of 6,600-volt single-phase alternating current, and for its high construction standards. Locally it was soon known for its large, handsome orange wooden cars. Obviously the territory served was one sorely in need of high-speed rail service to Chicago. Unfortunately, the South Shore (as it later became) had a serious defect from the very beginning in that passengers had to transfer at Kensington to the Illinois Central for completion of the trip to Randolph Street. Such transfers are always a source of infinite annoyance to commuters who want nothing more than to bury their heads in the morning newspaper.

In part this weakness was remedied in 1913 when the South Shore and the Illinois Central reached an agreement that the Illinois Central's steam trains would haul the South Shore's trailer coaches to Chicago, avoiding the annoying transfer of passengers. But this arrangement was not completely satisfactory either, even though passenger revenues rose sharply. It was not until the Illinois Central electrified its own suburban lines in 1926 that the South Shore could run its coaches all the way to Randolph Street without the eccentric indignity of having interurban equipment hauled into the city behind a steam engine.

Whatever the case, the line never did too well financially in the early years and it went into receivership in 1925. There was a quick rever-

sal of fortunes, however, when Samuel Insull acquired the line in a foreclosure sale. The name of the company was changed to the Chicago, South Shore and South Bend, which it retains to this day. A 6.5 million-dollar infusion of Insull capital, together with the completion of electrification, upgrading of the roadbed, purchasing of new all-steel cars from Pullman, and other improvements brought the South Shore right back on its feet. In one year, between 1926 and 1927, passenger revenues increased 100 percent.

For a number of years, all three of the Chicago interurbans were Insull properties, and all of them were vastly improved as a result of it. All three lines engaged jointly in traffic promotion. For a while an extremely able Insull lieu-

A night scene on the Chicago, Aurora and Elgin. The first car shown in this picture was from Aurora and the second from Elgin. The date is August 20, 1955, and the end of the line was a mere two years away.

(William D. Middleton)

CHICAGO SOUTH SHORE AND SOUTH BEND RAILROAD

CHICAGO TO HAMMOND, EAST CHICAGO, GARY, MICHIGAN CITY AND SOUTH BEND

CENTRAL STANDARD TIME   EFFECTIVE SEPTEMBER 25, 1927   SUBJECT TO CHANGE WITHOUT NOTICE

EASTBOUND

Miles		Gary Express	Marquette Limited	Gary Express	South Bend Limited	Gary Express	St. Joe Valley Limited	Gary Express Loc. So. Bend	South Bend Limited	Gary Express	South Bend Limited	Gary Express	South Bend Limited	South Bend Limited	South Bend Limited	South Bend Limited
		73 *	19 ● P	75 *	21 ●	77	23 ● D	79	25 ● B	27	83 ●	29	31 ●	33 ●	35 ●	37 ● *
		PM	PM	PM	PM	PM	PM	PM	PM	PM	PM	PM	PM	PM	PM	AM
0	Lv Randolph St. CHICAGO ILL.	2.31	3.00	3.30	4.00	4.31	5.00	5.32	6.00	6.30	7.00	7.30	8.00	9.00	10.00	11.00	12.00
0	Lv Van Buren St.	2.33	3.02	3.32	4.02	4.33	5.02	5.34	6.02	6.32	7.02	7.32	8.02	9.02	10.02	11.01	12.01
0	Lv Roosevelt Rd. (Central Sta.)	2.35	3.04	3.34	4.04	4.35	5.04	5.36	6.04	6.34	7.04	7.34	8.04	9.04	10.04	11.03	12.03
7	Lv Hyde Park (53d St.)	2.42	3.11	3.41	4.11	4.42	5.11	5.43	6.11	6.41	7.11	7.41	8.11	9.11	10.11	11.10	12.10
8	Lv Woodlawn (63d St.)	2.45	3.14	3.44	4.14	4.45	5.14	5.46	6.14	6.44	7.14	7.44	8.14	9.14	10.14	11.12	12.13
14	Lv KENSINGTON ILL.	2.54	3.23	3.53	4.23	4.53	5.23	5.55	6.23	6.53	7.23	7.53	8.23	9.23	10.23	11.21	12.21
16	Lv 124th St. "			f3.56				f5.57				f7.56					
16	Lv Parsons "			f3.57				f5.58				f7.57			f1026		
17	Lv Bridge "			f3.58				f5.59				f7.58			f1027		
17	Lv Ford City "			f3.59				f6.00				f7.59			f1028		
19	Lv HEGEWISCH "	f2.59		4.02		f5.00		f6.00		f6.59		f8.02		9.29	10.29	11.27	
19	Lv Burnham "	3.02		4.03		5.05		f6.03		7.02		f8.03					
21	Lv HAMMOND IND.	f3.03		f4.03		f5.06		f6.04									
23	Lv EAST CHICAGO "	3.07	3.33	4.07	4.33	5.09	5.33	6.08	6.33	7.07	7.33	8.07	8.33	9.33	10.33	11.31	12.31
24	Lv *Calumet "	3.13	3.39	4.13	4.39	5.15	5.39	6.14	6.39	7.13	7.39	8.13	8.39	9.39	10.39	11.37	12.36
25	Lv Cudahy "	f3.19	f3.45	f4.19	f4.45	f5.21	f5.45	f6.20	f6.45	f7.19	f7.45	f8.19	f8.45	f9.45	f1045	f1143	f1241
29	Lv Ambridge Ave. (Gary) "	f3.21		f4.21						f7.25		f8.25			f1051		
30	Lv Buchanan St. (Gary) "	f3.25	f4.25		f5.27		f6.26		f7.27		f8.27			f1053		
31	Lv GARY "	3.30	3.58	4.35	4.58	5.35	5.58	6.35	6.58	7.30	7.58	8.30	8.58	9.59	10.58	11.53	12.53
35	Lv Miller "				f5.03			f6.40	f7.03		f8.03		f9.03	f1003	f1103	f1158	
39	Lv Wickliffe (Ogden Dunes) "							f6.47									
40	Lv Wilson "				f5.13			f6.49			f8.13		f9.13	f1013			
43	Lv Baileytown "							f6.55	f7.14				f9.14	f1114			
45	Lv Mineral Springs "							f6.58									
46	Lv Port Chester "							f7.00									
46	Lv TREMONT (The Dunes) "		f4.18		f5.18		f6.18	f7.06	f7.18		f8.18		f9.18	f1018	f1118		
50	Lv Keiser "							f7.11									
54	Lv Lake Shore "		a4.25		a5.25		a6.25	f7.14	a7.25		a8.25		a9.25	a1025	a1125		
54	Lv Sheridan "							f7.18									
56	Lv MICHIGAN CITY "		4.35		5.35		6.35	7.30	7.35		8.35		9.35	10.35	11.35	12.32	1.25
57	Lv Shops "							f7.44									
62	Lv Springville "							f7.53									
65	Lv Wilhelm "							f7.57									
68	Lv Smith "							f8.02									
70	Lv Hillside "							f8.06									
73	Lv Sagunay "							f8.09									
74	Lv Lake Park "				f6.03			f8.13	f8.03		f9.03		f1003	f1103	f1202		
75	Lv Hudson Lake "				f6.04			f8.14	f8.04		f9.04		f1004	f1104	f1203		
76	Lv NEW CARLISLE "		f5.06		6.06		f7.06	8.22	8.06		9.06		10.06	11.06	12.05	12.59	f1.49
79	Lv Olive "							f8.29									
83	Lv Lydick "							f8.35									
85	Lv Fisher "							f8.38									
88	Lv Bendix Drive "		f5.21		f6.21		f7.21	f8.42	f8.21		f9.21		f1021	f1121	f1221	f1.10	f2.00
90	Ar SOUTH BEND "		5.30		6.30		7.30	8.52	8.30		9.30		10.30	11.30	12.30	1.20	2.10
		PM	PM	PM	PM	PM	PM	PM	PM	PM	PM	PM	PM	AM	AM	AM	

B—Carries baggage.   *—Daily.   a Stops to discharge passengers only.
f—Stops on signal (use light at night) to receive and discharge passengers.   D—Carries Dining Car.   P—Carries Parlor-Observation Car; light refreshments served.
The time from 12.00 o'clock, midnight, to 11.59 a.m., inclusive, is indicated by light-face type; from 12.00 o'clock, noon, to 11.59 p.m., inclusive, by heavy-face type.

The Chicago, South Shore and South Bend is the sole surviving Chicago interurban—the only interurban in the country for that matter. Whipping right along at 70 miles per hour, eastbound train No. 263, bound for Michigan City, Indiana, shows that aging electric equipment can perform with the best. This is 32nd Street in Chicago, on the IC's main line in 1977.

(D. R. Kaplan)

tenant, Britton I. Budd, was president of both the North Shore and the South Shore. Efforts were made to provide the highest possible engineering standards, equipment and operating procedures to obtain a first-class metropolitan rapid transit system. By 1930 there was nothing like it anywhere in the world, and thousands of Chicago-area commuters were enjoying interurban service that would have been undreamed of in 1910.

Sadly, the interurbans were all treated cruelly by the Depression. When Samuel Insull's financial empire began to collapse in 1932, the interurbans had to be thrown out as orphans of the storm. In the years that followed there was no way that they could look to some prosperous parent company to provide needed improvements and keep the capital rolling in. In another decade all of the roads were hurting and struggling along with outmoded equipment, declining revenues and dwindling ridership. In addition, that old nemesis the automobile was making inroads, and state funds for construction of highways and expressways eluded the interurbans. All of the interurbans did survive World War II with its brief resurgence of rail travel, but a few years later the handwriting was clearly on the wall.

The Chicago, Aurora and Elgin died first in 1957, killed with tremendous ferocity and suddenness by the opening of the first of the great Chicago expressways. The North Shore lingered a little longer, and in fact its route was never completely usurped by expressways. It had seen a tremendous surge of traffic during the War, when it had also carried countless thousands of sailors to the huge Great Lakes Naval Training Center. During the time of gas rationing it continued to be needed by thousands of other North Shore commuters who remained its loyal riders.

Conductor collecting tickets on the Chicago-South Bend train in 1966. The equipment is already outmoded, but it nonetheless looks meticulously well kept up and the passengers seem to be pleased with their surroundings.

(William D. Middleton)

Parlor and observation cars are strictly a thing of the past on the South Shore, but this ad from 1927 shows that in the last Insull years the line was doing all that it could to display the trappings of main-line railroad luxury.

(Author's Collection)

Definitely showing signs of wear in 1979, two South Shore trains wait for their passengers at Randolph Street Station. This is the Chicago terminal of the South Shore, as it is of the Illinois Central, although the two lines use different tracks and platforms in the station. IC passengers must pass through automatic ticket-collecting turnstiles, whereas South Shore passengers have their tickets collected on board.

(George H. Douglas)

A three-coach South Shore train operating between Roosevelt Road and Van Buren Street on IC electrified tracks, in the late 1960s. Framed in the background is famous old Central Station, still a lakefront landmark, but now in the last decade of its existence.

(William D. Middleton)

Here's a South Shore highball at Gary, Indiana, on June 14, 1966. The platform is at aisle level, but in its more suburban and rural environs passengers must still mount the stairs.

(William D. Middleton)

In South Bend passengers board right on the street in true streetcar fashion. This is the corner of La Salle and Michigan Streets, and the date is July 16, 1955.

(William D. Middleton)

The aging stone station at Michigan City, Indiana, is getting to look ancient. The South Shore continues to be lacking in the kinds of funds needed to rehabilitate its passenger facilities. They struggle along nobly nevertheless.

(Mike Cassidy)

The eight-car consist proves that this is the rush hour. Train No. 258 from Michigan City is snaking through Kensington and Eastern Junction where it joins the IC electrified line, the date being April 1, 1977. To the right is the 115th Street Kensington Interlocking.

(D. R. Kaplan)

The towns of northern Indiana are the only places in America where the true spirit of the interurban still lives and breathes. In the summer of 1980 a two-car South Shore interurban ambles right down the middle of the street in Michigan City, Indiana.

(Mike Cassidy)

Even in the dreary years of the Depression, the North Shore struggled nobly to upgrade its equipment and services. In the late 1930s it introduced its remarkable Electroliners, which once again testified to the speed and attractiveness of North Shore service.

But by the late 1950s the North Shore was on its knees also. It tried desperately to effect a cure for its lethargy by cutting off its commuter-rich shore line in 1958, keeping only the high-speed Skokie Valley Route, but, as could be expected, this medicine worked only temporarily. In a few years the North Shore was calling for total abandonment of its line, which finally came about in the wee small hours of January 21, 1963, when the last cars came to their berths in Milwaukee and in Chicago's Roosevelt Road Station, respectively. "The world's fastest interurban" would sing no longer along the electric lines of the North Shore communities.

This left only the South Shore, which endures to this day because of a rather curious set of circumstances. When Insull took control of the three Chicago interurbans, the South Shore was probably the one with the greatest number of difficulties, yet it was the South Shore that survived. It survived because it had a neat little margin of safety provided not by its passengers, but by its freight traffic. This was due partly to the function of geography in the rich industrial heartland around the southern tip of Lake Michigan, and partly to the fact that the original builders of the South Shore had provided for full-scale freight operations. Unlike other interurbans, the South Shore's entire route was built, even as it followed city streets, without any curves that could not accommodate long trains of conventional railroad freight cars. The South Shore was able to pick up and deliver from any point on its route every kind of freight business generally handled by American railroads. Even as early as the Insull years, the

Understandably it was freight that saved the South Shore from oblivion. In 1964 two former New York Central R-2 Class locomotives arrive at Burnham Yard with a freight train from Kensington.

(William D. Middleton)

Duneland

INDIANA DUNES · STATE PARK

by the

SOUTH SHORE LINE

Like all interurban lines from the classical era, the South Shore made every effort to publicize recreational and scenic attractions along its route. One of its best-known attractions was the Indiana Dunes State Park, advertised in this brochure from the late 1920s.
(Indiana State Library)

South Shore had built up enough of this freight traffic to pull off the dead weight of the money-losing passenger business. The North Shore had its freight too, but it was never sufficient to tip the scales.

All of the Chicago interurbans served their various territories extremely well in spite of their volatile and unpredictable financial circumstances. The ones that have passed on are mostly remembered with fondness and affection. This is due in no small measure to the strong sense of civic responsibility of Samuel Insull, who did the best that he could for the roads during the years of his rule. Under Insull management the interurbans built very charming and aesthetic suburban stations, often in a Spanish style. They pampered their patrons with magazines, outings, picnics, promotions, Christmas cards and all sorts of other imaginative efforts to fit the interurban network into the larger fabric of society. Insull was deeply committed to safety on his railroads and carried on a long, and mostly successful, campaign to warn the public about the hazards of entering on the right-of-way of electric railways where fast-moving trains creep up before one is aware of them. In the Insull years motormen on the trains were given missives to hurl out the window at trespassers to warn them of the dangers of being up on the track.

The Chicago interurbans had a great deal to do with developing the suburban territories through which they passed. They established real estate and referral services and took part in the cultural life of the communities along the line. Like interurbans generally, and only partly from motives of selfishness, they were always keen on developing the recreational facilities of the area—picnic grounds, forest preserves, and amusement parks—an interest that today is scarcely known to transportation companies of any sort.

It is rather interesting to note, for example, that the Ravinia Festival, one of the foremost centers of the arts in the United States, evolved from a smaller amusement center opened in 1904

Indiana Dunes State Park ❦ on the South Shore Line

"The Dunes" — What they are — What to do there   *And how to reach them conveniently and safely*

WHAT are the Dunes of Indiana? You have heard them talked about. But have you ever been in this "land of the whispering sands"? Some people have an idea that the Dunes country is nothing more than a vast sea of sand. Nothing could be further from correct.

There are sand hills, yes — huge, weird, fascinating mountains of golden sand. But while on one side of you there is a veritable desert, on the other there is a beautiful forest of trees, ferns and flowers!

"A little bit of everywhere brought together here at the southernmost end of Lake Michigan"—that, in a few words, describes the alluring Dunes country.

Would you like to visit the towering pines of the Canadian woods?
The famous Berkshire Hills of Massachusetts?
The cactus country of New Mexico and Arizona?
The valley of a quiet stream in Norway?
The tamarack lands of our northern states?
The broad, sandy beaches of Florida and Southern California?
The wilderness of the forest primeval?
The home of the trailing arbutus in old New England?
The great African desert of the Sahara?
The dune country of far-off Algeria?

You need not travel thousands upon thousands of miles to visit these wonders and beauties of nature. You need not take weeks and months of time. For they are here, at home. Fast South Shore Line service puts them almost at your door.

There are excellent reasons why people talk about the Dunes—why they come back again and again after their first visit. There is only one way to learn these reasons. That is to visit the Dunes yourself!

Like a Scene in Japan

More than 300 varieties of birds frequent the Dunes country. Wild flowers and trees grow there in great abundance —species that are found nowhere else in this region.

The State of Indiana has set apart a 2,000-acre tract of Duneland as a State Park. A map of it appears on the inside pages of this folder. You are welcome to this park at all seasons of the year. Ten cents is the only admission, and this small sum helps to maintain the park. The park entrance is at Tremont, "Gateway to the Dunes," on the South Shore Line.

There are twenty-five miles of sandy, gradually-sloping Lake Michigan beach. Swim if you like. At Waverly Beach, within the State Park, is a bath house. There, for a small charge, you can change to swimming clothes and rent towels and lockers. You can rent a bathing suit for 50 cents.

Take along your lunch—or pick up a delicious box lunch, reasonably priced, at Tremont station of the South Shore Line. Throughout the vast State Park there are attractive places to eat a picnic

The Lonesome Pine

Where the Trail Leads Upward

Beautiful Wild Flowers

A Quiet Lily Pond in the Dunes

lunch. There are numerous wells which provide pure drinking water. And there are crystal-clear springs which have been tested and marked by the State. Dunes Park is an ideal spot for a camp-fire—a marshmallow or "weenie" roast.

Above all, hike about the Dunes. That is the only way to see them—the only way to become familiar with the beauties they possess. There's something new to see at every turn! Popular hiking trails are shown on the map printed herein. Take your camera — "shoot" the beauties of Nature. No matter how tired you become, there is a restful, swift ride back home on the South Shore Line to look forward to.

"In the Dunes, as nowhere else in the world," says Prof. Henry C. Cowles, of the University of Chicago, "there is a procession from April to October of beautiful flowers. Within a stone's throw of almost any spot one may find plants of the deserts and plants of rich woodlands, plants of the pine woods and plants of the swamps, plants of the oak woods and plants of the prairies."

Some of the plants and flowers of the Dunes are ferns, sand cherry, bearberry, hepatica, lupine, puccoon, phlox, trillium, bird's-foot violet, orchids, four species of lady's slipper, wild roses, columbine, twin flower, harebell, goat's rue, butterfly weed, flowering spurge, prickly pear cactus, goldenrod, aster, sunflowers, yellow geradias, gentians.

You will see, in the Dunes, giant white pines, white oaks with trunks nearly three feet through the center, black oaks, pin oaks, tulip trees, beech and poplars, junipers, sassafras, ague trees, elms, silver maples, sugar maples, sand cherries, hickory, birch, sycamores, dogwoods, wild plums, wild crabapples, willows — a seemingly endless variety of trees and shrubs.

More than 300 varieties of birds have been seen in the Dunes. Among them are the kinglet, blue heron, wild canary, scarlet tanager, goldfinch, purple finch, wren, bobolink, meadow lark, cuckoo, dove, killdeer, mocking bird, thrush, phoebe, swallow, quail, sandpiper, owl, whip-poor-will, white and gray gull, wild duck, plover, thrasher, humming bird, oriole, indigo bunting, purple martin, bluebird, grackle, robin, warbler, to mention only a few.

Outing and Recreation Bureau

A FREE SERVICE FOR ALL THE PUBLIC

72 West Adams Street, CHICAGO
Telephone STAte 0080

This bureau is maintained jointly, as a service to the public, by the following companies:

Chicago South Shore & South Bend Railroad Company *(South Shore Line)*
Chicago North Shore and Milwaukee Railroad Company *(North Shore Line)*
Public Service Company of Northern Illinois
Chicago Rapid Transit Company
Shore Line Motor Coach Company
Northern Indiana Public Service Company
Commonwealth Edison Company
The Peoples Gas Light and Coke Company

Reminiscent of the Great Sahara   *Moonlight on the Beach*   *A Picturesque Dunes Blowout*

---

by A. C. Frost to provide business for his Chicago & Milwaukee Railway Company, which was the name used by Frost when, with George A. Ball of Mason jar fame, he bought up the old Bluff City Electric Company, shortly after the turn of the century. In the first few years of its existence, the Ravinia Festival was more like a traditional amusement park and included a baseball diamond with a permanent grandstand, an electric fountain, a theater with pipe organ, a refectory and dance floor, and a wooden open-air pavilion. By the time that Frost had to give up his grip on the Chicago and Milwaukee, the little park north of Glencoe had captured the affections of the local residents and the summertime activities were continued and expanded under local sponsorship. In later years the reorganized North Shore interurban had no financial interest in the festival, but the relations between the two remained intimate, with Ravinia getting prominent notice in the timetables, and with advertising posters in the cars announcing the park and its programs.

During the 1920s and 1930s the South Shore ran an Outing and Recreation Bureau in Chicago to inspire and stimulate public use of the splendid recreational facilities in the southern Lake Michigan area. Industry and pollution were a part of the picture even then, and it remains something of a mystery how primitive nature could survive in the shadow of a great metropolis.

(Indiana State Library)

The North Shore was always well-disposed toward all sorts of outings, parks, picnics, promotions—anything that would build good will and improve local traffic. The Chicago & Milwaukee was also the promoter of another, more typical amusement park at Highwood, known as Fort Sheridan Park. It included a dance hall, a beer garden, a theater, and an openair park, all well maintained and cared for, even if it never reached the artistic heights of the later Ravinia.

The South Shore also did all that it could to cater to the leisure-seeking multitudes, and accordingly, made efforts to promote vacation and leisure spots within its territory during the

Like all of the interurbans, the North Shore was keen on all sorts of promotions. It was keen on outings, picnics, amusement parks and the like. An early predecessor of the North Shore established one of Chicago's enduring institutions, the Ravinia Festival, south of Highland Park. Shown here in recent years, the Ravinia Festival continues to be a cultural gem of the Chicago area.

(Ravinia Festival)

The Ravinia Festival is known not only for the absorption of heavy culture, but for relaxation, and one imagines that this is just how the original interurban proprietors would have liked it.

(Ravinia Festival)

CHICAGO NORTH SHORE AND MILWAUKEE RAILROAD

NORTH SHORE
"WORLD'S FAIR"
LINE
Only Direct Way There

WORLD'S FAIR STATION
(Roosevelt Road)

●

CHICAGO MILWAUKEE

WAUKEGAN - ZION
KENOSHA - RACINE

SHORE LINE SUBURBS
SKOKIE VALLEY COMMUNITIES

●

FAST···FREQUENT

During Chicago's Century of Progress Exposition in 1933, the North Shore issued timetables advertising the fair, and referring to its southern terminal at Roosevelt Road as "World's Fair Station"—an easy way to get to the fairgrounds from all of the North Shore communities.

(Author's Collection)

1920s. These efforts came later to the South Shore than to the North Shore, but after Insull entered the picture the South Shore became exceedingly civic-minded. The South Shore was tireless in developing the dunes area of Indiana now known as the Indiana Dunes State Park. It contributed $25,000 toward the construction of a resort hotel and bath house at the Indiana Dunes, and in the 1920s printed thousands of very aesthetic posters and brochures extolling the virtues of this accessible natural attraction. In the year 1928 the South Shore scheduled some 250 special or chartered train movements which carried nearly 15,000 people to picnics, lodges, church gatherings, and other outings of all sorts. The South Shore published a monthly magazine entitled *South Shore Lines*, which it distributed widely to its patrons and friends. It also put out a number of special leaflets such as "Picnic Places Along the South Shore Line." It operated an "Own Your Own Home Bureau" and an "Outing and Recreation Bureau" in Chicago, both of which had the obvious effect of cementing ties between urbanites and the denizens of the greener lands out along the line.

The Chicago interurbans were technologically remarkable and built and operated to standards far above the norm for the nation as a whole. But more important for Chicagoans, they were always good neighbors. Too often they were out-of-pocket and couldn't serve as well as they might have liked to, but they did marvelously well. They all preserved the affection of the multitudes who rode them.

MINOR CHICAGO-AREA INTERURBANS

Name	Area Served	Dates of Operation	Remarks
Chicago and Interurban Traction (orig., Chicago and Southern Traction)	Halsted & 79th Street Chicago to Kankakee (54 miles)	1897–1927	Originally started as a storage-battery line to Blue Island; electrified in 1901, and completed to Kankakee in 1907.
Chicago and Joliet Electric Railway	Joliet to Chicago—outgrowth of Joliet St. Railway system	1901–1933	Became an Insull line in 1915. As with the Chicago and Interurban, suffered from lack of a high-speed entrance to Chicago.
Chicago and Illinois Valley (orig., Chicago, Oregon and Peoria)	Joliet eastward to Ottawa, Streator, and Princeton	1902–1934	An attempt to elongate the Chicago and Joliet Electric. Carried few passengers to and from Chicago.
Joliet, Plainfield and Aurora	Semi-circle around Chicago from Chicago Heights to Carpentersville	1903–1924	A number of smaller roads linked together to make this chain that was successful only until about 1914.
Joliet and Eastern Traction	Joliet to Chicago Heights	1909–1923	A meagerly trafficked route serving, with the JP&A, as part of a belt line around Chicago.
Aurora, Elgin and Fox River Electric	Fox River Valley	1896–1935	Served distant Chicago suburbia by extending the Chicago, Aurora and Elgin as well as Burlington, Milwaukee and North Western commuter lines.
Chicago, Aurora and DeKalb	Aurora to DeKalb (25 miles)	1910–1923	Brought small number of passengers from DeKalb to Aurora for transfer to Chicago on the Chicago, Aurora and Elgin.
Elgin and Belvidere Electric Co.	Elgin to Rockford and Freeport, a 78-mile route	1906–1930	A northwesterly line that served as a cumbersome extension from Chicago of the CA&E.
Fox and Illinois Union Railway	A 20-mile line linking Yorkville and Morris	1911–1931	Linked the Chicago and Illinois Valley with the CA&E. Continued small freight service with gas-electric locomotive until 1938.
Gary Railways	Served industrial communities southeast of Chicago and in western Indiana	1909–1947	Mostly these were electric street railways linking communities such as Gary, La Porte, Valparaiso, Hammond, Whiting, Indiana Harbor. Eventually came under Insull management. Finally replaced by busses.

CHAPTER 9

Commuter Paradise

The great streamlined trains of high pedigree no longer flash across the wide-open spaces of the United States. Since the decline of the long-distance train, the railroad have played a much less intimate role in the national life than they once did, and much of the public's old affection and good will for railroads and trains has eroded.

In one rather small area, however, the railroads still have direct contact with the general public. This is the area of the short-distance commuter travel in great metropolitan regions of the country, especially in a few cities of the East where the commuter lines were laid out in the days before the coming of the automobile. Chicago is one such metropolitan region, and it is pretty hard to deny that Chicago remains a showcase of commuter operation, just as it does for railroad activity in general. No American city is better served by commuter railroads than Chicago. Indeed, it would be hard to imagine what life would be like without those long-established suburban lines which daily keep hundreds of thousands of people from having to hustle their way along over-crowded expressways to the city's core. Chicago may not have the warm and inviting climate of Los Angeles, but it does have some of the amenities denied to those who live in that great exhaust-pipe wonderland of the West. One of these is a remarkable system of rapid transit, of which the railroad has been the keystone for many years.

The commuter lines in Chicago are the great and wonderful conveyances that they are because they were built a long time ago. If the need for them had had to wait for the twentieth century, they might never have been built. Most of Chicago's commuter lines were developed by railroads that went back to the very earliest days of rail activity in the city. In many cases suburban traffic was developed along the main lines, although other lines were later built to extend out to suburbs that were ready to burst forth. Mostly, though, the suburbs in the nineteenth century popped out where the railroad was operated, and countless Chicago suburbs are what they are because they happened to be along the railroad line back in the 1850s or 1860s. This was true of both close-in suburbs like Hyde Park, Kenwood or Beverly Hills, which were once part of the countryside and later became part of the city, and of far-out suburbs that happened to be on a principal railroad line—places like LaGrange, Hinsdale, Elmhurst, Arlington Heights, Highland Park, and many others. Chicago, they say, was built by the railroads. Ditto for its suburbs.

Even if it weren't for the solid historical roots of the Chicago suburban territory, Chicago was a natural to have become a great commuter wonderland. As opposed to New York City, which is an island, and somewhat difficult of access, and which dumps many of its commuters off on the Jersey shore where they are forced to continue their journeys through foul smelling tubes or by slow ferry connections, every Chicago commuter line had easy access to the city. When they were built, even the great expressways could offer them no competition in either comfort or speed. Some people fancy that they can't do without their car in the city for business and general flexibility, but except for those alleged virtues of the automobile, the commuter from the outlying suburbs who eschews the train for the highway is either a fool or an extravagant energy waster or both.

In the early years, of course, the railroad was not only the *best* way to get to the city, which it still is, but the *only* way to get there on a day-to-day basis. This became more and more obvious as the city spread its bounds and pushed further into the outlying territories.

The first railroad in Chicago to get into the commuter business was the Illinois Central, which started running a local train called "The Hyde Park Special" on July 21, 1856. Hyde Park in 1856 was a pretty little suburban community located on high ground—but near the lakeshore—six miles from Chicago. A young and enterprising Chicago lawyer had started the Hyde Park development and coaxed the Illinois Central to provide train service for himself and his neighbors who wanted to travel into the city. In those days the city of Chicago had its boundary at 22nd Street, and south of that one immediately encountered a distinctly arcadian setting, with picturesque groves and wooded areas. "Meadow larks sang in the clear morning air, and at twilight the deep croak of the bullfrog was heard, with crickets, whippoorwills and tree-toads joining in the chorus."

The Illinois Central's suburban service began with the Hyde Park Train in 1856. For a number of years this was the only suburban train and the passengers were few. By the time this pass was issued in 1873 there were other trains in local service, but the original name was still in use.

(Author's Collection)

The truth is, the "Hyde Park Special"—one or two cars pulled by a little woodburning locomotive—was not an immediate success. There just weren't enough people out that far to justify its existence. On the first day of the run an Illinois Central employee reported to the company headquarters in New York, "The Hyde Park Special train was put on this morning. . . . The first had 'nary' a passenger up or down." At first there were plans for four round trips daily between Great Central Station and Hyde Park, but in a few months this was cut back to three—a schedule which remained in effect for several years.

The Hyde Park area developed slowly, which was the reason for the lack of patronage for the special train, but before long there would be additional call for the IC's services farther south. About a mile south of the Hyde Park Station there was the famous junction with the Michigan Southern over which battles had once been fought. Here the Illinois Central built a "wye" to turn its trains and erected a small station that came to be called Woodlawn. Soon the Hyde Park Special was running out here and picking up additional suburban passengers, charging them the same fare as the Hyde Park passengers. Around the same time, a number of citizens who lived between Hyde Park and the city were also clamoring for intermediate stations. A Scotsman named Dr. J. A. Kennicott—who owned an estate at 48th Street and Lake Park Avenue—got the railroad to build a station for himself and his neighbors, calling this station Kenwood after his ancestral home in Scotland. Similarly, still farther in was another stop at Oakland, and this location, together with the other small communities of Woodlawn, Kenwood and Hyde Park, were organized into the town of Hyde Park in 1861.

In the following decade, and especially after the Great Chicago Fire of 1871, the Hyde Park area was subjected to very unusual demand for housing. Many of those citizens of Chicago who had been burned out sought new homes in this

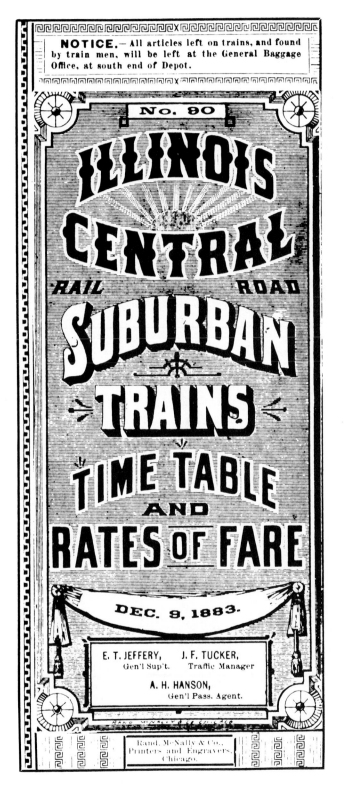

NO. 90

ILLINOIS CENTRAL RAIL ROAD

SUBURBAN TRAINS

TIME TABLE AND RATES OF FARE

DEC. 9, 1883.

E. T. JEFFERY,   J. F. TUCKER,
Gen'l Sup't.   Traffic Manager

A. H. HANSON,
Gen'l Pass. Agent.

Rand, McNally & Co.,
Printers and Engravers,
Chicago.

very pleasant pastoral setting to the south. In the decade of the 1870s, the number of suburban trains to Hyde Park stations increased from six to 36, and the population of the town of Hyde Park increased from 3,644 to 15,724. And the most phenomenal growth was still to come. The Illinois Central was to push its suburban service still farther southward, creating towns like Harvey and Homewood and ministering to Mr. Pullman's newly created model town. In the decade from 1880 to 1890, the Illinois Central suburban service expanded from 36 to 114 trains daily, and increased its number of annual riders from 1,500,000 to 4,000,000.

By 1900, the Illinois Central suburban lines had taken on pretty much their present-day dimensions. There was the main line to Homewood (later extended to Richton) and the two branch services, one leaving the main line at 67th Street for South Chicago and the other leaving at 115th Street for Blue Island. But long before all of these lines were finished, the original main line through Hyde Park and the Chicago near suburbs had already been built for heavy traffic—traffic as dense as anywhere in the United States. As early as 1880 the Illinois Central had to construct two additional tracks for suburban traffic between Randolph Street and Kensington (115th Street), thus providing two tracks for suburban service, two for freight, and two for long-distance service.

This multiple trackage, unbelievably extensive for the 1880s, made possible what became probably the largest movement of passengers on a daily basis ever achieved in America during the great Columbian Exposition of 1893, when the Illinois Central was required to carry nearly all of the people who wanted to visit the exhibits in Jackson Park in addition to its own daily passengers. There is nothing quite like it anywhere in the record books. Between May 1 and October 31, 1893, the Illinois Central operated 40,116 special World's Fair trains between Van Buren Street and Jackson Park. Company records show that in this period 8,780,616

By the 1890s the Randolph Street Station was taxed to the limits with suburban equipment. It is 5:35 P.M. on May 21, 1895, and six commuter runs are poised ready for departure to the city's southern precincts. Electrification was three decades off, but obviously it would have been a big help at this time.

(Illinois Central Gulf)

This little peanut roaster engine No. 1404 was built in 1883, and is seen in Chicago suburban service around the turn of the century. Doubtless she was hard put to pull this load of commuter cars.

(Bob Lorenz)

A southbound suburban train is stopped at 43rd Street around 1915. The locomotive is one of a number that the IC built in its own shops for suburban service. It is a 2-4-4T type built in 1887. These locomotives would continue in service until the arrival of electrified equipment a decade later. The cars in storage at the far left belong to the Kenwood "El" line.

(Illinois Central Gulf)

passengers were carried, in addition to the railroad's own regular suburban passengers. And all behind steam engines.

The great record-breaking day of the Exposition was "Chicago Day," on October 9, 1893, which was the 22nd anniversary of the Great Fire. On this single day the Illinois Central carried 263,282 passengers in special Fair trains and another 241,843 passengers in regular suburban service for a total of 505,035. That figure, which excludes the railroad's long-distance service from Central Station, represents the record for one-day movement of passengers by rail in America by a single railroad.

And it was all done before electrification with a fleet of noisy and smoky steam engines. It required a full mustering of Illinois Central resources from all over the system.* How this magic was accomplished remains partly shrouded

in the annals of history, but there is no mistaking the fact that the Illinois Central suburban service had come a long way since that little woodburning "Hyde Park Special" of 1856.

As far as regular daily commuting is concerned, the Illinois Central was to experience even more remarkable growth over the next four or five decades, as much of their territory became engulfed in the city itself and the outly-

*One engineer who shuttled tourists between Van Buren Street and Jackson Park was Casey Jones of ballad fame, whose identification was not always with the southern precincts of the Illinois Central as many believe.

258

ing areas filled in solidly with home buyers seeking green lawns at further and further remove from the city. This increasing density of traffic, along with extreme pressures on terminal facilities during rush hours, eventually became the forces that prompted the Illinois Central management to consider electrification of its suburban service in the early years of the twentieth century. Electrification was delayed somewhat by World War I, and did not arrive until 1926, but even this date was a fairly early one for American railroads. Indeed, the Illinois Central's electrification started a trend that later led to major suburban electrifications such as those on the Pennsylvania, the Lackawanna, the Long Island and the New Haven, all in the New York metropolitan area.

This is the terminal of the South Chicago branch of the Illinois Central's suburban line, probably about 1915. All the equipment is very characteristic of the IC's suburban roster before 1926. Engine No. 1411 was typical of those built in company shops for this operation, but behind it is No. 1406 which was built by the Rogers Locomotive Works in 1883, also of the 2-4-4T type.
(Illinois Central Gulf)

The electrified suburban service was many years in the planning, and was actually well under way before the War. But the project was a gigantic one and involved much more than the purchase of electrified equipment. For this high-speed service it was necessary to completely block access of the public to the right-of-way. This required the elimination of hundreds of streets and grade crossings, the erection and relocation of many terminal and servicing facilities, the construction of some 25 miles of new tracks, the construction of several thousand feet of retaining walls, the installation of new interlocking plants and a wholly new signaling system. Too, many stations had to be relocated. Every station on the line was, in some sense, new since it was decided to build platform access that would permit passengers to enter the cars without having to climb stairs, an obvious timesaving and safety feature.

All of these improvements were not without drawbacks, for the Illinois Central tore down a good many quaint and attractive suburban stations, putting up purely utilitarian structures that over the passage of years have not proved

Typical of the many wooden and threadbare IC stations in the city of Chicago is the station at 59th Street which has served thousands of students at the University of Chicago over the years.
(George H. Douglas)

In the last decade the old electrified equipment on the IC has been phased out with the financial help of the Regional Transit Authority, and some of the newer equipment is shown in servicing facilities south of the site of old Central Station. Tracks on the left take both main line and suburban equipment.
(George H. Douglas)

at 35th Street without further ado. This passenger was riding wholly within the first zone. The longer distance passenger went through a somewhat different procedure. Consider the passenger riding to Harvey, or Flossmoor. This passenger would have his ticket punched (not taken) at Randolph Street. After the train left 67th Street at the end of the first zone, the conductors audited the cars, collecting all tickets for destinations up through Kensington (115th Street). The ticket for the Harvey passenger, who is not in the second zone, would not be taken. He would be picked up on the next survey of the cars.

This system has been refined numerous times over the years, and at present the system is wholly automated. A passenger boarding the train at Homewood with a one-way ticket for downtown Chicago will run his ticket through a turnstile which reads the ticket, opens the gate, and returns the ticket to the passenger. When he

arrives at Randolph or Van Buren Street stations he again feeds his ticket into the turnstile, but this time the ticket is retained. If he has a weekly or monthly ticket, the highly sophisticated equipment returns the ticket to him every time he embarks or disembarks except on the last ride, when the ticket is retained.

In theory, conductors on the Illinois Central suburban trains should have to do no revenue work at all, and in very recent years the system has been further automated to eliminate agents at suburban stations. Passengers entering a station on the line are confronted by what looks like a streamlined soft-drink or coffee-vending machine—into which they may feed dollar bills or coins and push buttons for one-way, round-trip or commutation tickets (most multiple-ride tickets are bought through the mail or in the downtown terminals). These machines are convenient and economical, and they prevent the mugging of agents in the troubled near-in neighborhoods.

Unfortunately, automation is not perfect. Consider the commuter who arrives at the station at the last minute, hearing the sound of the approaching train. Let us say that he has forgotten his ticket or that the ticket machine is out of change or broken. This harried commuter may leap over the unguarded turnstile, briefcase in

A typical Illinois Central tableau. It is 8:36 A.M. at Homewood and a sizable number of commuters have assembled to wait the arrival of the next train to the Loop. With the usual luck all of them will be deposited at Randolph Street terminal by 9:22. The track on the right with its ground-level platform serves Amtrak's long-distance passengers.

(George H. Douglas)

Floosmoor is another Illinois Central community that once deserved something more genteel in the way of station architecture. But now the stop is for commuters only, so the IC has abandoned the main station in favor of a lowly platform shed. The station itself has been taken over by assorted entrepreneurs, as indicated by the sign in the window.

(George H. Douglas)

Floosmoor is a typical Illinois Central suburban community, and here, directly across from the railroad station, is what might once upon a time have been called "railroad square." But the ambience is strictly that of the affluent, with even the stores and apartments treated to facades of architectural fancy.

(George H. Douglas)

A two-car double-decker commuter train in off-peak operation has just left Van Buren Street Station on its way south. A fine view of the Michigan Avenue skyline on the left, including the Conrad Hilton Hotel, once the world's largest.

(Illinois Central Gulf)

hand, rather than watch his fellow commuters loading in the cars while he cools his heels in the station. In cases like these, the trainmen do have to do some revenue work. They are able to sell tickets in such unusual circumstances so that the passenger can get out through the guarded turnstile at Randolph Street. Persistent turnstile hoppers are not easily guarded against, but every station's turnstiles are monitored downtown by television. Regular freeloaders are quickly caught.

The Illinois Central electric service is as unique among railroads in 1980s America as it was in the 1920s. For years the service deteriorated, but with the coming of the streamlined, double-deck, air-conditioned coaches, a fresh face was put on the operation. Similarly, since the Regional Transit Authority entered the picture and began subsidizing the system, the line's dowdy and tatterdemalion stations have been given fresh coats of paint. They will never be objects of beauty, but they will continue to serve thousands of daily commuters agreeably and well.

If the Illinois Central has the mood and atmosphere of a city rapid transit system that just happens to belong to a railroad, the Chicago and North Western suburban service is all railroad. Indeed, to the line's nearly 100,000 daily commuters at the dawn of the 1980s, the Chicago and North Western is *the* railroad. Its service is strictly suburban in its flavorings, and the three flourishing routes—one westward to Geneva, one northwestward to Harvard, and one northward to Waukegan and Kenosha—service some of Chicagoland's most affluent suburban and exurban territories.

Suburban service on the Chicago and North Western probably cannot claim the antiquity of the Illinois Central's Hyde Park train, but there is some evidence of regular ridership on the old Galena and Chicago Union Railroad shortly after it reached the Des Plains River in 1848. Exactly when commuting in the modern sense began is hard to determine, but all three of the present suburban lines were ripe for commuter patronage from an early age. The Geneva or West Line is the original route laid out by the primeval Galena and Chicago Union Railroad. The route to Harvard was acquired somewhat later, in 1864, and was on the route of the "old Chicago and North Western Railway" between Chicago, Janesville, Fond du Lac and Green Bay. The present-day North Line, serving communities like Evanston, Winnetka, Highland Park, and Waukegan, originally belonged to the Chicago & Milwaukee Railroad, which had an independent existence for many years, and its own Chicago Station at Water and Kinzie Street. This line was consolidated into the Chicago and North Western Railway only in 1883, but it had been running regular trains to Milwaukee and towns in Lake County since 1855.

The present Chicago and North Western Railway is a strange amalgam of a large number of independent companies of the period of the 1850s to 1880s that all once had separate characters and separate identities, but which eventually were subsumed under the larger umbrella of the Chicago and North Western. One marked characteristic of the C&NW known to rail buffs all over the country is its left-handed operation. The Chicago and North Western is the only railroad in the country that runs its trains on the left side, a fact that is baffling to many. There can be little doubt that this oddity is closely connected with the rapid development of suburban service on the railroad, although the precise circumstances are lost in history.

Very early the Chicago & North Western's suburban traffic had become so dense that the line expanded its facilities at the Wells Street Station. The trains shown here use the suburban annex (the building at the right), which is beside the main branch of the Chicago River. The main station and the long-distance tracks are at the left, on the other side of the fence. The year is 1908.

(Chicago Historical Society)

Oak Park was quite a jaunt from Chicago in pre-automobile days. Here in 1903 two little girls, evidently dressed for travel, arrive from Chicago with their father on the left-handed Chicago and North Western. Henry P. Becklenberg's "Depot Hack" awaits at the far left, apparently to slim pickings.

(Historical Society of Oak Park and River Forest)

Steam train commuting at its delightful best. In the faraway civilized year of 1928, when the Chicago and North Western was at its apogee as a carrier to the elegant suburbs, a morning commuter run departs the beautiful stone station at Kenilworth. The tracks at the far right are those of the North Shore interurban, a brisk competitor in those days.

(Chicago and North Western)

Thereby hangs a tale—of sorts. Rail historians have long claimed that the C&NW is a "southpaw" railroad because in its period of rapid growth it was financed by British capital, which may have resulted in the purchase of switches and other equipment for the railroad when it was first double tracked. The implausibility of this explanation is that many railroads of this same period were built by British capital and did not end up with a left-handed operation. So the answer to the puzzle must involve some practical peculiarities of double tracking in the early days, and not a definitive management decision.

The first double tracking on the C&NW was obviously in the Chicago suburban territory, doubtless through the northern precincts of the city to Evanston, then out through Oak Park on what was then the main line. Certainly a single track sufficed for a while, but the suburbs grew rapidly, the need for a second track must have become readily apparent. Robert J. Casey and W.A.S. Douglas, in their history of the Chicago and North Western, *Pioneer Railroad*, express the opinion that simple matters of construction

in the early days were the determining factor in a purely incidental left-handed operation:

With no local precedent to guide them, the construction crews pushed westward from the Chicago terminal, hauling up supplies from behind as the rails went down ahead. They pushed ties, spikes and strap iron for rails from the right side of the flatcars as they went ahead, presumably because the surveyors' stakes had been planted on the left. And thus was established an unloading technique. The tracks went down, the trains moved, and presently stations were built. But materials still had to be hauled from town and they were still unloaded on the right hand side as one faced in the outbound direction. And for convenience the stations were erected close to the stockpiles.

When it came time to double track there was no place to lay the new line except on the right of way opposite the stations, whose usefulness to inbound

270

passengers was already fairly obvious. The original track, because it was nearer the station, was given the inbound traffic, and the new rails took what went out. That trains were thus made to run on the left-hand side was, of course, purely incidental.

We cannot be sure that this was the precise answer, but the explanation is very convincing. Double tracking in the suburban territories certainly was carried out with great rapidity, and in a period that is somewhat shrouded in mystery. In the Great Chicago Fire of 1871, much of the Chicago and North Western territory in Chicago was destroyed and had to be rebuilt in a helter-skelter fashion. The decade of the 1870s was one

in which the railroad, more than any other agency, was responsible for repopulating the outlying Chicago territories.

Consider, for example, the rapid growth of the North Shore line of the North Western. The line was an old one in a sense, having established the connection between Chicago and Milwaukee in 1855. But most of the communities along the line developed slowly, and none of them could really be considered Chicago suburbs at the time of the Great Fire. Even Evanston kept its clannishness and isolation as an enclave of righteous Methodism and militant Prohibitionism.

There was a big building boom on Chicago's north side after the Great Fire. During the fire itself over 1,300 acres were burned out, over 10,000 buildings were destroyed, and nearly 70,000 people lost their homes. As an example of the lightning regrowth after the fire, the town of Lake View, between Chicago and the Evanston boundary, grew into being almost overnight. The area of the city between Fuller-

In the mid-1950s the suburban coach yard of the Chicago and North Western was filled with musty old equipment, the product of railroad yesteryear. But there were many who loved these old cars, all of which have subsequently gone to the torch.

(Chicago and North Western)

The Chicago skyline was still in its infancy at the time this picture of a C&NW commuter run was taken in 1929. Under construction at top right is Samuel Insull's Civic Opera Building (since 1949 the Kemper Insurance Building).

(Chicago and North Western)

ton Avenue and Lake View filled right in—at least that part of it lying near the railroad tracks and the newly laid streetcar lines. Lake View was described as a "thickly settled" community by 1874 and Ravenswood and Rogers Park shortly thereafter. By the mid-1870s these suburban areas (all subsequently absorbed into the city of Chicago) were providing brisk patronage for the Chicago and North Western which offered fourteen daily trains, while building stations and laying track at a break-neck speed.

In the last quarter of the nineteenth century the lakeshore branch was providing regular daily commuting service to such previously isolated and stubbornly independent communities as Wilmette, Winnetka, Glencoe, and Highland Park. Lake Forest was far, far, out, but it, too, slowly became the home of people who were ex-urban refugees from Chicago. The town was at first a kind of "summer resort," a place where a few exclusive families could have a seaside retreat from the city. It was a long time before many in Lake Forest would regard themselves as daily commuters. Still farther north was Waukegan, the practical northern end of the commuter territory today. It, too, took a long

time to be drawn into the Chicago orbit. It was settled in the 1830s and first received railroad service in 1855, and was incorporated in 1859, but the C&NW didn't do very much for the city until around the turn of the century. The Elgin, Joliet and Eastern entered the city in 1889, and was responsible for giving the territory its industrial flavoring. The industrial boom in turn had the effect of making Waukegan into a residential town in the Chicago sphere of influence.

The history of the C&NW's Western division was somewhat similar. This was the very first of the railroad's lines, the original route of the Galena and Chicago Union Railroad, but it wasn't intensely built up as a commuter line until after the Civil War. However, the pattern of growth was pretty much like that on the North Shore. Both Oak Park and River Forest had modest development as suburbs during the

The year 1958 shows an intermingling of aged and modern suburban equipment coming out of North Western Station. But steam power has already breathed its last. Controlling the vast flow of traffic here is the Clinton Street tower, left center.
(Chicago and North Western)

1860s, and closer to the city, places like Austin and Maywood grew rapidly. Around this time, Elmhurst (originally called Cottage Hill) and Lombard (originally Babcock's Grove) were mere villages. But after the Fire, these villages grew with lightning swiftness. The real estate boom of the 1870s made far-out places like Glen Ellyn, Wheaton and Geneva respectable and prosperous Chicago suburbs.

The northwest line or Wisconsin Division grew pretty much in the same way. This line was originally the Anthony and Fond du Lac Railway, and came in as a part of the C&NW in the great consolidation of 1864. It brought with it rail access to Irving Park and Norwood Park (later annexed into the city of Chicago) and to

Des Plaines, Arlington Heights, Palatine and Barrington, all of which quickly assumed their present-day character as havens for daily commuters.

The Chicago and North Western suburban territory had taken on almost all of its present characteristics by 1900, even though there was much room for growth. The railroad management was proud of this territory, and in the early years of the twentieth century worked vigorously to promote it as a garden paradise at the city's periphery. They tore down old stations and built more substantial ones of brick or masonry. They ordered swifter and more powerful locomotives for the suburban service, and coaches of plush and stunning design, including some parlor cars and other private varnish for the city's elite who wanted to travel in the highest style to their country estates in Lake Forest or Fox River.

The Chicago and North Western's golden years as a commuter line were in the 1920s. By 1929 they could boast some of the most beautiful stations and the best rolling stock of any suburban carrier in the country. Unfortunately the Depression was especially cruel to the C&NW, and the company went into bankruptcy in 1935, and, even with the resurgence of traffic in World War II, it was strangled by its quixotic agricultural business, its hundreds of unprofitable branch lines, its sagging long-distance passenger business. The railroad just didn't have the business to upgrade the vital suburban territory, and by 1955 it was in disreputable condition. All of the equipment was pre-1930. The steam locomotives were expensive to repair and operate, although they may have had a certain appeal to rail buffs. The coaches were tattered and only a few were air conditioned.

But the service was just too big and too important to let die. Relief came after 1956 when a Chicago lawyer named Ben W. Heinemann became Chairman of the Board of the C&NW. Heinemann brought in as president Clyde J. Fitzpatrick, formerly Illinois Central's Vice President of Operations. In a few years these two latter-day railroad giants brought the C&NW back from financial oblivion, buying new equipment, discarding antiquated operating practices, and chopping off unneeded and unprofitable services. Very early on, Heinemann and Fitzpatrick decided that the North Western's long-distance passenger service was going nowhere and should be phased out, but that the suburban segment had a bright future.

The result was that all of the old pre-Depression equipment was junked and the North Western put in orders for 200 streamlined double-deck push-pull cars and diesel locomotives. The push-pull trains were obviously economical in a time of increasing labor costs. They did not require extensive crews for turning the trains at either end of the line. The cars were electrically heated and cooled, receiving power from a special electric generator on the locomotive. All of the under-body hardware was eliminated, meaning that there were no pipes to freeze in winter, no noisy generators for air conditioners in summer.

Not content with putting in the new equipment and establishing the right kind of new economics, the Heinemann management did something unheard of in railroading during the decline in the 1950s. They went out and sold their services, taking out advertisements in newspapers and on radio. The radio ads were planned to catch the Chicago area commuter just at rush hour as he was broiling and frying in his car on the over-crowded expressways, reminding him pointedly that he could be home in half the time if he rode the train.

Passengers came back to the North Western in droves. By 1963 the suburban service was in the black and by the late 1960s it was grossing about 20 million dollars a year (with profits of about ½ million). The trains are comfortable, efficient, and nearly always on time.

The man who gave a new birth to the Chicago & North Western's suburban service was Board Chairman Ben W. Heinemann. In the late 1950s, when rail men around the country were trying to rid themselves of burdensome commuter trains, Heinemann was rightly seeing that Chicago commuters would be delighted by modern, safe, fast and efficient rail service to the vast C&NW suburban territory.

(Northwest Industries, Inc.)

The engineer of the diesel. In the push-pull equipment on the North Western that has now become commonplace on other suburban lines, the engineer rides the diesel outbound when the train is being pulled. Inbound, with the diesel pushing at the rear, the engineer occupies a small compartment at the head of the front car.

(Chicago and North Western)

A major factor in the revitalization of the Chicago and North Western's suburban service was the purchase of these handsome double-decker coaches whose air conditioning and streamlined appearance brought the line's passengers back from the expressways in droves. By 1970, when this picture was taken, the coaches still appeared to be shop-new and were obviously getting first-class treatment from management.

(Chicago and North Western)

Oak Park, long a famous Chicago suburb, was a not insignificant distance from Chicago when this picture was taken about 1903. This is the Marion Street Station, built in 1893, a solid brick structure that would have served for many years had it not been a casualty of a modernization program in 1911 when the C&NW was elevated through town.

(Historical Society of Oak Park and River Forest)

It is 5:01 P.M. on July 25, 1980, and a long Chicago and North Western commuter train out of Chicago stops at Oak Park. On the platform at the left a small group of passengers traveling against the flow of traffic to Chicago awaits the inbound train which is almost 10 minutes late. The tracks at the right are those of the Lake Street elevated line which terminates here in Oak Park.

(George H. Douglas)

The C&NW's West Line to Geneva serves a number of venerable suburbs in addition to Oak Park: Elmhurst, Lombard, Wheaton, and Glen Ellyn, whose modern brick station sat for its portrait in 1969.

(Chicago and North Western)

This is the Chicago and North Western's Northwest Line, known to many oldtime railroad men as the Wisconsin Division, a term that is no longer appropriate since passenger service to Wisconsin is a thing of the past. The line's station at Mount Prospect is twenty miles from Chicago.

(George H. Douglas)

A rush-hour express gives the back of its hand to Palatine, Illinois, one of the long-established suburban communities on the "Wisconsin Division." It is 5:21 P.M., and this train has been stepping along at 60 miles per hour. It will make its first stop 5 miles to the west in Barrington. It left Chicago, 26 miles away, at 4:42 P.M.
(George H. Douglas)

The C&NW's North Line up the shore of Lake Michigan dates back to the 1850s, and continues to be a lush and profitable commuter line. Shown here on a spring morning in 1966 is the station at Glencoe, with a train stopping to pick up a load of commuters for Chicago. This train is pushing and has not yet come to rest, but the commuters know precisely where the doors will stop.
(Chicago and North Western)

Waukegan has been a Chicago and North Western town since 1855, but it didn't take on any significance as a commuter town until the 1890s. This Waukegan station, pictured at the turn of the century, shows that passenger traffic is significant and brisk at this date.

(Waukegan Historical Society)

The Waukegan station of today. Waukegan is the practical northern end of the C&NW's North Shore suburban service, although the railroad runs a small number of trains daily to Kenosha, Wisconsin. The train in the background, having ended its run from Chicago and deposited passengers by the station, is now moving into position for its southbound run.

(George H. Douglas)

Waukegan is a commercial and manufacturing community as well as a Chicago suburb. Looking into the downtown from the railroad station we see that clearly this is a small city with an independent life of its own. Curiously, it was not the C&NW that was responsible for the growth of Waukegan as an industrial community, but the arrival of the Elgin, Joliet and Eastern in 1889, a pure freight line which brought in manufacturing plants and a land boom in the early 1890s.

(George H. Douglas)

WISCONSIN DIVISION

Effective September 24, 1922

Chicago Passenger Terminal

Suburban Service

CHICAGO

IRVING PARK

PARK RIDGE

DES PLAINES

ARLINGTON HEIGHTS

PALATINE

BARRINGTON

CRYSTAL LAKE

and Intermediate Stations

CHICAGO & NORTH WESTERN RAILWAY

C. A. CAIRNS
Passenger Traffic Manager

A. R. GOULD
Asst. Passenger Traffic Manager

JNO. L. FERGUSON
General Passenger Agent

The Chicago and North Western of today is the second largest commuter operation in the United States in terms of the number of passengers served. It is second only to the Long Island Railroad in New York. But if it is second to the Long Island in mere numbers, it is second to none as an overall commuter operation. In terms of quality of service, efficiency and dependability, the Chicago and North Western runs the best large-scale commuter operation in North America.

Coming into Union Station two blocks south of the Chicago and North Western Station are two other commuter lines which, although much smaller, run the North Western a good race. The first of these, entering Union Station from the south, is the Burlington; the second, using the north stub of Union Station, is the Milwaukee. Both play important roles in the Chicago-area commuter scene.

The Burlington has always provided well for its Chicago commuters. The railroad never experienced the hard times in the 1930s that brought the North Western to its knees, and the Burlington was the first of the Chicago lines to

Hub of the Chicago and North Western's commuter empire is North Western Station in Chicago at the corner of Madison and Canal Streets. The ever-circling flock of taxicabs indicate that the evening rush hour is near, and vehicular passengers will mostly enter the station under the lighted sign. Many of the pedestrian passengers from the Loop enter the station through the walkway above left.

(George H. Douglas)

North Western Station is now given over entirely to commuters, and its various halls and approaches are lined with quick lunch counters, bars, paperback book stores, news kiosks, even airline ticket offices. The modernized interior shown here is the product of the early 1960s when the road was revamping its suburban service.

(Chicago and North Western)

become dieselized and to order the push-pull locomotives that later brought the North Western back from oblivion. The Burlington was the first railroad in the nation to get into streamlining in a big way, so it was no surprise in the late 1940s when the company ordered a new fleet of double-deck, stainless-steel coaches from the Budd Company for its suburban service.

Thirty of these new coaches were delivered in 1950, each 85 feet long, air conditioned, built of stainless steel and equipped with roller bearings, "tightlock" couplers, modern seats, vestibules and high-intensity lighting. Over the next seven years the entire fleet of suburban cars was replaced with this new equipment. For a while this new streamlined equipment ran behind old-fashioned steam locomotives, but on

It is almost, but not quite, the rush hour as afternoon commuters make for their cars at North Western Station. The leisured pace apparent in the stride of the commuters indicates that train time is still at least five minutes off. Before long there will be a scramble for seats and the pace will decidedly quicken.

(Chicago and North Western)

September 26, 1952, steam ran for the last time in the Burlington's suburban territory, and the diesel took over completely on the road that first introduced that form of motive power to American railroading. The entire suburban fleet has been upgraded and improved several times since, and it is only fair to say that the Burlington commuter has always been offered nothing but the best.

The Burlington has but one suburban line. This is the line they built hurriedly back in the

The Burlington was as proud as any Chicago railroad of its contributions to the development of its suburban territory, including towns like Riverside, La Grange, Hinsdale and Downers Grove. Here, about the turn of the century, is the entire crew of a local from Aurora, obviously prepared to deliver a full complement of commuters to Union Station.

(Burlington Northern)

1860s when their agreement with the Chicago and North Western ran out and they were forced to build their own spur into Chicago from Aurora. This remains the main line of the road as well as the commuter territory—the 38 miles between Aurora and Chicago. Over this stretch the Burlington runs about 30 trains each way on a usual weekday, over half of these during the rush hour. For many years, about half of the trains terminated at Downers Grove, but with the number of passengers on the increase, the Burlington decided to extend all of its runs the entire 38 miles to Aurora in 1952.

The Burlington management was very proud of its own Chicago suburban division from the beginning and officers of the road were actively involved in colonizing the land along the way. As laid out, the Burlington followed an old stagecoach route between Aurora and Chicago, and such towns as La Grange, Downers Grove and Naperville already existed, although they were still nothing but hamlets in the 1860s. Among the new towns created by the Burlington was Hinsdale, characteristically enough named for H. W. Hinsdale, a member of the Burlington's board of directors.

The Burlington constructed a great many solid and picturesque stations during the golden age of railroading. This station at Western Springs was built in 1891, and is pictured here around 1910. This is the Burlington's main line; in fact, it is the railroad's only line out of Chicago.

(Burlington Northern)

Downers Grove was still a suburban terminal and steam still reigned supreme when this photograph was taken in 1946. But these 2900-series Pacifics would soon become a memory when the suburban territory was dieselized a few years later, and all the runs would terminate at Aurora.

(Burlington Northern)

Steam train commuting—how delightful, with open observation platform, and all. In the late 1940s a two-car Burlington local from Aurora prepares to disappear into the inky darkness of Union Station as a main-line Pennsylvania diesel emerges at the right.

(Bob Lorenz)

The delightful little stone station at Highlands has been painted and photographed by many and loved by thousands. The station was built by some local residents in the 1880s, and it is as charming and sightly as it was then. This picture of it was taken in March 1980.

(George H. Douglas)

Hinsdale was strictly a country delight when this picture was taken in 1883. But the town was then, as it is now, a Chicago bedroom suburb, and one of the finest. This scene looks northward over the Washington Street crossing.

(Burlington Northern)

Hinsdale as it appears in 1980. The railroad square is typical of Chicago suburbs, but the station now performs only minimal railroad functions, most of its space being rented to other establishments—a savings and loan, ice cream parlor, an optical shop and various outlets for antiques, trinkets and the like.

(George H. Douglas)

A two-car mid-day train has just discharged its passengers at Hinsdale. The rush hour will show crowds 10 times this size. The rear marker indicates that the train departed Union Station at 10:30. The timetable says that it is 11:02 A.M., and so it is.

(George H. Douglas)

It is 4:35 P.M. at the Burlington suburban coach yards south of Union Station. Four trains are poised here waiting for the opportunity to feed into the station. Within seven minutes all of these trains will be gone, every one of them loading homebound commuters.

(George H. Douglas)

Hinsdale was long to remain a kind of preserve of Burlington high brass. J. M. Walker, an attorney for the line and later president, took an active interest in the community and had a large estate there, as did a later president, Robert Harris. The developers of Hinsdale, including the Burlington executives and William Robbins, a St. Louis banker who established residence there in 1864 when he was assured that the Burlington was going to build that way, hired a notable landscape architect to lay out the town so that it was destined from the beginning to be one of the most gracious and charming Chicago suburbs. Hinsdale avoided the geometrical banality that stamped so many older settlements in the Midwest, with their strict squares and rectangles. The homes were set out along gracefully curved roads which offered a leisured bucolic ambience that for over a century would attract the city's prosperous and elite citizenry.

Another Burlington suburb, Riverside, somewhat to the northeast of Hinsdale, has received even more notoriety nationwide, probably because it was designed by America's best-known landscape architect, Frederick Law Olmsted. Olmsted, too, avoided the grid pattern of the older suburbs, and elected curved lines and rusticity. But much as it seemed otherwise, the community was planned in every detail, including every kind of essential service—water, drainage, lighting, recreational facilities, schools, and public areas. The meandering Des Plaines River provided a natural focus for a park area, and here, and along the town's leisurely streets and walks, 60,000 shrubs and trees were planted, all well thought out as to type and aesthetic appeal.

Between Riverside and Hinsdale, the Burlington has served some other important Chicago commuting towns, most notably La Grange and Western Springs, and in the twentieth century Clarenden Hills, Downers Grove and other far-distant communities have been added to the Burlington's sphere of commuting towns. The communities continue to be well served with streamlined push-pull trains, pleasant stations and a scenic right-of-way. The Burlington, for over a century, has run through one of the most delightful little commuting territories in the country.

The Milwaukee Road has two suburban lines from Chicago—a North Line to Fox Lake, a distance of 49.5 miles, and a West Line to Elgin, 36.6 miles. There are about 20 trains each way

A timetable for Burlington's weekday westbound commuter service in 1978.

(Author's Collection)

← ———————— MONDAY THROUGH FRIDAY — WESTBOUND ————————→

	201	203	205	207	209	211	213	215	217	219	221	223	225	227	229	231	233	CHICAGO	235	237	239	241	243	245	247	249	251	253	255	257	259	261	263	265	267
	AM	AM	AM	A M	AM	PM	PM	PM	PM	PM	PM	PM	PM	PM	PM	PM	PM	Lv. Union Station Lv.	PM	PM	PM	PM	PM	PM	PM	PM	PM	PM	PM	PM	PM	PM	PM	PM	AM
	6.25	7.45	8.45	10.30	11.30	12.30	1.30	2.30	3.30	4.05	4.30	4.40	4.52	4.54	4.59		5.03	Union Station	5.09	5.10	5.16	5.20	5.22	5.24	5.33	5.44	5.48	6.10	6.30	7.30	8.30	9.30	10.30	11.30	1.15
	6.29	7.49					1.34			3.34	4.09	4.34	4.39	4.44			4.58	Halsted St. (at 16th)				5.26							6.34						
	6.33	7.53	8.52	10.36	11.36	12.36	1.38	2.37	3.38	4.13	4.38	4.43	4.48		5.02	5.06	5.10	Western Ave.				5.30							6.38		8.37		10.36	11.36	1.20
	6.38	7.58	8.57	10.41	11.41	12.41	1.43	2.43	3.43		4.43	4.48	4.53		5.07			Cicero				5.35						6.20	6.43	7.40	8.42	9.40	10.40	11.40	1.25
	6.41	8.01	9.00	10.43	11.43	12.43	1.46	2.45	3.45		4.46				5.10			Clyde				5.38						6.45		8.44		10.42	11.42	1.27
							1.48		3.47		4.48				5.12			La Vergne				5.40						6.47		8.46				
	6.43	8.03	9.02	10.45	11.45	12.45	1.50	2.47	3.49	4.21	4.50				5.14			Berwyn	5.22			5.42					5.58	6.24	6.49	7.44	8.48	9.44	10.44	11.44	1.29
	6.45	8.05	9.04	10.47	11.47	12.47	1.52	2.49	3.51		4.52				5.16			Harlem Ave.	5.25			5.44					6.00	6.26	6.51		8.50		10.46	11.46	1.30
	6.48	8.08	9.07	10.49	11.49	12.49	1.55	2.52	3.53	4.24	4.55				5.19			Riverside	5.29			5.47					6.03	6.29	6.54	7.47	8.53	9.47	10.48	11.48	1.32
							1.57		3.55		4.57				5.21			Hollywood	5.32										6.56		8.55				
	6.51	8.11	9.10	10.52	11.52	12.52	1.59	2.55	3.57	4.27	4.59				5.23			Brookfield	5.35			5.51					6.06	6.32	6.58	7.50	8.57	9.50	10.50	11.50	1.34
							2.01		3.59		5.02				5.25			Congress Park	5.38										7.00		8.59				
	6.54	8.14	9.13	10.55	11.55	12.55	2.03	2.58	4.01	4.30	PM	4.57		5.10	5.27			La Grange, La Grange Rd.	PM	5.34		5.57			5.51	6.09		6.35	7.02	7.53	9.01	9.53	10.53	11.53	1.36
	6.56	8.16	9.15	10.57	11.57	12.57	2.05	3.00	4.03	4.32			5.00	5.13	5.29			La Grange, Stone Ave.		5.38		5.59			5.57	6.14		6.40	7.07	7.56	9.06	9.56	10.57	11.57	1.39
	6.58	8.18	9.17	10.59	11.59	12.59	2.08	3.03	4.06	4.35			5.03	5.16	5.32			Western Springs		5.42		6.02							7.09		9.08				
	7.00						2.10		4.08				5.06		5.35			Highlands		5.46		6.04			6.00	6.17			7.13		9.12				
	7.01	8.21	9.20	11.02	12.02	1.02	2.12	3.06	4.10	4.38			5.08	5.20	5.37		5.26	Hinsdale				6.06	5.45		6.19			6.43	7.11	7.59	9.10	9.59	10.59	11.59	1.41
							2.14		4.12				5.11		5.39		5.29	West Hinsdale				6.08	5.49		6.21				7.13		9.12				
	7.04	8.24	9.23	11.05	12.05	1.05	2.16	3.09	4.14	4.41			5.13	5.23	5.41		5.32	Clarendon Hills				6.10	5.52		6.23			6.46	7.15	8.02	9.14	10.02	11.03	12.03	1.43
	7.07	8.27	9.26	11.08	12.08	1.08	2.19	3.12	4.17	4.44			5.16	5.26	5.44		5.35	Westmont				6.13	5.56		6.26			6.49	7.18	8.05	9.17	10.05	11.06	12.06	1.45
	7.09	8.29	9.28	11.10	12.10	1.10	2.21	3.14	4.19				5.19		5.47		5.38	Downers Grove, Fairview Ave.				6.16	6.00		6.29			6.51	7.20		9.19		11.08	12.08	1.47
	7.11	8.31	9.30	11.12	12.12	1.12	2.23	3.16	4.21	4.47		PM	5.11	5.50	5.27			Downers Grove, Main St.			5.35	6.18					PM	6.13	6.53	7.22	8.08	9.21	10.08	11.10	12.10	1.49
	7.14	8.34	9.33	11.15	12.15	1.15	2.26	3.19	4.25	4.50			5.15		5.54	5.31		Belmont			5.40		5.50	6.21					6.56	7.25	8.11	9.24	10.11	11.13	12.13	1.51
	7.17	8.37	9.36	11.18	12.18	1.18	2.30	3.22	4.29	4.54			5.19		5.58	5.36		Lisle			5.45		5.55	6.24					6.59	7.28	8.14	9.27	10.14	11.16	12.16	1.54
	7.22	8.42	9.41	11.23	12.23	1.23	2.35	3.28	4.36	5.00			5.26		6.06	5.43		Naperville			5.52		6.02	6.30				6.15	6.29	7.06	7.33	8.19	9.30	10.19	11.21	12.21	1.59
																		West Eola (No passengers)					6.05	6.16	6.43	6.24									
	7.36	8.56	9.55	11.37	12.37	1.37	2.49	3.42	4.50	5.14			5.40		6.00			Ar. Aurora Ar.	PM	PM	PM	PM	PM	PM	PM		6.41	7.17	7.47	8.33	9.43	10.33	11.35	12.35	2.13
	AM	AM	AM	AM	PM	PM	PM	PM	PM	PM			PM		PM		PM		PM	PM	PM	PM	PM	PM	PM		PM	PM	PM	PM	PM	PM	PM	AM	AM

■ These trains will arrive and depart from the center platform at Western Avenue.

New Year's, Memorial Day, Independence Day, Labor Day, Thanksgiving and Christmas, trains will run on Sunday Schedule. Special Afternoon Schedules in effect Christmas Eve and New Years Eve. Consult Agent for details.

With Chicago's skyline glittering in the background a rush hour commuter express is leaving Chicago's Union Station. This is an express to Downers Grove, and, after it threads through the heavy traffic of the Chicago yards, it will step right along, covering the 21 miles in 24 minutes. You can't match that on any expressway.
(Burlington Northern)

With tracks aplenty gone to weed, a present-day Milwaukee commuter train leaves Union Station for the suburbs. In the summer of 1980 when this picture was taken the Chicago skyline is still not static, with new construction going on at the far right. This train is about two minutes out of the north stub of Union Station.
(George H. Douglas)

Glenview station serves both long distance and commuter passengers on the Milwaukee. This picture was taken in June of 1961 to commemorate a demonstration run of the new bi-level push-pull equipment just introduced to the line.

(Milwaukee Road)

on both lines, although not all of the trains go the whole distance to the ends of the lines. On the North Line many of the trains running on a local schedule end at Deerfield, 23.9 miles from Union Station. The Milwaukee suburban territory has boomed tremendously since World War II, and the prospects of the lines have brightened even as those of the mother railroad have dimmed.

The Milwaukee, like the C&NW and the Burlington, use push-pull equipment, and they have 22 locomotives and 103 bi-level cars, all manufactured by the Budd Company. Additional equipment purchases for these lines will, of course, not come from the bankrupt Milwaukee but from the Regional Transit Authority, but it is expected that the two lines long operated by the Milwaukee will continue to be an important part of the Chicago commuting scene.

The Milwaukee got into the commuting business in a rather peculiar way. The two routes now so heavily used by Chicago commuters were not originally intended for commuters at all. The North Line was the Milwaukee's attempt to cash in on the Chicago market by leaving its own bailiwick and dipping down into Illinois. It was completed in 1872 as main line competition with the C&NW between Milwaukee and Chicago. In 1880, the

Milwaukee, which was in the process of moving its base of operations from Milwaukee to Chicago, leased from the Chicago & Pacific Railroad the present line to Elgin so that it could also enjoy a more direct route west to cities like Omaha, Denver and Kansas City. The acquisition of this long-distance line slowly but unwittingly brought the Milwaukee into the commuter business in Chicago.

For a while the Milwaukee also had a third commuter line in Chicago, a spur up through Evanston, which went as far north as Wilmette by 1888. In the 1890s this line had some rather brisk traffic, but the railroad never adequately exploited these possibilities and by 1905 the line passed from the hands of the Milwaukee. The part of the line within the city of Chicago became the route of the city's elevated line to Evanston.

The two remaining lines grew slowly, with the West Line only beginning to realize its great potential after the Second World War. Around the turn of the century, most of the Milwaukee's

A typical Milwaukee commuter run steams through Bensenville
around 1940. The old ten-wheeler pulling her was built in the
Milwaukee's shops in 1907 and scrapped in 1948.
(Bensenville Community Public Library)

Bensenville has been a Milwaukee suburb since before the turn of
the century. The distinctly rural ambience shown here gives some
idea of the once far away suburbs which are now completely surrounded by the city. This picture was taken in 1908.
(Bensenville Community Public Library)

commuter business was on the North Line in the towns of Morton Grove, Glenview, Northbrook and Deerfield. Beyond these towns, the territory was strictly countrified. At the same time the Milwaukee had a big business in the near-city communities of Grayland, Irving Park and Montrose, at times giving the Chicago and North Western a good run for its money. North and west of Deerfield, the North Line of the Milwaukee retains an overall rural atmosphere, but many citizens of towns like Lake Forest, Libertyville and Gray's Lake regard themselves as (and in fact are) daily commuters to downtown Chicago.

In the early days, most of the commuter business on the Milwaukee's west line was to villages and towns that have long since been annexed to the city. Among those were Humboldt Park, Galewood and Mont Clare. All of these were distinct communities in the last quarter of the nineteenth century, Humboldt Park, for example, being a German community with German-language signs and newspapers. Around this time, River Grove (or River Park as it was originally called) was the practical western terminus of the suburban service. West of here there were only a few trains a day. With the passing of years, service to towns such as Franklin Park, Mannheim, Bensenville, Roselle and Bartlett became more important to the line.

Probably the youngest Chicago territory to blossom was that part of the Milwaukee's West Line that lies between Bensenville and Elgin. This territory literally sprang to life after World War II, especially when the opening of O'Hare International Airport in 1955 pumped new commercial and residential vitality into an area that had been strictly out in the country. This made true commuting towns of Bensenville, Wood Dale, Itasca, Roselle and Bartlett.

As history has proved, if only recently, the two Milwaukee suburban lines are very well located for future growth and development, and even if the Milwaukee itself is sold for scrap, its name will continue to mean something to thousands of daily commuters in the Chicago area.

The last of the major commuter operations in Chicago is the Rock Island, whose trains leave from the La Salle Street Station. In fact, the Rock Island commuter trains are the sole remaining tenants of La Salle Street Station, the long-distance passenger trains having moved to

Union Station with the coming of Amtrak in the early 1970s.

The Rock Island operates two suburban lines, one called the Main Line between Chicago and Joliet, a distance of 40.2 miles, and the other, known as the Suburban Branch, which leaves the Main Line at Gresham Junction (88th Street) and proceeds to Vermont Street in Blue Island, at which point the tracks rejoin the Main Line. Some of the trains on the Suburban Branch terminate at Vermont Street, but outside the rush hour others proceed onto the Main Line. The Rock Island carries about 26,000 daily commuters, about two-thirds of these on the Suburban Branch, the others going to more distant suburbs such as Midlothian, Oak Forest, Tinley Park, and Joliet.

Financial difficulties kept the Rock Island from modernizing for many years, but with aid from the RTA it has acquired the same streamlined push-pull service as the Burlington, the Chicago and North Western, and the Milwaukee. In service on the Rock Island are 73 bi-level cars, some of Budd and some of Pullman Standard construction. The RTA has also purchased for the Rock Island 17 new 3,200-horsepower diesels especially designed for push-pull service, replacing conventional diesels that were hand-me-downs from main-line service. Before 1978, the Rock Island was a veritable museum of railroad antiquity, but with public money flowing in, the service has taken its place among the more substantial carriers.

The Rock Island has been on the verge of oblivion as a carrier for many years, but back at the end of the last century the road took its Chicago suburban service seriously and developed the territory with real fondness and loving care. As on the Burlington, railroad executives were deeply involved in suburban real estate, most especially along the line known as the Suburban Branch, which was built in the 1870s and which resulted in the development of

The Rock Island, like the Illinois Central, developed a suburban territory much of which was eventually swallowed up in the City of Chicago. The South Englewood Station shown here about 1890 served a community that was strictly independent and strictly arcadian. The station name no longer exists on the Rock Island and the area has been ravaged by urban sprawl.

(University of Illinois Library)

communities like Morgan Park and Beverly Hills (which only much later became a part of the City of Chicago).

Before the 1870s the Rock Island had an important part in the development of several charming suburbs, including Englewood and South Englewood, which were right on the railroad's main line out of town. In 1852, when the Rock Island started operations in Chicago, the city did not extend beyond 39th Street, so that Englewood (sometimes called "Junction" because of the multiplicity of railroads that crossed there) was definitely considered out in the country. But by 1875 there were some 3,000

Much of the southwest part of Chicago remains very nicely suburban to this day, and for years dwellers of the city's outlying neighborhoods were able to enjoy the delights and challenges of steam train commuting. Posing for a wintry portrait is a Rock Island commuter train at 99th Street in the 1940s.

(Albert Joseph Vogele)

people in this area, which was fast becoming a residential suburb of Chicago. These people were served by 28 trains a day, which may now seem to be an enormous number for the size of the community, but in the middle 1870s the railroad was the only way to get to town. The streetcar lines were a few years off, but by 1890 their coming would bring additional thousands of middle and working class families, many of them Irish and German, to the Englewood area.

The twentieth century saw the Englewood-63rd Street neighborhood become strictly urbanized. After the long-distance trains ceased calling at the great Englewood Junction, the area no longer provided enough daily riders to warrant a stop by the Rock Island commuter trains. The once-famous commuter and long-distance station is now slated for demolition.

The Rock Island's most enduring and important commuting district lay to the south of here, most especially Washington Heights on the Main Line and Beverly Hills and Morgan Park on the suburban line. Washington Heights, whose earliest land boom came in the 1860s, only a decade after the coming of the railroad, was from the beginning earmarked as a comfortable

294

The Rock Island built a number of picturesque stations in its suburban territory, many of them unique and individualistic. Those that did not pass the test of time have mostly been replaced by cinder block nonentities or grandiose lean-tos, but a fair number of interesting specimens survived. One that didn't is this station formerly at 103rd Street and Hale.

(Andrew C. Koval)

The Rock Island commuter train starts its run in 1949 from La Salle Street Station. Obviously this is a midday picture, since the coach yards to the right are filled.

(Bob Lorenz)

and scenic suburban community. The territory occupied a ridge from 40 to 100 feet above the surrounding area, and by Midwestern standards this was positively mountainous. Rock Island investors and officers were among those most active in this real estate speculation. The developers subdivided the land into lots, planted shade trees, put in six-foot sewers, and, to attract people "of modest means," sold houses on convenient time payments.

By 1873 the Washington Heights region was rapidly filling up and pushing westward. This was what prompted the Rock Island to construct its other line to cater to the newer subdivisions, which eventually came to be known as Beverly Hills and Morgan Park. Once again a mad speculation for land quickly filled up the territory, although Morgan Park was not annexed to Chicago until 1914. These neighborhoods remain among the more suburban-appearing parts of Chicago, and this is due in no small measure to the fact that the village plats used curved streets to make a strong contrast with the rectangular grid pattern of other parts of the city, and because the rolling terrain offers dramatic scenery to many of the homeowners.

The Rock Island continued to upgrade the quality and frequency of service to southwest Chicago during the last few decades of the nineteenth century, eventually being responsible for the development of Blue Island, a community that had been settled in the 1830s and which had maintained a separate identity over the years. In its residential suburbs the Rock Island did everything it could to encourage patronage. While developing Morgan Park, it offered all new residents a guaranteed ride of 10 cents during their first two years of residence. Morgan Park had a total of only 187 residents in 1880, but by 1890 it had grown to over 1,000.

By the turn of the century the suburban district as far as Blue Island had taken on much the same character it has today, although it had not yet been completely filled in. The Rock Island now began its further colonization in the

This delightful station at Morgan Park (115th Street) still stands now that RTA funds are moving to maintain and improve the Rock Island suburban service. This station and many of its breatheren, have been given fresh coats of paint. Some even have remodeled interiors.

(George H. Douglas)

territory between Blue Island and Joliet. Some of the towns in this area are well built up and hug the city belt—Robbins, Midlothian and Oak Forest. From here the line strikes out into open country, hitting such quasi-suburban communities as Tinley Park, Mokena, and New Lennox, before coming to rest in Joliet, 40 miles from La Salle Street Station.

The Rock Island remains a delightful little suburban line. Through Morgan Park and Beverly Hills there are stations every half mile or so. In some cases old stations have been replaced with contemporary brick ranch-style structures. But a number of Victorian gingerbread stations or others of eccentric design remain, and the RTA has been active in repainting and refurbishing them. For example, the station at Vermont Street in Blue Island, where the Suburban Line rejoins the Main Line, has recently been treated to a completely remodeled interior, which has not interfered with the traditional structure.

The old ballad about the Rock Island line being a mighty good road may no longer have any meaning for the network that once served the vast Midwest so well, but the little suburban line out of Chicago still holds attraction for riders of the rail.

There are no other important commuter operations in the Chicago area, although a few very small services remain. A few generations ago the Chicago and Western Indiana was operating a steam suburban train out of Dearborn Station for Dolton, serving such intermediate stops as Auburn Park, Oakdale, Fernwood, Roseland and Sheldon Park. Until the middle 1960s the New York Central operated a small-scale suburban service along its main line to Elkhart, Indiana, and before the mid-1950s this service was fairly extensive. The former Pennsylvania operated a fairly efficient commuter service to Gary, Hobart and Valparaiso, Indiana. Until the beginning of the Depression the Illinois Central even had a little steam commuter service to the western Chicago suburbs!

Is there a Beverly Hills in Chicago? Yes, there is, and it remains one of the neatest little suburban areas within the confines of a great metropolis. There are five stations in Beverly Hills— this eccentric little charmer being the northernmost, at 91st Street and Beverly Avenue.

(George H. Douglas)

There remain two small-scale commuter operations in Chicago, remnants of long-distance services that at one time were extensive. The Gulf, Mobile and Ohio (once the Alton and now the Illinois Central Gulf) has its own route between Joliet and Chicago's Union Station. Taking the route once followed by the line's streamliners *Abraham Lincoln* and *Ann Rutledge*, and shadowing the Chicago Sanitary and Ship Canal towards town, the ICG now runs one train a day each way, picking up passengers in Lockport, Lemont, Willow Springs, Summit, Glenn and Brighton Park—a weekday reliable for three hundred passengers.

Another one-train-each-way service is offered by the Norfolk and Western (formerly the Wabash). This makes several stops within the city of Chicago and the suburban communities of Oak Lawn, Chicago Ridge, Worth, Palos Park, and Orland Park. The service provides for nine hundred daily commuters and the equipment is

It is 4:36 P.M. on a drizzly summer afternoon and the first big express of the afternoon has left La Salle Street Station on its way to Joliet. First stop will be Vermont Street Blue Island, 15 miles away, after which the train will make all the main-line stops to Joliet.

(George H. Douglas)

Naturally, toward the end, the C&WI dieselized its little line to Dolton, which was some 17 miles from Dearborn Station. Shown here at 79th Street a diesel with more than sufficient power pulls a lone mid-day coach which has just passed under the Rock Island main line at this point.

(Andrew C. Koval)

For a number of years the New York Central maintained a fairly elaborate commuter service in the Chicago area along its main line around the southern shore of Lake Michigan. Shown here is one of their typical short-haul trains leaving Englewood Station in 1949.
(Bob Lorenz)

completely up to the high standards of the other major Chicago commuter lines. The nine or ten-car train leaves Orland Park at 6:50 A.M. and arrives at Union Station at 8:00. In the evening it departs at 5:30 and arrives at Orland Park at 6:30. The run has a large number of regular and loyal riders. A second train is now being considered for the line.

Whatever else can be said about Chicago as a commuterland, the results are locally spectacular for an industry that nationally is beset by the severest of financial difficulties. No other city can presently match Chicago as a rail commuter town. Public money has taken over in recent years to modernize the equipment and improve all kinds of services. It's still a great show, with long years of experience and railroad know-how behind it. It's one of Chicago's great public treasures.

CHAPTER 10

Decline and Regrowth

They don't talk much anymore about Chicago as the railroad capital of America. The railroads themselves have fallen on evil days in the last few generations. Thus, it is only natural that the country's great rail metropolis should lose some of its luster as a showcase of railroad progress and vitality. The newspapers are filled with items about railroad bankruptcies, a few involving some of Chicago's oldest and most celebrated lines. Imposing stations have given way to the wrecker's ball, and long-distance travel by rail has fallen off to a trickle. Giant rail yards, once an ensign of railroad power and authority, are thinned out, sometimes to only half of their former capacity. Hundreds of miles of freight sidings lay unused, their rails rusted, with thick undergrowth covering these once vital arteries and capillaries of a magnificent transportation system.

In the late 1970s there began some talk of a revitalization of the railroad, even of a possible return to the steam locomotive, as many oil wells around the world gurgled and sputtered their last. No vast and revolutionary changes were immediately apparent for the railroads, but strong indications of an upturn are there. Clearly, the railroads have the physical facilities, the well-planned and well-chosen real estate that could enable them to swing into action if needed for the nation's betterment.

Some would not have seen any such glimmer of a blue sky up ahead in the late 1960s and early 1970s. Railroads seemed then to be falling apart physically as well as financially, and the industry found itself going from one downturn to another. Nothing offered more dramatic evidence of this darkening picture than the tragic

blow to the widely trumpeted merger of the Penn-Central, amidst high hopes and expectations. In early 1968, the two great giants of the East joined forces amid fanfare and public acclamation of a new era in railroad prosperity and amalgamation. Less than two and a half years later the great conglomerate and house of cards fell apart with a thunderclap, leaving the public to wonder if the railroads had any steam left in them at all. If two giants like the Pennsylvania and the New York Central could fall to the ground with a thump, as they did in the summer of 1970, was there any hope that less mighty and prestigious roads could save themselves from oblivion?

The shifting railroad scene was dramatized in the public's eyes by the creation around this time of a government-sponsored plan to save rail passenger service from extinction. By 1970 it appeared that passenger travel by rail would soon be a thing of the past unless public funds were found to keep it going. Not everybody wanted to save the railroad passenger business, but even the least-farseeing congressman could see that there was some virtue in providing alternate relief to overburdened highways, crowded airways and noxious fuel emissions. After extensive efforts of congressional and U.S. Transportation Department leaders, President Nixon signed into law legislation providing for a National Railroad Passenger Corporation (NRPC), which soon came to be referred to as Railpax. There were a lot of wrinkles to be ironed out, but this new corporation—with the name later changed to Amtrak—took over intercity and long-distance rail travel on May 1, 1971.

Amtrak had its problems from the begin-

300

It is the summer of 1971 and the noble edifice of Chicago's Grand Central Station has its rendezvous with the wrecking crew. It may be that a few years later this station could have been preserved, but apparently the various landmark and architectural historical societies had not yet gotten their act together at this time.
(Chicago Historical Society)

ning. It had to honor labor agreements already in force; it had to contract with the railroads (at least in the beginning) for train crews and station operation. The starveling infant had other yokes around its neck: it had to show a profit and (what would be most troublesome in time) it had to operate over rails that were all too quickly being given over to deferred maintenance and freight-operating standards. But there were some good things, too. Amtrak could immediately provide a national reservations system, a national policy on such things as travel agents' commissions, credit cards, fares, and food service. Because many unprofitable runs were immediately eliminated, Amtrak

started life with a pool of the best equipment available in the country at the time. Soon they would be able to buy some new equipment of their own.

Still, May 1, 1971, the day appointed for Amtrak takeover of intercity passenger traffic (commuter lines were exempted), was hardly a red-letter day for train lovers, or for a city like Chicago. For it was not at once a matter of upgrading, but of lopping off, of pruning out the deadwood. And this was a day which saw the elimination in Chicago of 77 of its 121 scheduled intercity passenger runs. The railroad capital of the nation took it on the chin, because in one fell swoop it had to suffer the humiliation of absorbing 30 percent of the national quota of lost runs.

In the blink of an eye, so to speak, some of Chicago's favorite name trains disappeared. Into the pages of history went all the trains of the Baltimore and Ohio (which a few years before had abandoned Grand Central Station for North Western Station). The *Capitol Limited* vanished forever from the Chicago scene. Gone, too, were the *San Francisco Chief*, the *Nebraska Zephyr*, the Milwaukee Road's *Hiawatha*s (although the Milwaukee route to Minneapolis-St. Paul was taken over by Amtrak), all of Chicago and North Western's remaining 400 streamliners, all of the Grand Trunk's international runs—the *International Limited*, the *Maple Leaf*—thus ending Chicago's rail connection with Canada. The mighty trunk line of the Penn Central from New York to Chicago shrank down to a mere thread with the loss of trains like the *Manhattan Limited*, the *Pennsylvania Limited* and the *Admiral* (the *General* and the *Trail Blazer* had already faded into the pages of history). The *Twentieth Century Limited* had died in 1967, but Amtrak salvaged the *Broadway Limited*, thus preserving the New York—Chicago run through Pittsburgh. Illinois' primeval railroad, the Illinois Central, lost the *Panama Limited* (later restored by Amtrak), the *City of Miami*,

the *Hawkeye* (the IC's Iowa train to Sioux City), the *Governor's Special* to Springfield — the successor to the *Green Diamond*.

Many famous trains had disappeared even before Amtrak takeover. The Erie-Lackawanna had ended its long service into Dearborn Station a year before. The Chicago and North Western had effectively been out of the long-distance passenger business for some time. The Rock Island didn't have many trains left in 1971 and it was too poor to buy its way into Amtrak (a cash payment was expected of railroads that wanted Amtrak to relieve them of the passenger burden). For a time it kept its trains in Peoria

As is so often the case in the cities of today, the destruction of interesting historical buildings serves no useful purpose. Here is the site of Grand Central Station in 1980—a lonely parcel of land, a roost for pigeons, a haven for blowing papers, a depository for beer cans. Looking northward toward Harrison Street, along one of the station's former platforms.

(George H. Douglas)

302

and Rock Island. In general Amtrak salvaged the lines and the trains it thought could make money, hoping to profit on dense urban corridors around the country—New York to Washington, Chicago to St. Louis or Detroit or Minneapolis. Gone forever would be the ambling "country gentlemen" trains that once made rail travel so charming.

This period of belt tightening and passenger train elimination had an enormous impact for another reason. It led within the period of one decade to the closing (and in some cases demolition) of some of Chicago's great and distinctive railroad stations. Grand Central Station, always the least trafficked of all the stations, was the first to close its doors. And, in spite of some weak efforts of environmental and architectural protection groups, it succumbed to the wrecking crews in the summer of 1971. Its site at the corner of Harrison and Wells, a lonely roost for idle pigeons and a haven for wind-scattered papers and empty boxes in full view of the Eisenhower—Congress Expressway, is a pathetic reminder of one of the city's lost architectural treasures.

The much less attractive La Salle Street Station, a few blocks to the east, continued to function because of the heavy load of Rock Island commuters, but the long-distance trains were mostly gone by 1971. The Illinois Central Station at 12th Street would continue to serve Amtrak for a very brief time—between May of 1971 and March of 1972. Amtrak had to figure out how to get the Illinois Central trains over to Union Station where it was concentrating all passenger services. It did so by using the old St. Charles Air Line, linking up with the Burlington's access tracks into Union Station. With this problem solved, Central Station, too, was a target for demolition, although this was not carried out until the spring of 1974.

The Central Station demolition involved both the station itself and the complex of office buildings that surrounded it. These buildings had for a long time housed the Illinois Central's executive offices, although they were abandoned by the railroad for more plush and modern

quarters at Two Illinois Center in the fall of 1973. Tumbling down with the famous old clock tower, for many years a landmark in this part of Chicago, were two ten-story office buildings north of Roosevelt Road that went back to the time of the construction of the station 80 years before, and the 7-story Dowie Building on the south side of Roosevelt Road, connected to the main building by a bridge at the third-floor level. Curiously, this little Dowie Building was the oldest structure in the 1974 demolition, since it had originally been a part of the Ashland Block in the Loop and had been moved to two other locations before 1907, when it was purchased by the Illinois Central and moved to this last site at 109 East Roosevelt Road. The razing of Central Station in no way

It is 8:15 a.m. on May 25, 1969, and the Concourse Building of Union Station gives way to the wrecker's ball. A skyscraper, the Marsh and McLennon Building, rose on the spot, although all the old functions of the Concourse Building are still carried on underground in an inglorious fashion.

(Chicago Historical Society)

The Illinois Central terminal and office building, built in 1893, reached the end of the run in 1974. Never a highly regarded architectural monument, the station was nonetheless an important visual landmark near the lakefront in Grant Park.

(Illinois Central Gulf)

Central Station was built to house both the IC's long distance trains and the general offices of the road. But several years before these offices came tumbling down, the Illinois Central had moved on to newer and more luxurious quarters on North Michigan Avenue.

(Illinois Central Gulf)

Hundreds of railroad structures in Chicago have given way to the ravages of time, and others look as if they are about to. This precariously perched interlocking tower controls the approach to the La Salle Street Station, and, if anything, looks as weathered and tattered as the old station itself.

(George H. Douglas)

Long one of the best-known railroad stations in America, especially to the railroad photographer, is Englewood Station, where the lines of the Rock Island, the New York Central and the Pennsylvania (and others) intersected. The station is now deserted and unused, the victim in part of urban blight. It now awaits the wrecker's ball. November 15, 1979.

(George H. Douglas)

The Dearborn Station is still standing in 1980, although closed for almost a decade. The train shed has been demolished, however, and this picture gives some idea of the demolition process in the spring of 1979.

(George H. Douglas)

The Dearborn Station hasn't fallen yet, but in its crumbling condition, after the removal of the train shed, it has the appearance of a superannuated palace of the doges or of some Florentine bishop.

(George H. Douglas)

affected the Illinois Central's suburban service at 12th Street, which had always been served by its own separate station.

The coming of Amtrak brought an end, but not demolition, to old Dearborn Station over at the corner of Polk and Dearborn Streets. This was the oldest of the great Chicago stations, having been built in 1885, and its age and small capacity had condemned it to a decline in the years before the coming of Amtrak. The Monon and Erie had already deserted the station by the time that Amtrak entered the picture, and the Wabash had been merged with the Norfolk and Western—thereafter the old Wabash commuter run would use Union Station (the Wabash trains to Decatur and St. Louis were eliminated by Amtrak). This left the Santa Fe, the C&EI and the Grand Trunk Western as tenants at the end of Dearborn's long years of service. But by 1967 the Santa Fe had discontinued 3 of its 7 trains into the station. The Grand Trunk Western had three trains on the route between Chicago and Detroit or Toronto, and their planned demise brought about the end of international rail service between Chicago and Canada. It has not been restored.

Appropriately enough, the very last train to leave Dearborn Station was the Grand Trunk's Train 156, a remnant of the old overnight train called the *International*. The Grand Trunk's last train was scheduled to leave at 9:00 P.M., but it was delayed an hour and 50 minutes so that it could add equipment from the inbound *Maple Leaf* and *Mohawk*. All of the remaining Santa Fe trains had left earlier in the day. But this was not precisely the bitter end of train operations at Dearborn Station. The Santa Fe trains that had set out from the West Coast on April 30 did not arrive in Chicago until May 2. So the very end of all official train movements came at 9 P.M. on May 2, when the Santa Fe's *Grand Canyon* arrived from California. The arrival board was brushed clean, the clocks stopped, the doors chained shut, and Dearborn Station, after 86 years, faded into the mists of railway history.

The Dearborn Station has not been demolished as of this writing. After the loss of the Grand Central, certain architectural and

A lonely and pathetic old baggage wagon stands in front of the Dearborn Station during the process of renovation in May of 1979. In this process the interior of the station was gutted and the train shed was removed. The station is now a mere shell of its former self, but it is still a place of Gothic romance.

(George H. Douglas)

historical groups began to express an interest in Dearborn Station and eventually the station passed from ownership of the Chicago and Western Indiana to the City of Chicago, which has cooperated with developers who have planned an elaborate housing project in the area, using the old station as a kind of historic centerpiece. It was of some help that the station was added to the National Register of Historic Places in 1976. In 1979 the station's old shed was torn down, and the City of Chicago is making no definite promises to anybody about what will happen to the station. Certainly many Chicagoans who walk along Dearborn Street for many blocks to the north will miss the quaint old clock tower if and when it encounters the wrecker's ball.

The great decline of passenger traffic into and out of Chicago in the years after the Second World War made it seem at last a possibility to have a single union station as was once dreamed of by Daniel Burnham, and for which generations of Chicago politicians had been clamoring. The truth is that by 1960 Union Station would easily have been capable of handling every long-

The long-distance trains have long since fled the La Salle Street Station, but the Rock Island (now RTA) commuter trains have kept the station open for a while, although as these grass-covered roadbeds show, the station has been the subject of neglect and unstudied abuse.

(George H. Douglas)

When the Dearborn Station was closed in 1971 a great many of its name trains disappeared for all time. The Erie-Lackawanna, like a number of other railroads, didn't even hold out until the end. Here, on January 4, 1970, the road's *Lake Cities Express* departed Dearborn Station for the last time, thus ending the Erie-Lackawanna connection between Chicago and New York.

(Erie-Lackawanna)

distance passenger train for the city. Extensive commuter operations at La Salle and North Western stations, and great expense to the railroads of making the switch, kept everything from being moved to Union Station at the end of the passenger train era. But with the coming of Amtrak, Union Station was able to consolidate all of the long-distance passenger runs and its already existing commuter operations of the Burlington and Milwaukee—all without overtaxing its facilities in the slightest.

Union Station was able to take on this extra burden even while losing its great Concourse Building with its remarkable vaulted ceiling and metal latticework. The causes of this destruction actually dated back a few years, and were, in a sense, the last part of the gigantic building project (one that began in the early 1960s) to construct some fabulous skyscrapers over the traditional Union Station air-rights—a precedent set in the late 1920s with the building of the Daily News Building (now Riverside Plaza Building). Two very attractive buildings, designed by the distinguished architectural firm of Skidmore, Owings and Merrill, were built from 1963-65 and 1965-67 in the blocks just northeast of Union Station between Canal Street and the Chicago River. These came to be known as Gateway Center. A few years later, however, real estate values being what they were, and the Penn Central Railroad—50 percent owner of Union Station—being in a state of penury, the above-ground rights to the Concourse part of Union Station were sold to construct a third such building—now known as Marsh and McLennon Plaza. The Concourse Building met its fate in 1969.

The old functions of the Concourse Building still go on at Union Station—but all underground. In place of the vast and impressive vaulted hall, the east half of Union Station is now an underground labyrinth of news and popcorn stands, commuter bars, cheese stores and various sellers of gewgaws and trinkets—all very simple and easy to understand for the daily commuter, but sometimes a bit confusing for Amtrak's long-distance riders looking for their gates.

In general, though, Union Station continues to serve Chicago rail passengers well. The headhouse is still there, somewhat tarnished but impressive, although its interior cavern is regularly compromised by the presence of automobiles being raffled for charity, knick-knack stores and soft drink machines. One may still dream, if one wishes, of some ancient Roman emperor swishing by in his toga on the way to his bath. Television and movie makers are still sufficiently impressed by the big dome to set up their cameras to capture live human drama and big city railroad ambience.

East of the headhouse, in the center part of the complex, Amtrak has done some remodeling of ticket offices, baggage-handling facilities, lounges and the like, attempting to give the place the modern feel of an airport terminal—an attempt that is only half successful (but still worth doing). Union Station remains one of the most colorful and breathtaking railroad stations in the United States.

After more than a decade of deterioration and abandonment, American railway passenger service got a new breath of life with the coming of Amtrak. This picture from 1972 shows some spanking new Amfleet equipment on display at Central Station before Amtrak discontinued use of that station in favor of completely unified operations at Union Station.

(Amtrak)

309

For a while Amtrak managed to muddle through with the best equipment from the pools of cars turned over to them from the participating railroads. But in the years since 1971 they have ordered much new equipment, such as these bi-level Superliner cars which are used in a number of long-distance runs from Chicago.

(Amtrak)

As of the spring of 1981 the Chicago and North Western Station still stands, performing noble service as a strictly commuter station, although it is presently threatened by real estate scavengers who want to rip it down for an office building of the kind that brought an end to the Union Station's Concourse Building. Whatever the fate of the station itself, the passenger function will continue to be performed even if in less-dignified subterranean surroundings.

Long-distance train service out of Chicago has greatly diminished since the Amtrak takeover in 1971. Amtrak has done its best with the extensive Eastern urban corridor between Boston and Washington. A few name trains still exist and can be seen daily in Union Station. The *Broadway Limited* continues to follow the old Pennsylvania main line between New York and

Chicago. But it is just a ghost of its former self. The trip takes 20 hours instead of the 15½ that it took in 1950. The Pennsylvania's tracks are hardly in a condition to receive high-speed passenger trains. Gone, too, are the beautiful Tuscan-red cars of the "all-room" *Broadway* as designed by Raymond Loewy. In general Amtrak tries hard, but they have abandoned all of the old railroad flourishes. Basically they compete with bus lines in an attempt to serve "everyman."

Amtrak equipment is not what you would call elegant, but it is modern, clean and comfortable. The seats recline, the water runs, the toilets in the washrooms flush, and when the trains run on time (not strictly a matter under Amtrak control), the passengers are happy.

(Amtrak)

Unfortunately, Amtrak has not done as well in culinary matters as it might, and in recent years it has replaced many of the traditional dining cars with so-called cafe cars where sandwiches and light meals are heated in microwave ovens. But some of the Superliner trains still have traditional dining cars, as shown here, and these serve reasonable food in comfortable surroundings. This is a double-level car, seating 72 people at 18 tables, the food being prepared on the lower level and sent up on dumbwaiters.

(Amtrak)

This very pleasant and modern waiting room is supposed to be reserved for long-distance passengers of Amtrak, but doubtless a number of unclassified passengers and other station users filter in from time to time. This is the lounge as it appeared on June 2, 1975, in mint condition.

(Amtrak)

The baggage carousel at Union Station is reminiscent of airline baggage facilities dreaded by the multitudes. In general, though, Amtrak does better with checked bags than the airlines, maybe because they don't have a great many.

(Amtrak)

Amtrak's passenger servicing facilities occupy the space once given over to the Pennsylvania Railroad's coach yards south of Roosevelt Road and along the West bank of the Chicago River. The Amtrak service building, built in the 1970s, appears in the center of the picture with the airport-style control tower.
(George H. Douglas)

The Broadway's old competitor the *Twentieth Century Limited* bowed out for good in 1967, but Amtrak has kept up the line through Cleveland and Buffalo to New York with one good train a day—the *Lake Shore Limited*, an old New York Central name. It is reputed to be a bit better than the *Broadway*. Amtrak has service to Boston and Washington, too, although for the latter, interestingly, they selected none of the former major routes, but the old Chesapeake and Ohio route through White Sulphur Springs and Cincinnati.

Another great Chicago train that has survived is the *Panama Limited* to New Orleans (Amtrak briefly killed it when they first selected a daytime schedule for the New Orleans route). Gone are the "King's Dinner," and most of the other amenities. Breakfast is cooked in a microwave oven using frozen materials that have been put together in some central kitchen. The equipment is new, and nice, but undistinguished.

Amtrak wanted to keep the name the Santa Fe *Chief*, but after a while the Santa Fe balked at this impertinence and the *Chief* disappeared from the time cards. Still, Amtrak is following the old Santa Fe Trail to Southern California through Kansas City, Dodge City and Albuquerque. This once-a-day train is now called the *Southwest Limited*. But Amtrak has been able to keep other traditional railroading names such as the *San Francisco Zephyr* and the *Empire Builder* to Seattle.

It hardly needs to be said that Amtrak has done best with its corridor services in the Midwest, as in the East. They have bought French-built Turbo trains for the routes between Chicago and Milwaukee and between Chicago, Bloomington, Springfield and St. Louis. These are well-patronized, even though track conditions forbid that they operate at the speeds for which they were designed. They also operate a modest sort of corridor service between Chicago and Detroit, between Chicago and Kansas City (through Quincy and Galesburg), and between Chicago and Carbondale through Champaign-Urbana.

Altogether, Amtrak serves Chicago fairly well, considering the restraints under which it operates. With fuel shortages on the increase, there just might be a new flowering of inter-city rail passenger traffic.

One form of passenger service with a bright future is the suburban service, even though it will have to continue to be supported by public money. In this field Chicago is second to none. By the end of the 1970s no city in North America was better served by commuter lines than Chicago. The various lines are well placed (mainly because they built the suburban communities in the first place), the equipment is modern and up-to-date, and the trains arrive mostly on time, which is what a commuter wants. With oil prices skyrocketing, the Chicago suburban lines may be in for a new influx of passengers.

Chicago, of course, remains a great center for the railroad industry in more ways than one. Even if by chance there were some nationalization or unification of rail services, Chicago will remain a place of freight yards and transfers because of the singular location of the city and because of the pattern of rails laid down long ago. In addition, the city continues to be an important headquarters, a home to railway executives, planners and staff functionaries of all sorts. The walker on Michigan Avenue can hardly help but notice the Santa Fe sign atop the Railway Exchange Building, and yes, the Santa Fe's executive offices are still there.

The Illinois Central gave up its old office complex at 135 East 11th Place (Central Station), but it is still in Chicago, in much fancier quarters on North Michigan Avenue. The Burlington merged with its two parents the Great Northern and the Northern Pacific. With the corporate headquarters moved to St. Paul, the old Burlington Building on West Jackson Boulevard was eventually sold. The Milwaukee has kept its offices in Union Station in spite of recent trying times. The Rock Island moved in the late 1970s from the old rookery of the La Salle Street Station to presumably more sump-

To replace delapidated and outmoded facilities, Amtrak has had to do a considerable amount of its own building in the Chicago area. Here an addition is being made to the engine house in the Amtrak complex south of Union Station.

(Amtrak)

The passenger train may actually survive. If Amtrak could run this French-built turboliner (here leaving Union Station for Detroit) at the speeds for which it was designed, the train might regain some business from the extremely expensive airlines.

(Amtrak)

One kind of passenger business that is still very much alive in Chicago is the commuter business. Here, with equipment that was spanking new in 1974, is a two-car bi-level commuter train inbound to Union Station on the Milwaukee. In the left background is the world's tallest office building, the Sears Tower, and beneath it the Kemper Insurance Building (before 1949 the Civic Opera).

(Milwaukee Road)

tuous quarters on Michigan Avenue, but their continued penuriousness did not make expectations of high life possible at the new address.

Chicago continues to be a town wealthy in professional and executive railroad talent.

Much of the color of railroading was lost with the disappearance of the steam locomotive. A few generations ago, Chicago, with its thousands of locomotives throbbing and puffing just south and west of the Loop, was distinctively and vividly a railroad town extraordinaire. The sounds are now stilled and the dramatic evidences of the railroad's might are partially obscured. But in a somewhat subdued way they are still there—the massive yards out around the city's periphery where the diesel engine is humming by day and night, where freight cars from every railroad can be spotted along the city's network of expressways, where the Illinois Central's silent electric trains can be seen fleeting along the lakefront with pantograph bristling along the overhead wires, where the blinking of block signals can be seen during the dim evening hours—all signs of the continued power of this great mode of travel.

In Chicago the railroad perseveres as an endless form of fascination and a reassuring testimony to the muscle and sinews of American commerce and industry.

Chicago's commuter rail lines have been partially revitalized by an influx of public funds, most of it very well spent. This is the old Rock Island Station at Vermont Street, Blue Island, painted, repaired and given a completely modern interior with the use of funds from the Regional Transit Authority. How much more sensible to save these picturesque structures than to rip them down.
(George H. Douglas)

With the construction of modern skyscrapers Union Station stands in a more pleasant and seemly environment than it did years ago. After over a half century of service, Union Station continues to thrive amidst modern plantings and well-planned vistas.

(George H. Douglas)

Under constant threat of extinction in 1980, as are most innercity rail structures, the Chicago and North Western Station continues functioning as the noble public edifice it was when it opened in 1911. This picture shows the Clinton Street entrance to the Station with a broad expanse of the train shed at left.

(George H. Douglas)

A steam train under the shadow of the Sears Building? Impossible? Not at all. This is a special steam fan trip which has left La Salle Street Station jammed with railfans and aficionados. Not very far out of the terminal the train has already stopped to accommodate the numerous photo bugs who naturally want to capture everything. June 24, 1973. Love of trains continues at fever pitch in Chicago.

(Chicago Historical Society)

After long years of wandering to world's fairs and railway exhibitions Chicago's first locomotive got a permanent home in the Chicago Historical Society, which had to knock out a wall to get the locomotive into its second floor exhibit room.

(George H. Douglas)

It appears that Chicago officialdom has not forgotten the agency that created the city. In 1973, at the corner of Canal and Kinzie Streets, the site of the city's first railroad station, a group including Mayor Richard J. Daley (with trowel at center) prepare to lay a plaque commemorating the 125th anniversary of the first train trip out of Chicago on October 25, l848. At the left is Jim Adams of the Midwest Railway Historical Society, also chairman of the Pioneer Anniversary Commission.

(Midwest Railway Historical Society)

Another famous train that is on permanent exhibit in Chicago is the *Pioneer Zephyr*, the streamlined train with which the Burlington introduced the diesel to long-distance passenger service in 1934. The train is on exhibit outside the museum of Science and Industry, along with several steam locomotives (not shown) and the captured German submarine U-505 of World War II fame.

(Burlington Northern)

Evidences of railroad wealth and diversity are found everywhere in Chicago, which has not only the stations, the trains, the rail yards but many of the executive offices as well. This is the Railway Exchange Building on Michigan avenue, which contains, among others, the executive offices of the Santa Fe, whose sign is highly visible along the avenue and in Grant Park. The building was designed in 1903 by Daniel Burnham, who once had his offices on the top floor.

(George H. Douglas)

The tracks of the Illinois Central continue to wind their way right into the very heart of downtown Chicago. For years this was thought to be an aesthetic blight, but here they are benign and unobtrusive, as much a part of Grant Park as the flowers and the trees.

(George H. Douglas)

Bibliography

The following is a brief bibliography of various books dealing with Chicago and the railroad. The list is in no sense intended to be complete, but contains the principal sources used by the author, and other works that may prove of interest to the general reader.

Ackerman, William K., *Early Illinois Railroads*. Chicago: Fergus Printing Company, 1890.

Alexander, Edwin P., *Down at the Depot: American Railroad Stations from 1831 to 1920*. New York: Clarkson N. Potter, 1970.

—————, *The Pennsylvania Railroad, A Pictorial History*. New York: W. W. Norton, Inc., 1947.

Andreas, Alfred T., *History of Chicago*, 3 vols. Chicago: A. T. Andreas, 1884–86.

—————, *History of Cook County*. Chicago: A. T. Andreas, 1884.

Angle, Paul M., ed., *The Great Chicago Fire*. Chicago: Chicago Historical Society, 1946.

Beebe, Lucius, *The Overland Limited*. Berkeley, California: Howell-North Books, 1963.

—————, *The Trains We Rode*, 2 vols. Berkeley, California: Howell-North Books, 1965.

—————, *Twentieth Century: The Greatest Train in the World*. Berkeley, California: Howell-North Books, 1962.

Bross, William, *The Rail-Roads, History and Commerce of Chicago*. Chicago: Democratic Press, 1854.

Brown, Dee, *Hear That Lonesome Whistle Blow: Railroads in the West*. New York: Holt, Rinehart & Winston, 1977.

Brownson, Howard Gray, *History of the Illinois Central Railroad to 1870*. Urbana: The University of Illinois, 1915.

Buder, Stanley, *Pullman: An Experiment in Industrial Order and Community Planning*. New York: Oxford University Press, 1967.

Burgess, George H., and Miles C. Kennedy, *Centennial History of the Pennsylvania Railroad Company, 1846-1946*. Philadelphia: The Pennsylvania Railroad, 1949.

Butler, Charles, *Travel from Detroit to Chicago in 1833*. Chicago: Railway Library vol. 3, 1912.

Casey, Robert J., and W.A.S. Douglas, *Pioneer Railroad: The Story of the Chicago and North Western System*. New York: Whittlesey House, 1948.

Chamberlain, Everett, *Chicago and Its Suburbs*. Chicago: T.A. Hungerford & Co., 1874.

Chicago-Aurora Centennial, 1864-1964. Chicago, Burlington & Quincy Railroad, 1964.

Chicago Historical Society, Collection of Illinois Maps.

Chicago, Illustrated and Descriptive: A Description of the City as it Appears in 1882. Chicago: N.F. Hodson & Co., 1882.

Chicago in 1860: A Glance at Its Business and Houses, Its Trade, Its Manufacturers, and Commerce. Chicago: W. Thorn & Co., 1860.

Chicago and Interurban Trolley Guide. Chicago: The Chicago and Interurban Trolley Guide, 1907.

Chicago and North Western Railway Company, *Yesterday and Today: A History*. Chicago: Rand McNally & Co., 1905.

A Comprehensive Local Transportation Plan for the City of Chicago. Chicago: City Council Committee on Local Transportation, 1937.

Condit, Carl W., *Chicago: Building, Planning and Urban Technology, 1910-29*. Chicago: University of Chicago Press, 1973.

—————, *Chicago: Building, Planning and Urban Technology, 1930-70*. Chicago: The University of Chicago Press, 1974.

Corbin, Bernard G., *The Burlington in Transition*. Red Oak, Iowa: Corbin Publications, 1967.

Corliss, Carlton J., *Main Line of Mid America: The Story of the Illinois Central*. New York: Creative Age Press, 1950.

—————, *Trails to Rails: A Story of Transportation Progress in Illinois.* Chicago: Illinois Central Railroad, 1934.

Cromie, Robert, *The Great Chicago Fire.* New York: McGraw Hill, 1958.

Currier, Frederick A., *A Trip to the Great Lakes.* Fitchburg, Mass.: Sentimental Printing Company, 1904.

Davis, James Leslie, *The Elevated System and the Growth of Northern Chicago.* Evanston: Northwestern University Department of Geography, 1965.

Dorin, Patrick C., *Commuter Railroads.* New York: Bonanza Books, n.d.

Drago, Harry Sinclair, *Canal Days in America.* New York: Clarkson N. Potter, 1972.

Droege, John A., *Passenger Terminals and Trains.* New York: McGraw Hill Book Co., 1916.

Dubin, Arthur D., *Some Classic Trains.* Milwaukee: Kalmbach Books, 1964.

Dunbar, Seymour, *A History of Travel in America,* 4 vols. Indianapolis: The Bobbs Merrill Co., 1915.

Edmonson, Harold A., ed., *Journey to Amtrak.* Milwaukee: Kalmbach Books, 1972.

Federal Writer's Project, *Illinois: A Descriptive and Historical Guide.* A. A. McClurg & Co., 1947.

Ferguson, William, *America by River and Rail; or Notes by the Way on the New World and Its People.* London: J. Nisbet & Co., 1856.

From the Lakes to the Gulf. Chicago: Illinois Central Railroad, 1884.

Gates, Paul William, *The Illinois Central Railroad and its Colonization Work.* Cambridge: Harvard University Press, 1934.

Graham, Jory, *Chicago: An Extraordinary Guide.* Chicago: Rand McNally & Co., 1968.

Grow, Lawerence, *On the 8:02: An Informal History of Commuting by Rail in America.* New York: Mayflower Books, 1979.

Hamton, Taylor, *The Nickel Plate Road.* Cleveland: World Publishing Co., 1947.

Harlow, Alvin F., *The Road of the Century: The Story of the New York Central.* New York: Creative Age Press, 1947.

Hayes, William Edward, *Iron Road to Empire: The History of 100 Years of the Progress and Achievements of the Rock Island Lines.* Simmons-Bordman Publishing Co., 1953.

Hilton, George W., *Monon Route.* Berkeley, California: Howell-North Books, 1978.

History of the Illinois Central Railroad Company and Representative Employees. Chicago: Railroad Historical Company, 1900.

Holbrook, Stewart H., *The Age of the Moguls.* Garden City, N. Y.: Doubleday & Co., 1953.

—————, *The Story of American Railroads.* New York: Crown Publishers, 1947.

Hubbard, Freeman H., *Railroad Avenue.* New York: McGraw Hill Book Co., 1945.

Hungerford, Edward, *Men of Erie.* New York: Random House, 1946.

—————, *The Story of the Baltimore and Ohio Railroad.* New York: G. P. Putnam's Sons, 1928.

Husband, Joseph, *The Story of the Pullman Car.* Chicago: A. L. McClurg & Co., 1917.

Illinois Central Railroad, Annual Reports, 1854–.

Illinois Central Railroad, *Organization and Traffic of the Illinois Central System.* Chicago: Illinois Central Railroad Company, 1938.

Industrial Chicago. Chicago: Goodspeed Publishing Co., 1894.

Jackson, Elizabeth Coleman and Carolyn Curtis, *Guide to the Burlington Archives in the Newberry Library, 1851–1901.* Chicago: The Newberry Library, 1949.

Johnson, Arthur M. and Barry E. Supple, *Boston Capitalists and Western Railroads.* Cambridge: Harvard University Press, 1967.

Johnson, James D., ed., *A Century of Chicago Streetcars, 1858–1958.* Wheaton, IL: The Traction Orange Co., 1964.

Johnson, Rossiter, *A History of the World's Columbian Exposition,* 4 vols. New York: D. Appleton & Co., 1897.

Kirkland, Joseph, *The Story of Chicago.* Chicago: Dibble Publishing Co., 1892.

Kogan, Herman and Lloyd Wendt, *Chicago: A Pictorial History.* New York: E. P. Dutton & Co., 1958.

Lowe, David, *Lost Chicago.* Boston: Houghton Mifflin Co., 1968.

Lyon, Peter, *To Hell in a Day Coach.* Philadelphia: J. B. Lippincott Co., 1968.

Marshall, James, *Santa Fe: The Railroad that Built an Empire.* New York: Random House, 1945.

Masters, Edgar Lee, *The Tale of Chicago.* New York: Putnam's, 1933.

Mayer, Harold M. and Richard Wade, *Chicago, Growth of a Metropolis.* Chicago: University of Chicago Press, 1969.

Mayer, Harold Melvin, *The Railway Pattern of Metropolitan Chicago.* Ph.D. dissertation, University of Chicago, 1943.

Meeks, Carroll, *The Railroad Station.* New Haven: Yale University Press, 1960.

Mencken, August, *The Railroad Passenger Car.* Baltimore: The Johns Hopkins Press, 1957.

Middleton, William D., *North Shore: America's Fastest Interurban.* San Marino, California: Golden West Books, 1964.

————, *The Railroad Scene.* San Marino, California: Golden West Books, 1969.

————, *South Shore: The Last Interurban.* San Marino, California: Golden West Books, 1970.

Mohr, Carolyn Curtis, *Guide to the Illinois Central Archives in the Newberry Library 1851–1906.* Chicago: The Newberry Library, 1951.

Moses, John and Kirkland, *History of Chicago,* 4 vols. Chicago: Munsell & Co., 1895.

Official Railway Guides, 1868–. New York: National Railway Publications Co.

Our Suburbs. Chicago: Chicago Times, 1873.

Overton, Richard C., *Burlington Route: A History of the Burlington Lines.* New York: Alfred A. Knopf, 1965.

————, *Burlington West: A Colonization History of the Burlington Railroad.* Cambridge: Harvard University Press, 1941.

Pierce, Bessie Louise, *A History of Chicago,* 3 vols. New York: Alfred A. Knopf, 1937–57.

Plumbe, George Edward, *Chicago: The Great Industrial and Commercial Center of the Mississippi Valley.* Chicago: Chicago Association of Commerce, 1912.

Putnam, James William, *The Illinois and Michigan Canal.* Chicago: University of Chicago Press, 1918.

Quaife, Milo M., *Chicago's Highways Old and New.* Chicago: D. F. Keller Co., 1923.

Rehor, John A., *The Nickel Plate Story.* Milwaukee: Kalmbach Books, 1965.

Reminiscences of Chicago During the Civil War. Chicago: The Lakeside Press, 1914.

Reminiscences of Chicago During the Forties and Fifties. Chicago: The Lakeside Press, 1913.

Riegel, Robert Edgar, *The Story of the Western Railroads.* New York: Macmillan, 1926.

Salisbury, R. D. and W. C. Alden, *The Geography of Chicago and Its Environs.* Chicago: University of Chicago Press, 1920.

Schroeder, Douglas, *The Issue of the Lake Front: An Historical Critical Survey.* Chicago Heritage Committee, n.d.

Scribbins, Jim, *The Hiawatha Story.* Milwaukee: Kalmbach Books, 1970.

Smith, Henry Justin, *Chicago's Great Century, 1833–1933.* Chicago: Consolidated Publishers, 1933.

Szwajkart, John, *Train Watcher's Guide to Chicago.* Brookfield, Illinois: Self-Published, n.d.

Valle, James E., *The Iron Horse at War.* Berkeley, California: Howell-North Books, 1977.

Ward, Martindale C., *A Trip to Chicago: What I Saw, What I Heard, What I Thought.* Glasglow: A. Malcolm & Co., 1895.

Waterman, A. W., *Historical Review of Chicago and Cook County,* 3 vols. Chicago: The Lewis Publishing Co., 1908.

Westing, Frederick, *Erie Power.* Medina, Ohio: Alvin F. Staufer, 1970.

Whitaker, Rogers E. M., ("E. M. Frimbo"), *Decade of the Trains: the 1940's.* Boston: New York Graphic Society, 1977.

White, John H., Jr., *Early American Locomotives.* New York: Dover Publications, 1972.

————, *"The Pioneer," Chicago's First Locomotive.* Chicago: Chicago Historical Society.

Wood, David Ward, *Chicago and Its Distinguished Citizens.* Chicago: Milton George & Co., 1881.

Index

All place names are in Illinois unless otherwise noted.
Italic page numbers indicate illustrations.
† Indicates map.

OVERSIZE   40.186
385   Douglas, George
D   Rail City Chicago USA